YESTERDAYS

Memoirs from the Gray Hawk Writers

Alan Brody, Editor

Alan Brody

Pat Davis

Tom Davis

Joseph Dobrian

Marilyn Holland

John Hudson

Sandra Hudson

David Jepsen

Mildred Lavin

Jeanne Liston

Michael McNulty

Don Ross

Gordon Strayer

Ocie Trimble

Bob Wachal

*Members from
the Early Years*

Dean Andersen

Sam Becker

George Bedell

Mirriel Bedell

Lane Davis

Bob Kremenak

Nellie Kremenak

Hal Mulford

Clayton Ringgenberg

For information or permissions contact:

Alan Brody
319-512-1030
Brody.Alan@gmail.com

Or

John Hudson
319-341-7166
JohnBHudson2011@gmail.com

First Edition

ISBN-10: 1500606049
ISBN-13: 978-1500606046

Contents

Introduction

In a long ago time (slightly before the end of the last Millennium), the chapters of their excellent lives entering periods of denouement that inevitably lead to a final chapter, a doughty band of "Gray Hawks" began to gather in unassuming corners of what would become America's first UNESCO City of Literature, and constituted themselves *The Gray Hawk Memoir Writers Group*.

Since those early days, this band has met every second Thursday to read their writings and provide each other with encouragement and friendly critique. They have in common the willingness to share, through writing, some of the stories of their lives.

The history of the group began in 1999 when Professor Emeritus Sam Becker, then head of the University of Iowa Retirees Association (Gray Hawks), challenged his colleagues not to sit down quietly waiting to pass on, but instead to take up still unfinished business as volunteers and historians to pass on their experiences to the next generation. Gordon Strayer proposed memoir writing as an interest group for the Gray Hawks, and Sam ran with the idea.

The Gray Hawk Memoir Writers Group is now over 15 years old. We meet every two weeks, someone reads a favorite sample from a published memoir, and then each member reads a piece of personal writing. John Hudson chairs the meetings, reminding us regularly to follow the meeting guidelines his wife Sandra researched and developed in the early days of the group, at least when he is not getting carried away himself. He calls us to order when we linger too long over pre-meeting coffee and gossip, and wields a timer that rings to announce we have exceeded the nine minutes allowed for our reading, or the five minutes allocated to discussion of each piece.

We have had a total of 27 members since the group's founding. Five of the current active members have been with the group since its beginning. Is their advanced age a sign that writing from the heart, among good-hearted company, is good for the heart?

Our writers come originally from different places, have passed through often very different lives and careers, and have very different styles. Perhaps under the influence of years spent in Iowa, however, they seem to share, in the way of "attitude," a spirit of Midwestern common sense leavened with good humor.

The Gray Hawk Memoir Writers Group encourages a focus on memoir writing, but the guidelines allow members to use the meetings to share other types of writing if they desire. We have reprinted those guidelines at the end of the book. They have served us well, and others with similar aspirations to share their lives may find them useful.

The items published in this collection are but a few selected from those read in our more than 350 meetings over the group's first 15 years. The group endorsed the idea of doing a publication early in 2007, and gathered a set of materials at that time. But with the shared knowledge, from military and civilian experience, that the one who volunteers usually takes the bullet, no one stepped forward once the scale of the editing and publishing work became clear.

Four years later Mildred Lavin took the initiative to volunteer an "editors group" made up of her, Sandra Hudson, Mike McNulty, and Alan Brody. As "the kid" in this group, I was volunteered to be the editor, perhaps as punishment for being the one who originally broached an idea originating from my wife (not a member) that we owed it to the world to publish the work of the memoir group as a book.

By way of payback, I roped Sandra Hudson in to take charge of the biographies and photographs. Sandra's ever-supportive husband John, one of the memoir group's founding stalwarts (along with Sandra), took on responsibilities for electronic typesetting and publication arrangements, as his punishment for having said just enough in a meeting to establish that he knew more about the current state of the self-publishing industry than anyone else in the group. Joseph

Dobrian, a member of the memoir group since 2011, and John Hudson volunteered to help me with copy editing.

And so with such help, we are pleased to share—for our children and grandchildren who come after us and wonder what kind of lives we lived, for our friends and neighbors in Iowa City and the "Hawkeye State" of Iowa, and for any others whose curiosity invites them to spend a few hours with our work—some of the stories that we Gray Hawk Memoir Writers have been sharing with each other, every second Thursday.

Alan Brody, Editor
Iowa City, Iowa
April 14, 2014 (Our 15th Anniversary)

1

Section I

Members As This Book Took Form

Alan Brody

Alan on safari at Woodland Heights

Our writers group looks forward to Alan Brody's memoirs and to his op-ed pieces in the *Iowa City Press-Citizen*. His writing provides cross-cultural perspectives from his career experiences with the Peace Corps and UNICEF, and his 40-year marriage with his Ghanaian wife Mary. When Alan reads, we never know where we will end up that day: across the world in an African or Chinese village; engaged in conversation with a deposed Afghan president; battling AIDS in Swaziland; back in time to Yale or Harvard classrooms of the 1960s and 70s and Iowa's School of Journalism and Mass Communication a decade later; or into his 1950s childhood in a small western Pennsylvania town. Wherever we accompany him, we know we will always find a new insight, a felicitous phrase, and something to surprise us.

On Becoming a Gray Hawk

Do not go gentle into that good night.
Rage, Rage against the dying of the light.
— Dylan Thomas

I have a photograph of my first child taken in Ghana in 1973, not long after he learned to walk. He stands in front of a cake made in the shape of a Teddy Bear. There's a single tall candle sticking up from the center of the cake, borrowed from the packet of candles we kept in the storeroom as insurance against the frequent power outages we experienced. It was his first birthday, and he was about to learn that he could receive claps and cheers if he blew out the candle.

In the night he would have to learn a second lesson: that blowing out exactly the same kind of candle, but not on a birthday cake, would plunge the house into darkness, and elicit groans of "Oh, no!" with no claps and cheers.

This first-birthday metaphor applies to me this month, January of 2008. A year ago I joined the Gray Hawk Memoir Writers Group in Iowa City. Those who welcomed me to join them must look at me as "the kid." Just past 60, sporting a belly still with capon lined, carrying literary ambitions, I must make them look at me from time to time, shake their heads, and say, "So much to learn." As I was with my son when he turned one, they are to me, infallibly kind, humoring my efforts to earn a clap or a few cheers, and understanding and polite about the flickering of the light, when I blow on the wrong candle in the descending night.

Members who formed the group share history and special bonds. In the course of nine years, yielding to the writer's impulse, they have shared with one another thoughts and experiences that they might otherwise have carried in silence to the grave: memories of joys from some long ago time, or of the still fresh hurt of a bruise that everyone else has long forgotten.

I can imagine what their interactions were like, in the early days of the group, from my observations of my friend McNulty, who joined the group soon after I did. I've known him for almost 30 years, and many times watched him in his capacity as a geography professor stand before crowds of hundreds and hold forth with all the panache of an Irish storyteller. How surprised I was then, the first day he read to the Gray Hawks, to hear his voice quaver. Talking about the geography of the world is something different, and requires less courage I think, than those first steps to reveal, before others, the geography of one's soul, and the stories of one's family.

A few have left the group, permanently. Those who I never knew are the ones who made room for me. A few others come less and less often, as the challenge of getting out and about becomes more onerous with age. They grow more thin and fragile, the way I remember my father changed at 75, his step growing more tentative, and the suits he had worn all his life suddenly grown too large.

Others come religiously. Always at least some of the stories are very good, and there is never predicting whose reading will make a particular day memorable. One day, Don seems lost in a pedestrian list, then appears another day and soars with a story that cuts to the quick of human relationships and the cruelties of youth. Bob, reveling in his reputation as curmudgeon, proves in this company to be a gentle giant of laughter and good cheer. Tom struggles in the aftermath of a stroke, fortunate in the assistance of his wife Pat, to share with us the words and wit and limericks that but for this effort would remain locked up inside. The two of them make the rest of us feel blessed by their devotions. Ocie, a man whose life one senses has been full of friendships, writes in longhand on his yellow legal pads, still harvesting and sharing with us the pleasures of a lifetime of merry mischief. Hal can bring to life, on a quiet Iowa afternoon, the feelings and confusions of going to war almost 65 years before, and make us understand what those words "the greatest generation" mean. Sandra and John are not shy about their 50-year love affair, as they continue to dance through life, and sometimes on the page. Gordon with Christmas approaching brings back the magic of Santa's presence in his youth, and Marilyn takes us back to the candy store of all our youths, the marvelous struggles to choose what one's penny should buy as an Iowa City long disappeared suddenly comes to life again. And then Mildred, who reads marvelous narratives that make us wistful for the goodness and zest she brought to her sweet life, one day reads us a letter she wrote 70 years ago, when she was only 12. The voice we hear in the girl of that time, and the voice of the woman at the table with us every other Thursday afternoon, sound exactly the same, unchanged by time.

Sam Becker, who issued the challenge for the formation of this group and was for a long time a regular member, has only come twice since I joined. Once he came to read a piece about his wife and her response to the birth of a child needing special care. He paid tribute to her special character and the differences she made not only in the life of that child, but to the life of her entire community by her response to that challenge. The second time he came was the week that his ailing wife had died. He didn't read that week. He just came to be with friends, I think, this special group of friends that he knew would understand exactly how he was feeling.

How fortunate I feel, to have been invited to become a part of this very special group of people, to participate every other Thursday in their "continuing education" class, as I take lessons in how to go gently, fully conscious and with grace, into that good night.

I Think I Can…

My father was at the Atlantic Grill on Seventh Street the September evening I arrived in the world. The Atlantic was the only place open on a Sunday evening in those days when Pennsylvania Blue Laws enforced the Sabbath. He was eating a peanut butter sandwich, I was later told.

"It's going to be a long night," the doctor must have advised him once they settled his wife Anita in the labor room of the Indiana, Pennsylvania, Hospital. "You have plenty of time to get a bite to eat."

In those days doctors knew everything, and my father was feeling hungry. I assume my brother Steve, not yet three, was at Pop and Mom's house (my grandparents to be). Why did my father choose a peanut butter sandwich at the Atlantic Grill instead of stopping in for home cooking?

Perhaps breaking of bread with a little peanut butter topping at the Atlantic Grill was his last feeble protest in the face of the doubling of paternal responsibilities about to fall upon his life. No historian recorded definitive answers. The year was 1946. The birth was to be in a hospital, a doctor would supervise. Would all go well?

"The only certainty is continuing uncertainty," I would write 48 years later during an assignment in the fractured state of post-Soviet Afghanistan. That I lived to write such a useful mantra at least answers one question: all went well that September 1946 morning. I crossed the boundary into life, was snipped from a jointly owned umbilical cord, and had a healthy shout-out with my first breath in life responding to the doctor's smart slap to my butt.

Life does not always go so well, as my anxious mother well knew. She lost her first-born child Harry Robbins. Growing up I saw no framed pictures of him around our house. The memory of loss remained too raw and overwhelming for my mother, for this child who had thrived for almost two years before a freak accident took him away from her.

The baby was sound asleep in one of those new products of the type forever being marketed to improve American lives, a "snuggly" blanket sewn up on three sides the better to protect baby from the cold. This sleeping baby one evening woke up and crawled to the bottom of the snuggly, and got tangled there during a time when parents were out for just 10 minutes. Leonard and Anita, coming back full of happiness, found Harry there already dead, smothered. Anita's life came crashing down around her. "Taken from her" were words others might use. She, on the other hand, would pay for that cup of coffee for the rest of her life, nickeled and dimed by guilt and unhappiness, and through her, my father also would pay.

My mother didn't approve of the Atlantic Grill where my father stopped that Sunday evening. The place was best known for its Coney Island hot dogs, and as a hangout for the local boys who drank beer in the afternoons. Leonard had gone to school with some of them. Perhaps he missed their banter. But my mother and grandmother always told my nativity story with a hint of disapproval, as they declared, "Your father was having a peanut butter sandwich at the Atlantic Grill when you arrived."

"That awful place always smells like stale beer," my mother would add.

My father would put on a slightly sheepish expression in hopes to please those demanding ladies. "It was the only place open," he would say.

I don't know what got into me to come into the world faster than expected, leaving my father stuck to explain his whereabouts. Perhaps the lifelong tendencies towards procrastination that now frustrate my wife were counterbalanced, on my first journey into the world, by desire to confound a know-it-all doctor. Whatever the case, I crossed the boundary into this world by 7:05 p.m. that September 8th. As my brother Harry, wherever he is today, would have to agree, the rest was for chance or the stars to determine.

To say one cannot predict where life will take us doesn't mean we don't try to steer the car, pick-up truck, or donkey cart we find ourselves in at any time. Society places some at the wheel or reins, of course, and others in roles of passengers or back-seat drivers. My mother, a pianist, had graduated from the Yale Music School in 1939, then promptly gave up her career to marry my father and move from New England to his small western Pennsylvania hometown. We children of that generation of women who had earned the right to an education, but not the right to use it, became the vessels into which those mothers poured all their ambitions and frustrations.

Aunt Manila (my grandmother Gertrude's sister) had given my brother "Stevie" a book containing the illustrated score for a song. My mother would sit on the piano bench, Steve and I on each side of her, prop that book up in front of her and play "Would You Like to Swing on a Star?" The song suggested we had opportunities to "carry moonbeams home in a jar, and be better off than we are …"

The illustrated alternatives to "swinging on a star" were to be a stubborn mule out of school, a fat dirty pig who doesn't care a fig, a jailbird fish who can't write his name or read a book, a cacophonous crow who can't sing a note, or one of the many monkeys outside the zoo ("every day you meet quite a few").

Of course, I wanted to sit beside my mother on a swing, and swing on a star, carry home moonbeams that appeared to turn into jelly beans in a jar, and be better off than I are …

"We say 'I am'" my mother would correct my grammar, "and 'you are.'" I didn't know at the time that we were being prepared for the College Board exams and the results that in another 15 years would get first my brother and then me admitted to Yale.

In addition to "swinging on a star," we were preparing to pull a train that would carry gifts to all the little girls and boys on the other side of a mountain. My mother was training us to be like "The Little Engine that Could." All I had to do was huff like the steam engines that still pulled the trains of those days, and click like the sound of steel wheels on the rails of the train we took each year to visit my mother's relatives in Worcester, Massachusetts. "I think I can, I think I can..." was the sound those old-fashioned trains made.

Fifty and more years later, working for UNICEF, up until midnight to meet a deadline for an emergency funding proposal, or awake early, before four, writing a children's book to inculcate resilience in Swazi orphans, the rhythm of that "I think I can" train would still be clicking away in my head.

I still hear it clicking on a September morning as I begin this memoir, the day the Beatles' line "when I'm 64" transforms for me from future to present tense. I tap at my keyboard to that earlier contrapuntal rhythm from my childhood, "I think I can," chipping away at the massive block of time and memory that the life I've lived has left behind in me, like a sculptor sitting before a massive block of marble, chisel in his fingers, trying to extract semblance of life from stone.

Dining with Haji Qadir[*]

By May of 1994 life in Jalalabad had settled down enough for us to hold a weeklong workshop there. We were training health workers for the eastern provinces on the new, regional-based health care framework and immunization strategy that I and the European Commission's representative in Peshawar had helped the Afghan factions develop over the previous three months.

The technical aspects that our workshop covered were straightforward, the politics more complex. We were bringing together professionals from the urban-based government health ministry structures left over from Communist rule with the Mujahideen affiliated "cross-border" vaccination teams. Western donors had been bankrolling those teams since 1987 to travel monthly from Peshawar to rural areas within Afghanistan. The latter groups were themselves now split into factions that mirrored the civil war that broke out among the Mujahideen after the fall of the Communist government in 1992.

The Minister of Health in the deeply split national government was a member of one of the neutral factions, and traveled from Kabul to open the workshop and launch the new health framework and vaccination strategy. We flew in vaccination program managers from other regions to learn from the experiences.

It was an emotional event for many of the Afghans, for it was the first opportunity in more than two years for public health professionals to meet with their friends and colleagues from other regions. They hoped it would prove a harbinger of better times.

The self-appointed governor of the Eastern Region and head of the Nangahar Shoura, Haji Abdul Qadir, understood the political significance of this gathering, and organized a formal dinner for the guests at the governor's residence.

---

[*] Excerpt from Alan Brody's longer memoir about his 1993-95 work in Afghanistan, entitled "Afghanistan Revisited: The Certainty of Continuing Uncertainty."

I had been hearing stories about Haji Qadir, a mysterious man with a smoothly bald head, ever since my arrival in Peshawar 14 months before to serve as UNICEF Afghanistan's planning officer and deputy head of office. The U.N. coordination and security personnel found Haji Qadir difficult to pin down. He had a habit of disappearing from Jalalabad for long periods, especially when security circumstances in the province got complicated and they most needed to see him. It was rumored that he had cancer and that these long absences were for trips to Pakistan for chemotherapy.

Haji Qadir was conveniently away on one of those rumored trips in May, 1993 when unknown attackers ambushed and killed Commander Shamali, his chief rival for power in the Jalalabad Shoura. As I heard it, the attackers in a matter of less than two hours killed the whole party traveling with Shamali as well his brothers and cousins scattered in their homes and businesses around Nangahar, about 40 persons in all. Whoever was responsible, that nearly clean sweep of an entire family did reduce risks of revenge killings, at least until a new generation of small children from the Shamali clan would have time to grow up.

Haji Qadir remained away from Jalalabad for some time after that slaughter, amidst rumors of his death from cancer. Factions jockeying to fill the power vacuum brought the Nangahar Province Shoura perilously close to political disintegration and outbreak of a civil war in the entire eastern region that Haji Qadir had dominated. Then Qadir suddenly reappeared, miraculously robust again, his presence pulling the province and the region back from the brink. The killings of members of the Shamali clan were forgotten, for the time being at least, and Haji Qadir assumed undisputed leadership of the Nangahar Shoura.

I had not been to the governor's residence before. As we came through the gate, we drove up a paved driveway lined with stately palms, leading to a series of low, whitewashed buildings. The whole place seemed clean, swept, watered and green, a haven from the streets of the dry, dirty city of Jalalabad outside, where roads were potholed, buildings pocked with bullet holes, men's dusty faces lined with struggle, and the few women in public places moved about furtively, covered toe to head in black burkhas, even their eyes shrouded by netting.

The governor's dinner party was largely an Afghan affair, with the Minister of Health from Kabul as guest of honor. We were about 14 present, including some prominent Nangahar citizens, the guests from the other regions, a Somali colleague from the World Health Organization, and I the only non-Muslim. We were all men, of course.

The "table" was laid on a cloth spread over carpets that covered the floor of the dining room. We sat cross-legged around it, snacking on nuts and dates with sweetened tea. An Afghan doctor working with the UNICEF Jalalabad office sat near me, translating when I was addressed. Otherwise, most of the conversation went by me.

Young men brought in the main courses and laid them on the cloth, trays of grilled lamb and chicken kebabs, accompanied by large serving dishes of steaming Afghan rice mixed with raisins and fried lamb, spiced with pine nuts and cardamon seeds—delicious! We were served by the governor himself, Haji Qadir in his Afghan robes, his bald head shining with a look of remarkable health. He would get up, pick up a serving plate and come round to each of his guests, insisting we must each have more, and kneeling beside us to serve, he the consummate host, acting out the egalitarian traditions of his people's hospitality.

I marveled at this brief taste of Afghanistan as it must have been before it fell into 15 years of continuous war. How much had been lost!

Not long afterwards, Haji Qadir would host a gathering of leaders of the warring factions from around the country. Perhaps the guests at the dinner party I attended that evening reported back to their respective regional warlords about the excellent food, and these reports softened up these commanders to accept invitations for a Jalalabad jirga. Once gathered, however, old disputes reemerged, and we heard that some leaders were threatening to walk out. At that point, hundreds of Jalalabad women widowed by the jihad against the Soviets appeared in their black burkhas at the governor's palace and blocked its exits. They would not allow any leader to leave, they said, until all had signed a peace agreement.

Haji Qadir's bodyguards were backing up the women, of course, but that was never mentioned. For another man to force them into agreement would have besmirched the Afghan honor of these powerful men. To compromise in deference to widows of the jihad, on the other hand, would perhaps find praise in the eyes of Allah. Under such duress, the leaders came to an agreement, and for a few months the fighting stopped, at least until the July 1994 appearance of the Taliban in Kandahar initiated a new phase of war.

Haji Qadir held on to his position until 1996, struggling to juggle new challenges as the Pakistan-bankrolled Taliban movement and an increasing presence of Arab visitors destabilized the region. Eventually he fled to Pakistan, but influential men there did not appreciate his conspiracies. He went on to Dubai to look after business interests, and later joined with Ahmad Shah Masood in the Northern Alliance. He would reemerge after 9/11, when American air power helped that Northern Alliance to dislodge the Taliban from Kabul, and Haji Qadir reappeared in Jalalabad in late 2001 to take the reins of power there again.

Afghanistan's American-installed President Hamid Karzai would eventually make Haji Abdul Qadir a vice-president, taking him away from his powerful regional base to the capital Kabul. There, on unfamiliar ground, he would fall victim in July 2002 to another kind of cancer eating away at the soul of Afghanistan, the bullets of assassins.

On Revisiting My Wedding Photo

Almost 35 years ago, I and my wife made a journey to the City Council Chambers in Accra, Ghana to undergo a civil wedding ceremony. That act would legitimize our marriage in the eyes of the U.S. Government, which refused to recognize our existing marriage under African customary law and tradition. It would also make our nine-months-old son eligible for American citizenship, and thus entitle me to a dependent's allowance for him from my employer, the U.S. Peace Corps.

I use the word "undergo" because it reflects my then libertarian perspectives on society, government, and personal freedoms. What business had the State, I wondered, in matters of my relations with a spouse?

The $75 dependent's allowance would increase our monthly income by 75 percent, and keeping open my beloved son's future citizenship options also weighed in on the side of pragmatic compromise. My wife in her own way no doubt was providing her own subliminal encouragements for my going through with this civil marriage. She had already experienced the vagaries of African customary law in earlier arrangements that had placed her at age 18 in the position of number three wife and number one baby producer to an older man who could send her away at any time, merely by saying "I divorce thee" thrice, a choice he made 10 years and five births later.

And so on May 17, 1973, a rotund Accra City Council clerk in white shirt and a bow tie registered Francisca Mary Blay and Alan M Brody as duly wedded. A photographer with an old box camera encouraged us to memorialize the event by posing for a wedding picture on the front steps of the City Council building built in the British colonial days. And thus our images were fixed to this day in silver halide chemical reactions.

The skinny young man in that photo was 50 pounds lighter than the person I carry around today. He wears black plastic-framed glasses to match hair black and bushy and a moustache. He is wearing what the Ghanaians called a "political suit," a style made popular some years before by the African socialist leaders Kwame Nkrumah and Julius Nyerere, though elsewhere around the world it was known as a "Mao suit."

Perhaps with that mode of dress I hoped still to assert, in the face of such a bourgeois institution as marriage, the continuing fundamental disenchantment that had led me in the first place to refuse to serve society in the roles laid out for me. It had been two and a half years since I quit Harvard Business School for a life of voluntary poverty in Ghana, and for the intermittent epiphanies that personal freedom, risk, pursuit of integrity, and the existential purity of the Ghanaian smile inevitably would bring.

In the wedding picture, I am not looking into the camera. My head is turned to the left, looking at the woman beside me in her Ghanaian, full-length dress, and the handsome, almost regal, nine-month-old boy she cradles against her side in the crook of her left arm. I have taken out this photo recently as part of preparations for an Iowa summer writing workshop and its exercises in observation and memory. "Look beyond the subject," our teacher urges each of us, "look at the rest of your photo, look for something there you have never seen before …"

We are posing on cement steps in front of the City Council building, and directly behind us is the frame of an open door and wooden steps. The steps lead to the second floor offices where we just completed our ceremony and inscribed our names in the Register of Marriages. In the very center of the photograph, hanging from my wife's right forearm, is a sizeable purse, but I happen to know this is a mere fashion statement, and contains nothing. Beyond my child, to the far side and behind my wife's left elbow, is a pillar that must be part of a colonnade running along the front façade of the building, reflections of past delusions of colonial grandeur of the defunct British Empire.

And now I see in my wedding photo, never noticed before, that behind the pillar is an open doorway and in the darkened room within, barely visible, is the curved edge of a porcelain toilet bowl.

It is exactly the kind of little surprise that life used to bring me every day in Ghana. No doubt the City Council's official wedding photographer posed many of his clients on those steps, and it would never enter his mind to just shut the door. Why indeed would one bother? Few Ghanaians could afford such a sculptural touch in their own homes, and I suppose in his mind a porcelain toilet was a sufficiently "morden" object—like the oft-misspelled signs for a "Morden Bakery," and "Morden Hair Stylists"—to pass muster as a symbol that we had arrived.

The little boy in that photo is a father now, just turned 35 years old, with his own wife who has blessed him with smiles and gifts of love and two small children of his own. And in the comforting march of time, Francisca Mary and I, still together and more in love today than ever, have arrived after many journeys to a house near Iowa City, and the woods that surround it, and the company of wildlife that share the abundance about us, and four porcelain toilets.

Pat Davis

Pat Davis' memoirs are always poignant and frequently witty. Our writers group anticipates her trademark, the zinger conclusion. Pat writes about the everyday life experiences that come out of 53 years of marriage, four sons, two grandsons, and events both during and after college.

Small World

When I was accepted as a freshman at the Eastman School of Music to major in Music Education I knew I would have some catching up to do. But even after a couple of months there I knew I was way out of my league.

First of all I had graduated from a very small high school where there were few activities and little competition. Most of the kids at "the Eastmans," as we jokingly called it, were in the upper quadrant of their classes and were involved in many high school activities. It was going to be an uphill climb.

After a while I stopped climbing. I wanted out of there. I finally agreed with my parents I would stick it out for two years. So I did. I learned a lot and made some great friends but time was flying. I wasn't sure where I was going and talked often with a classmate who had also had enough.

One day, walking back to the dorm, we met up with Alice Tucker, a graduate student who was listening to our gripes and plans to leave. Our problem was where to go. She recommended her undergraduate school, Northwestern University in Evanston, Ill. She said it had a great music ed program and she was sure we would enjoy the different environment there. In particular, walking to classes in the morning we would not have to pass grungy bars where scary old drunks were already lined up to get in at 8 a.m.

It took some coaxing but my parents finally relented. Both my friend Gelene and I were accepted and we were delighted. It was a fantastic change. I was euphoric. Not only was the campus on the shore of Lake Michigan but Chicago was only an el ride away.

In the spring of my first year there I met an ex-Navy man who had returned from the Korean conflict and we began dating. His name was Tom Davis—that's the Tom Davis I've been with for 53 years now—and he had started his schooling at Northwestern but then left to join the Navy. He was following his father's advice that there were no foxholes in the Navy, and signing up before his name could be drawn to be drafted into the Army. He was returning now to start his sophomore year after his four-year absence.

One night we were sitting in a Howard Street bar getting to know each other better. He asked, "How did you choose Northwestern?" I told him my story.

He smiled and I wondered why he looked so smug. He finally said, "I used to date Alice Tucker." Small world.

Don't Register for Wedding China

Tom and I were college sweethearts at Northwestern University. Music majors taking some classes together, we became acquainted, started to date, fell in love, and ultimately became engaged.

When the preparations for the wedding began Tom's mother said, "Don't register for china." The story then came out that Tom had been engaged before he was called away to serve in the Navy (or "at War" as his mother always said). While stationed in Japan Tom had sent to his fiancée a complete set of china, with 12 place settings, of the finest Japanese dishes selected by a Japanese friend. At his mother's suggestion, he had sent her an identical set.

Tom's fiancée, named Ruth, won the Miss Wyoming title while he was away, and then fell in love with her manager. The "Dear Tom" letter reached him while he was still in Japan. The Japanese dishes were returned to Tom's family home and, sadly, arrived on Christmas morning. I always asked "What year was she Miss Wyoming?" but never got an answer.

No one in the family ever brought up the name Ruth. When we visited Casper (Tom's hometown) we never saw her. When we went back to Casper for Tom's 40th high school class reunion I asked, "Is Miss Wyoming going to be here?" Tom said no, she was in the class behind him. We arrived at the Casper Cattlemen's Club for the Friday night party and Tom was surrounded by old friends. This was his first attendance at a class reunion. I was approached by an attractive blond woman who asked, "Is Tom Davis here? I was told he was coming." I pointed to a group of people and said, "He's right over there." Then I went to the bar. It was Ruth, and (looking sad) Tom said he didn't recognize her. (Right.)

At any rate, as a newlywed-to-be I acquiesced to the suggestion of not registering for china, but when I finally saw the dishes I wished I had held out for my own. They were attractive but nothing I would have selected.

Yesterdays

We had to live with these dishes, kept special for holidays, etc. When Tom's parents passed away, we received the other 12 place settings. And I am talking about serious dishes now, like 24 each of dinner plates, salad plates, bread and butter plates, soup/cereal bowls, small sauce dishes, cups and saucers. For each of the serving dishes there were two of each including large platter, small platter, vegetable serving dish, covered vegetable dish, creamer, and sugar bowl. This collection filled all the cabinet space of any 1950s kitchen and still needed extra space. But practicality won out, and occasionally we did use them. They were very handy, whenever we were entertaining 24 people!

When we decided to move into a condominium I said, "I'm not taking those dishes." Our two married sons said they would like some of them. The oldest (Terry) said he could use eight place settings but they had space for no more. The next son, Tim, said 16 place settings would be great as his business required them to entertain larger groups. Terry's mother-in- law, who lived in Des Moines, was driving to Florida and volunteered to take Terry's service for eight to him. And, as luck would have it, my brother (Jack) was in the Midwest researching a book on monasteries, and volunteered to take Tim's dishes back to Buffalo, N.Y.

On the way back to Buffalo, Jack stopped at Gethsemane Monastery in Lexington, Kentucky, to meditate and to remember one of his life-long heroes, Thomas Merton. Merton had entered his religious life here at Gethsemane. After four days of meditation, Jack felt he should leave something there in the way of thanks, but had nothing with him to contribute. Suddenly, as he described it, he miraculously thought of the dishes and of Thomas Merton's international fame, and he proudly donated two of the dinner plates to the monastery.

When he told me about it I was speechless. When I finally could talk again I asked him, "How could you give away something that did not belong to you?"

"Don't you get it?" he replied, "Merton was international and the dishes are Japanese!" He was totally nonplused and insisted, against my protestations, that it was absolutely the right thing to do. "Besides," he rationalized, "I wasn't charging you freight for taking the dishes with me."

When son Tim found out about the missing dishes he was enraged. You would have to know Type A Tim to realize that this was going to be a problem. And it *was*. At least twice a month Tim brought up the damn dishes. No one can go on as long about the morality of something as Tim, particularly when he feels he has been wronged.

After several months (and many conversations with Tim) my brother's new book arrived, with its descriptions of monasteries where people could spend weekends or longer, seeking spiritual renewal. The first thing I did was to look up the monastery in Gethsemane, Kentucky. With address in hand, I began writing my letter. I told the Abbot/Retreat master of my brother's act and described the situation as "a blip on the family radar that would not go away."

About ten days later a large box arrived from UPS and in the box were the dishes. This was about a month before Christmas and I immediately knew what Tim's big surprise would be this year. Finally, some relief from the dish outrage! Included in the box was a letter from the Retreat master who was very gracious. In the text was a phrase "He must have gotten caught up in the moment, we do not use china dishes here in our rustic setting." But the line that I found most amusing was "just forgive and forget."

Forgive, probably. Forget? Never.

Don't Call in Sick

After college graduation I had to make some decisions. The first was where I was going to live. For the previous two years I had been in the Chicago area at Northwestern University and really loved the excitement of the city. I decided to stay on, and found a place to live, and my first job in a company called Star Employment. We would call companies to see if they needed personnel and then, for a fee, would try to match them up with our clients.

It could have been a very lucrative job but I hated it. So, I identified another job advertised at Star, interviewed for it, and got it. This new job was at the Toni Company, a division of The Gillette Company in the Merchandise Mart. Toni Home Permanents was fairly new on the market at that time and had become very popular. All my friends will remember the Toni Twins who were TV favorites for the product.

My boss was P. V. Elson. She was a great person and I enjoyed working for her. My job was in customer service. If a shipment was delayed or broken, or any of the other seemingly impossible but very probable things that happened to our products between our warehouse and their business, my job was to try to solve it. I talked to the customers personally and then would follow up with a letter to verify our agreement on the scope of the problem. I couldn't type at that time but in those days there was something wonderful called the typing pool. We would dictate our letters on a tape, send the tape to the typing pool, and the next day the letter was on my desk, ready to sign and mail.

One day a customer called and told me that some of our products had ruptured on the shelves of his drugstore. He was very upset because of the mess and also because the store had just been remodeled. I talked to P. V. about this customer and she told me to talk to "legal." Legal at that time was a couple of women attorneys (Teddy and Evelyn) who were noted for their brusque approach to everything. The only thing they said to me was, "Let us see the letter before you send it." I promised that I would.

My boss P. V. prided herself on her efficiency. She liked to keep things moving in her department, and if any fellow worker got behind or was ill, she would ask a co-worker to clean up their desk. And as fate would have it, I had called in sick on the day that the letter I had dictated for our unhappy drugstore owner was sent back to my desk from the typing pool. A co-worker assigned to my desk signed and mailed all of the correspondence at hand. Of course the "don't send" letter went out. Teddy and Eleanor were furious. The system had worked against us.

I was to be leaving the Company in a few weeks to get married and move to Iowa. I only had a short time to quietly avoid Teddy and Eleanor. I would peer through the door into the Company cafeteria, and if they were there I'd have to find my lunch somewhere else.

Our first Christmas in Iowa we got a card from P. V. Elson who wished us well and let me know that the owner of the drugstore was suing the company.

"Merry Christmas," she wrote.

Driving Practice and the J Handle

Boys love cars and love driving them, or so I always thought. When our oldest son, Terry, showed no interest in getting his learner's permit at age 14, I didn't push it. When he turned 15 I asked him when was he going to sign up for Driver's Education. "Not right away," he said.

I was puzzled, and a bit concerned. He needed to take the course at West High School to get a good discount for insurance purposes. He also needed to learn from a professional driving teacher. At the end of his junior year at West High School I said, "You need to sign up for driving class in the summer session." He said he didn't want to do that. I insisted.

This is when he told me that in order to learn to drive he would need to get some glasses as he couldn't see very far. I was shocked! I took him to the optometrist and sure enough, he needed glasses.

So he started wearing glasses and was delighted to point out what he could now see. Then the fun began. He went to class every day, but I had to go out later and practice with him. It was not a relaxing experience. He loved to drive down the center of the road. We spent hours over in Mosquito Flats, whose lanes provided a good practice area in those days when there were not so many homes in the neighborhood.

It was during those often-frightening trips that I discovered the "J Handle." When accompanying my student driver, I found myself gripping the handle located above the passenger right side window, quietly mumbling the words, "Oh Jesus!" more frequently than you're ever likely to hear them in church.

Terry passed his driver's test but didn't like to drive. I didn't like to ride with him, either. His wife still complains about his driving. Thankfully, the other boys went through their driver education rituals without any problems. I do remember spending a lot of time practicing with them, however, and not enjoying the ambiance of West

High School's parking lot. I often found myself using the J Handle when we were driving on city streets.

Last winter, when riding with my daughter-in-law Becky and her friend Kathy, the subject of teenage drivers came up. Kathy mentioned that her daughter was learning to drive and she was finding it rather stressful. I looked up over the passenger side window and said, "You don't have a Jesus handle!" They didn't know what I was talking about. I had to explain to them how when driving with an inexperienced driver I used to grab the handle above the door and whisper, "Oh Jesus."

I talked to the boys about this last year, and none of them ever heard this handle had this particular name. I suspect that's because none of them had yet had to ride with a teenage driver.

Last month my husband Tom got permission to drive again, post stroke. He first had to pass two tests administered by occupational therapists. The first test involved knowing the rules of the road and the ability to apply them. Also included were tests on depth perception and driving simulation. The second test involved actual driving. An occupational therapist from a company based in Des Moines came over and took him driving. They used her car because she had a brake on her side so she could exercise some control if necessary. They drove about 50 miles in this area including town and county roads. She passed him on the first try. The final decision remained with his doctor who gave him the go. It was pretty exciting. At last, after over a year, he could go it alone.

I must confess, however: the first time he took me for a ride to the grocery store I grabbed the J Handle and softly murmured, "Oh Jesus."

Blest Be the Tie that Binds

When our youngest son Dan and his fiancée Shana decided to get married they were living in Seattle, Washington. The wedding was to be held in Foxboro, Massachusetts to accommodate Shana's mother who is terrified of flying, and her 80-year-old grandfather who was not well enough to travel to the West Coast. The plan worked well for our family since Dan's brothers and their families were all on the East Coast.

My husband Tom and I went to Boston a few days early as we had never spent much time there. We had a wonderful three days of exploring and meeting up with Dan, Shana, and our son Marty. We then went off to Foxboro.

The wedding was held in a steak-house restaurant. On first glance we wondered why this particular place was chosen, but on further investigation, decided it would be fine. The restaurant had a private dining room in the rear of the building, and beyond that an outdoor patio with a lovely background made up of a high stone wall with a waterfall. This imposing wall completely blocked sounds of traffic from the busy surrounding streets.

My sister-in-law and I met with the wait staff, decided how to arrange the tables, and waited for the guests to arrive. The justice of the peace arrived in her robes and chatted with the groom for a few minutes to iron out some last-minute details.

One such detail was the groom's open collar. Our son Marty told us that Shana was supposed to bring Dan a tie for the ceremony, but she forgot. Marty looked around and determined that the restaurant manager's tie was the perfect match with Dan's suit, and he asked to borrow it.

It seems this didn't happen every day. "My daughter gave me this tie for Father's Day," he protested. But Marty had his way, managing to borrow the tie with promises to return it.

As part of the ceremony the couple exchanged vows that they had written for the occasion. Shana deviated from her script, however. "I'm sorry I forgot your tie," she said.

It was a lovely evening, with dinner and dancing and at the end of the evening the restaurant manager got back his necktie. For Shana and Dan, still together, that was the beginning, not the end of it.

"Blest be the tie that binds!"

Rest in Peace

About a year ago Tom and I began to seriously consider dying. I don't mean that we planned to end our lives together or anything like that. We just decided to call a local undertaker and discuss the motions of dying and what the family had to do.

Ken Holmes, a Certified Preplanner, came to call. Yes, I said "Certified Preplanner." Don't ask where he got the title. It came on the letterhead. Ken asked lots of questions about our obituaries, our past careers, and would we consider a plan to pay up front so that our boys would be free of the decisions that had to be made at the time of our separate exits from this world. The discussion took about an hour and was quite informative. He promised to follow up with a letter and he did. The problem is that I cannot find the letter. That's the sort of thing that makes us think we need a Certified Preplanner. I'm sure he would send a copy but at this time I'm going on my memory.

First of all, dying is expensive. If Tom paid up front and used all of the help provided by Lensing's Funeral Home he could die for about $7,000. That would be the price if he paid in full in the next few months. I could die cheaper because I could pay in installments (as I recall). So, my exit would cost about $6,000. This, of course, is if we were to be cremated. Exiting in a bronze/wooden casket would be much more costly. We talked about this information and ended up doing what we do very well. Nothing.

In the meantime I have been reading obituaries. They are really quite interesting. Some seem to glory in the end of the person's life and make statements like "The Lord came and took him to heaven." Or, "The Lord wrapped his arms around him (her) and took her peacefully away."

The phrase about the Lord wrapping his arms around grabs my interest. What do the Lord's hands look like? Does this depend on what the deceased worked at during his lifetime? Do they have that manicured look like those of a surgeon or a well-heeled attorney? Or, are the fingernails dotted with perpetual grease like an auto mechanic? Are the Lord's arms encased in a silk shirt with long white sleeves or (depending on the deceased) a denim work shirt? I'm not really thinking that the Lord would be wearing a tank top or a strapless shirt for a female but it could happen, particularly if the Lord was busy doing other things when it was time to wrap arms around someone.

One obituary left me feeling the surviving family was quite angry with the death of the dad. The obit said there would be no visitation or memorial. This left me with sad feelings about the deceased. Where could friends go to say goodbye?

I'm also amazed in the number of children, grandchildren, and sometimes great grandchildren, all named individually. What if someone were left out of the naming? Is this the reason some obits are run several times and called "corrected" obituaries? Last week I read an obit that included naming the family dog. Is this going too far?

The latest obit I read said "died peacefully in her sleep." To the casual observer this may be the case but perhaps things are not what they seem. A co-worker of mine awoke one morning to discover her mate of many years lying beside her stiff and cold. She mourned, "He was only 53 years old," but a snide voice said, "He lived 100 years, at least it felt like that…"

What may seem a quiet exit from our world could be taking place on the other side as a tug of war between Lucifer and Michael the Archangel making lists of good and bad behavior, fighting over where the spiritual remains would be sent. Could you envision a block of small bricks making a wall of nasty transgressions? And small pebbles dropping into a calm pool to verify good deeds?

A friend of mine has no belief in the afterlife. She maintains that when you're dead it's all black. That's all. I think that is too trivial. Most religions keep us hooked on bettering our lives to attain some measure of rewards. And we have all met those whose rewards on earth we would like to cut short, individuals who we maintain should "burn in hell."

I am writing my own obituary. All the facts and information will be correct and concise. I hope to have a short visitation so my remaining friends could come by and visit with the boys. There will be no memorial.

Rest in Peace.

Tom Davis

Thomas L. Davis' timely limericks were known to delight Rotarians weekly. That tradition is carried on in our writers group. We credit Tom's sense of meter and rhythm to his career as a professional musician and music professor. His performances delighted our community for nearly four decades. Tom founded the University Of Iowa Percussion Department, initiated the Jazz Studies Program, directed the Hawkeye Marching Band, and the Alumni Band.

Hail, Iowa City

Throughout my professional career I made every effort to meet deadlines and to be as organized as my abilities would allow. There is one incident, however, which is a glaring indication that I was not always as successful as I might have wished.

It was on a cold February evening in 1983 that I received a telephone call from the President of the Board of Directors of the Iowa City Community Band. He wished to know if I would be interested in being commissioned to compose a march to be used as a signature concert opener for the band. At first I was rather reluctant to accept this offer, as my compositional efforts had been largely in the areas of jazz tunes and percussion solo and ensemble works. After a few moments of conversation and a bit of thought, I agreed to accept this challenge. I had been in bands all my life and I was very familiar with the march form. "They're not asking me to write a symphony," I reasoned, "this will merely be a march." The board president informed me that the band would like to introduce the march on the concert scheduled for the 4th of July, 1983. When I hung up the phone I was so excited that I got out my manuscript paper and began working on an introduction. In ten minutes, I had it! The rhythm of the introduction went "Daa-Daa-Du-Dat-Daa, Daa-Daa-Du-Dat-Daa" and I had the title of the march: "Hail, Iowa City, Hail, Iowa City."

Before going further with the saga of the march, I wish to delve into the history and structure of the Iowa City Community Band. The band was formed in the early 1950s and was sponsored by the City of Iowa City and by the American Federation of Musicians. In those early years, the members were actually paid a small wage to rehearse and perform once a week and to play one concert a week for eight summer weeks. The most unusual aspect of this band is that it has never had a permanent conductor. Each week of its annual season is directed by a different conductor. Early in its history, the Board of

Directors developed a roster of conductors and to this day, the system is still in effect. The band members are no longer paid, the board members are all volunteers, and the conductors receive a small stipend for their efforts in selecting and rehearsing the music. I conducted my first concert with the band in July of 1959 when I was added to the roster of conductors. I suppose that it is this long association with the band that led to the offer of a commission to compose the march.

In addition to my regular teaching duties, in March of 1983 I took the U. of I. Percussion Ensemble on a concert and recruiting tour of Eastern Iowa schools. During spring break of 1983, my wife Pat and I went to Jamaica for a warm weather vacation. When spring break was over, my Jazz Department at the School of Music hosted the Iowa High School Jazz Championships. In late April two of my Doctor of Musical Arts candidates defended their essays. In May I presented a clinic for the Iowa Bandmasters Association entitled "How to Keep Your Percussion Section Organized." In June, I organized the percussion sections for the three concert bands, orchestra, and jazz bands of the University's All State Music Camp.

Obviously, time had been marching on. On Wednesday, June 30, 1983 Pat arrived home from a luncheon with her friend Marge, who had just attended a meeting of the Chamber of Commerce. Marge said to Pat, "It was announced at the Chamber meeting that Tom's march will be premiered at the Community Band's concert on Sunday. I'm looking forward to hearing it." In her own special way, Pat asked me, "What march?" In my own special way I thought, "Holy Sousa!"

On Thursday afternoon, July 1, I began writing the rest of the march. I kept the introduction I had written in February. The first and second strains went reasonably well, and then I got to the trio. (The trio is the part of the "Stars and Stripes Forever" that all Americans so dearly love.) "Hail, Iowa City" again reared its ugly head! "Daa-Daa-Du-Dat-Daa, Du-Daa-Du-Daa-Du-Daa." (Hail, Iowa City, our home so tried and true, Hail, Iowa City, our hats go off to you.) At that point the musician took over and the poet failed and there were no more lyrics.

By Friday noon, July 2, the march was complete. All of the parts for the individual instruments had to be extracted from the score and sent to Kinko's for reproduction. It was a very long evening.

The score and parts to the march were delivered on Saturday morning, July 3, in time for the rehearsal at 10:00 a.m. On Sunday, July 4, at 4:00 p.m., the march was introduced. Since I was unable to complete the lyrics to the trio, I gave up on "Hail, Iowa City" as a title and settled for "The Iowa City Community Band March." To this day, the band's announcer continues to chide me for my less than innovative title. In this he is relentless but nevertheless, I am thrilled to have been incited to contribute to and be a part of this remarkable community band. Hail, Iowa City!

Here is a closing limerick:

Here's what I've learned throughout the years
Meet that deadline when it appears
Do not delay
Do it today
That march is music to my ears.

Ode to the Lowly Limerick

When you read my memoirs you know sometimes my memoirs end with an appropriate limerick. The members of the Gray Hawk Writers Group know this as well. Webster defines a limerick as a kind of humorous verse of five lines of which lines 1, 2, and 5 rhyme with each other and lines 3 and 4, which are shorter, form a rhyming couplet. The limerick is named for a county in Ireland.

Webster does not mention anything about rhythm. Rhythm in a limerick is very important. Since my career was as a percussionist, I am fairly conversant with rhythm. Lines 1, 2, and 5 of a limerick not only must rhyme but also must have the same rhythm. Also lines 3 and 4 share the same rhythm.

My fascination with limericks started when I was in junior high school. They were easy for me to create. Back then my limericks were not meant for mixed company. In fact, in today's vernacular they were not politically correct. For reasons unknown to me my fascination with limericks took a 40-year hiatus.

In 1985, when I joined the Iowa City Noon Rotary Club, because of my profession I was assigned to the Music Committee. These Rotarians love to sing. The format for their Rotary Meeting goes somewhat like this: They open by singing two verses of "America" followed by the pledge of allegiance. Next comes introductions of visitors and guests, followed by announcements. Next comes a singing of a Rotary song followed by a 20 minute programmed guest speaker. The responsibilities of the Music Committee are to provide a song leader and a piano player to accompany the singing at each Rotary meeting.

When I joined that club, the chief song leader was in a habit of telling a joke or a shaggy dog story before he led the singing of the Rotary song. He was a great storyteller. He had the timing of Jack Benny and the delivery of Jay Leno. The Rotarians loved his stories. In a year or so of my membership, I was appointed assistant song leader so I would lead the singing in the Chief's absence. Now I cannot tell a joke as well as the Chief. He was a very hard act to follow. So I made up my mind not to tell jokes. Instead, I would make up a limerick. To keep them on their toes I would try to make my limerick current. Gradually I think they began to appreciate my limericks. Following are a few of my favorites.

> The word yoyo is spelled y-o-y-o
> In Cincinnati, Ohio
> The date today
> Is the fourth of May
> Tomorrow is Cinco de Mayo.

I wrote this one in the fall, during the football season on a Thursday. The previous Saturday Iowa played Wisconsin, the following Saturday they were to play Minnesota.

> Limousines are driven by chauffeurs
> Who often wear shiny black loafers
> If they persevere
> Maybe this year
> Our Hawkeyes will badger the Gophers.

This one I e-mailed in January from Florida to the Music Committee to read for me in my absence. (Sorry about the last line. I've been wanting to use that post card cliché for a long time.)

> I send you greetings of good cheer
> Florida's nice this time of year
> By word of mouth
> It's warm down south
> Having a great time, wish you were here.

One year 1 even held a limerick contest for Rotarians. I decided to give the first line of a limerick and they had to provide the other four lines. I gave them this first line in September.

I once saw the falls at Niagara …

I gave them until the first week of November to turn in their limericks. The prizewinner would be announced in the second week of November. The prize was a book by humorist Ogden Nash containing the world's most popular limericks. Surprisingly I got over 65 entries. I even entered one myself. I used the members of the Music Committee as my judging panel. I typed each entry on a 3x5 card and assigned it a number and removed the author's name so the entries would be anonymous. Most Rotarians are good rhymers, but they have no concept of good rhythm. Lo and behold, the Committee chose my entry to be the winner. This would never do! I should not win my own contest. So, I announced the winner to be the runner up. Now it can be revealed. Here is the true winner of the Iowa City Noon Rotary Club's Official Limerick Contest.

I once saw the falls at Niagara
While purchasing stock in Con Agra
If the market goes down
It won't cause me to frown
I simply will feed it Viagra.

The Hawkeye Marching Band
and the Peace Sign

When I came to the University of Iowa in the summer of 1958, my job description was Assistant Director of Bands and Instructor of Percussion Studies. As there were very few percussion students, the major portion of my time was spent in the band department. In the fall, of course, my time was spent almost entirely with the marching band during the football season. Having spent my collegiate years at Northwestern University, a perennial doormat of the Big Ten in football, I thought I had died and gone to heaven when Iowa went to the Rose Bowl at the end of my very first semester with the Hawkeyes.

During the 1950s and 60s, Big Ten marching bands were presenting half-time performances that consisted of precision drill routines, concert formations, formations that made a picture, and musical arrangements fitting a particular theme. For example, near the end of October, a band might do a Halloween show. The first drill routine could be to the tune of "That Old Black Magic," followed by a formation of a skeleton to the tune of "Dry Bones." (The arms and legs would move—we called that an "animated formation.") Such a show might conclude with a drill routine to the tune of "Bewitched, Bothered, and Bewildered."

By 1962 I had been promoted to Co-Director of the marching band and had learned quite a bit about crowd psychology. I learned that you cannot be subtle with a football crowd. If I called for the band to form a Xerox machine while playing "Someday My Prints Will Come," no one would get the pun. I learned that the football crowd wants to be entertained, not educated. If I wrote a concert arrangement of Bach's Toccata and Fugue in D Minor, it would be met with polite applause at best. If I wrote a concert arrangement of Bill Hailey's "Rock Around the Clock," I might get a standing ovation. One very interesting thing I learned about the crowd reaction to a half-time show was that if the football team was ahead at the half, the band got a better reaction than if the team was behind. That's show business for you.

In the spring of 1967, my Co-Director, Fred Ebbs, left Iowa to become Director of Bands at Indiana University. The University of Iowa then hired Frank Piersol as Director of Bands, and I was appointed Director of the Hawkeye Marching Band. In those years, Big Ten marching bands made only one trip to an away conference game each season. These trips were planned well in advance—usually a year or two out. Entirely by coincidence, Iowa's band trip for the 1967 season was scheduled for Indiana. As you can well imagine, I worked my tail off to build the best half-time show that I possibly could for the Indiana trip. After all, I was facing my former boss!

On game day in Bloomington, Ind., the Iowa band played first, as is the custom. We received a standing ovation. The Indiana band received polite applause. I was thrilled, the Iowa band was thrilled, and it was a very successful trip for us.

In the fall of 1968, the Indiana band was scheduled to make its only trip to Iowa City. Once again I would be facing my old boss. And again, I worked my tail off to build the best half-time show I possibly could. The Iowa band members were most enthusiastic about facing the Indiana band one more time.

Let's remember that the decade of the 1960s—and particularly the latter part of that decade—was a volatile time on college campuses. Opposition to the Vietnam war was the primary cause for this heated agitation. Oddly enough, several subtle changes occurred in Big Ten football stadia. During the pre-game band performances, members of the ROTC usually marched with rifles, accompanying the colors to midfield before the playing of the Star Spangled Banner. All at once the members of the ROTC carried no rifles. Those rifles would have represented the image of war. Soon after, the ROTC contingent no longer carried flags onto the field. Now, the American flag stood in the center of the top of the East stands during the playing of the national anthem. And finally the ROTC itself was nowhere to be seen.

Images of war were much too incendiary. The themes and content of marching band half-time shows were under careful scrutiny.

For the Iowa-Indiana game of 1968, I chose what I thought would be a very safe and innocent theme. The title of the show was *Tunes of the Times*. The opening drill was to the pop tune entitled "Goin' Out of My Head." The first formation was of a hot air balloon and the music was "Would You Like to Ride in My Beautiful Balloon?" by the Fifth Dimension. The last formation was to be the controversial Peace Sign.

I decided that I should run this Peace Sign idea past the "authorities." My boss had no problem with it, the Athletic Director had no problem with it, and my wife, Pat, had no problem with it. When I told her I thought I should ask the Head of University Relations, she said "Don't ask!" Dummy that I am, I asked—and the Head of University Relations said "No! No Peace Sign! No Way!" So instead, we made a formation of the Golden Gate Bridge and played and sang the Simon and Garfunkel tune "Bridge Over Troubled Water." It brought tears to my eyes, as they did it so beautifully.

On game day, Iowa was leading by a field goal at half-time. As was the custom, the visiting Indiana band performed first. I do not recall the exact title of its half-time show, but it was patriotic in nature. For the finale of their show, they marched out six American flags accompanied by ROTC members carrying rifles, made a formation of the Peace Sign and released six dozen doves to fly about the stadium. The Indiana band got a tremendous standing ovation and the Hawkeye Marching Band got polite applause.

Here is a closing limerick:

> Here's what I've come to understand
> Things don't always go as planned
> Go with your hunches
> Roll with the punches
> And do your best to beat the band.

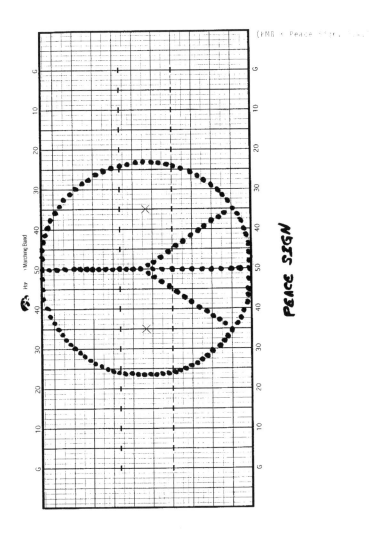

Tom Davis and the Peace Sign.

Joseph Dobrian

Joseph Dobrian is CEO of Dobrian, Frances, Bowie & Long, an editorial services firm with offices in New York City and Iowa City. He came of age in Iowa City, but lived most of his adult life in New York, where he built his practice. He writes about diverse subjects, including real estate, finance, fashion, and sports. He has acted off-Broadway, hosted a TV talk show, and was the Libertarian Party's candidate for Mayor of New York City in 2009. His by-line appears frequently in *The Wall Street Journal*, and he's published plays, poetry, and social commentary. His books include the novels *Willie Wilden* and *Ambitions*, and the essay collection *Seldom Right But Never In Doubt*.

Where's Mine?

Most children have to deal with being bullied or harassed, at least a little. But in elementary school in particular, in every class, there's going to be one kid who's at the very bottom of the pecking order: the one whom anyone can pick on who feels like indulging in a little cruelty for its own sake.

Know this; believe and understand this: *That kid is never blameless.*

The butt of the classroom won't be the crippled kid, the deformed kid, the mentally slow kid, or the kid who's the wrong ethnicity. Only the lowest of the low will harass someone for something he can't help, and such malefactors are usually disciplined or shunned by their peers. The butt of the classroom is a different animal.

There's always a reason why the butt of the classroom (it's usually a boy) gets picked on, and it's always something he could change. He might have a disagreeable personality. He might have an uncontrollable temper. He might have poor personal hygiene. He might be weak and ineffectual to a point where the other kids just lose patience with him. Whatever the reason, if he's the picked-on kid, it's going to be his own fault to some extent. We cannot deny this fact. It's critical that we face it.

During my years of elementary school, I was that kid. I still have nightmares about it. I was not just casually picked on in class. Invariably, four times a day, walking to or from school, I'd be accompanied by about half-a-dozen kids who'd torment me in various ways: usually just teasing or name-calling, but sometimes there'd be physical assaults as well. I remember being spat upon occasionally.

In my second-grade class, the most visually noticeable kid was a boy named John. All the boys wore jeans, including John, but John always had a clean, pressed, long-sleeved white shirt. He also wore polish in his hair, the way grown businessmen did in those days, and you sometimes saw older kids, high school kids, polishing their hair, but kids of seven or eight, no.

John carried himself in a slightly aristocratic way. He wasn't un-friendly, or stuck-up, but he was a little reserved, with a straighter posture than most kids, and maybe a more cultivated way of talking. I was not particularly friendly with John, but at least he never picked on me.

In the spring of my second grade, John's eighth birthday came up, and he invited all the boys in the class to his party. It was a typical Saturday afternoon kids' birthday party, but with this difference: At this party, quite a few of the boys thought to add to the fun they were having, by having a little fun with me. They'd surreptitiously punch me or poke me, or whisper little insults at me, and I can't remember the exact details, but they were bad enough that John's mother had to intervene a couple of times.

What was particularly painful was the knowledge that John's mother was being drawn away from the main business of administer-ing the party, in order to attend to this little subplot—and I blamed myself, and was deeply ashamed of myself, for two reasons.

First, I should not have been the boy who attracted this kind of attention. If I was, it was my own fault. It was due to some flaw in my-self—and I was sure that it was some flaw that I could have corrected if only I'd had the self-knowledge and the self-discipline to do it.

Second, why did I not take care of business? Why did I not turn myself into a dangerous person who could and would retaliate with devastating effect, if some other kid started with me? Why did I not learn how to just drive my fist into a kid's face so that his nose would come out the back of his skull?

I came home from that party feeling as low as I'd ever felt in my life up to then. And I'll repeat: my anger was not so much directed at the other boys. I understood that these were normal children. They were doing what boys their age will do.

It's *fun* to gang up on some other kid. It makes you feel like you're part of the community, and it's a way of reminding yourself, "At least

I'm not that kid." Ganging up on someone is an important part of life, at that age, and I suppose it always will be, as long as there are children.

Now let's fast-forward a couple of years. John didn't host a party in the third grade, as I recollect, but he did in fourth grade.

It's not like I was thinking about it, let alone looking forward to it. But one afternoon, in school—it was right after lunch, and the kids were coming into the classroom but the teacher hadn't called us to order yet—John in his white shirt and polished hair was going around the room, handing out small white envelopes. Obviously party invitations; there was no way they could have been anything else. John handed an envelope to every boy. Except one.

As he was sitting down at his desk, I leaned over and asked him, "Hey, John, where's mine?" I asked him again, a little louder, "Hey, John, where's mine?" There's no way he didn't hear me, but he didn't even look in my direction.

What was obvious to me, was the reason why I was being publicly shunned. Almost certainly, it was because he and/or his mother had decided that the party would be considerably less enjoyable if I were included.

That was my fault, and mine alone. I accept that. If I'd been John, or his mother, I'd have wanted to exclude me, too.

But what in God's name were they thinking? John was a bright kid, and his mother was a cultured, sophisticated woman. Did it simply not occur to them that it wouldn't be quite the thing, to physically hand out formal invitations to a party to every single boy in the classroom with the exception of one? Really?

If you want to exclude one kid from your party, there are ways. There are telephones. There's a perfectly good postal service. Failing both of those, you have a car and two good legs, and you can deliver the invitations to every boy's home. But, no. For some reason, no.

Ever since then—and almost 50 years have now passed—that incident has stuck with me. And still, if I ever wanted to take revenge on anyone, for any wrong or slight that I've suffered in life, John and his mother would be at the top of my list.

Unfortunately, I never will, because I don't know whom to blame for it.

For example, could the mother have been completely innocent? Could she have written out an invitation for me, which John then decided not to pass along?

Or might John have been innocent? Maybe his mother said to him, "Honey, we just can't invite that boy again; he'll ruin the party for everyone because the other kids will be picking on him."

I want to be fair. I would not want to punish an innocent party. And that is why this little incident—this trivial incident, which a saner and more decent person than myself would have forgotten about long ago—will never be avenged.

But I will always wonder: Did John feel any pang of conscience, when I asked him, "John, where's mine?" Or did he feel that I deserved to be snubbed, and snubbed publicly, and did he take pleasure from doing so? Or—what is probably the most likely—did he simply not think about it at all? Would he even remember it, today, if I were to see him and bring it to his attention?

He would probably just ask, "Gosh, why would you want to dwell on a thing like that?" And I daresay a lot of other people would ask the same question. I would be the bad guy, you see, for having carried this grievance around with me. And maybe I am.

Probably many other people have had a "Where's mine" experience, at some point in life. Perhaps one important step toward growing up is realizing that if you didn't get one, it's your own damn fault. Curing the fault, though: that's the killer.

County Fair, At Last

County fairs were just not the sort of thing my family was interested in, when I was growing up. We lived in a state that was practically a byword for agriculture, but we were academics: concerts, libraries, and museums were more our thing. It didn't occur to me until later in life that I should have insisted on at least one trip to the Johnson County (Iowa) fair, just to see what it was about. But in retrospect, maybe it's just as well to have experienced a county fair for the first time at age 53. When you're older—contrary to popular belief—you get more curious, not less, about this sort of event.

In particular, I'd like to go back next year to learn something about judging livestock. I don't have the first notion of what makes a rabbit, a hog, or a chicken a prize-winner, and I should at least have an idea, in case I'm ever called upon to feign intelligence of the subject. This time, I was only able to wander and observe.

Evidently, many of the livestock exhibitors at the fair were young folks, members of various 4-H or FFA chapters. I'm afraid that until I saw them tending their beasts, at this fair, I'd had the idea that raising livestock must be pretty uncomplicated work, and not very interesting, but these kids seemed just as proud of their accomplishments as any football player or bandsman or debater, and no wonder. And I saw a couple of them in tears when their animals were eliminated from competition.

The poultry might have been the most interesting of all the livestock exhibits, if only there'd been someone there to educate me about the various birds, because I know nothing whatever about chicken-farming and couldn't begin to explain why some people might raise one breed of bird, and some another. It was in the poultry shed that I got a sample of the kind of people you deal with around these parts. I could identify the more common types of hen—the Rhode Island Reds, the various Plymouth Rocks, and so on—but I was especially interested in a pair of brown speckled chickens with black tail-feathers and no combs. They had much larger and stronger-looking feet than most chickens, and they looked almost like birds of prey. I asked a fellow standing nearby if he could identify the breed, and he admitted he couldn't—"But I know the owner." And then he absolutely called the owner on his cell phone, to ask what sort of chicken we were looking at.

The owner didn't know, either. He said we'd have to ask the breeder when he showed up, later in the day.

Pigs, apparently, live a pig's life. Those that I observed at the fair were crowded together, three or four to a stall, covered with flies, and while almost all of them were peacefully asleep, sometimes one lying across another, they didn't look very comfortable. It appeared that they knew they were in hot, cramped, and stinky circumstances, and had decided that the best way to survive the experience would be to sleep through as much of it as they could. I've been told that swine are much more intelligent than they look, and this was evidence of the truth of that generalization.

Cows don't interest me much, although I've been told they're harmless and easy to work with. Up close, until this visit to the fair, I'd only ever seen the more common breeds: Angus, Guernsey, Jersey, none of which run to any exceptional size. This was my first exposure to the Brown Swiss, and until I stood next to one I had no idea that any cows that big existed. They look almost like fabulous creatures, or something a cave-man might have hunted. However, the Brown Swiss are not for eating: They're dairy cattle, and their milk is particularly suited to cheese, so I'm told. They're also supposed to be exceptionally docile, but stubborn. If I were that big, I'd be inclined to stubbornness too—just because I could get away with it.

Goats are among the most sociable of animals, and they'll often show their friendly intentions by butting you gently on the leg. They seem to enjoy being petted like a dog or cat, and they'll sniff your hand as a dog will—but then they'll want to chew on you. Contrary to myth, goats won't eat everything, but they'll certainly test their teeth on just about anything. Being chewed by a goat doesn't hurt. Their teeth aren't sharp enough, and they're never really earnest in their efforts. Goats are pretty easy-going, and some people think their milk is more healthful than a cow's; I'm surprised that more people don't keep them as pets. As it is, they appear to have it pretty easy: just hanging out and getting shorn every now and then.

Horses are not as uniformly friendly as goats, but they always arouse my sympathies because most of them are dumber than bricks and probably don't understand that their entire purpose in life is to be hassled by humans—so if they're not friendly, it's no wonder. I generally get along with horses, even those from whom I've been warned not to expect any affability. What a lot of people do wrong is to stroke the horse's nose. Some horses tolerate this—no doubt they've resigned themselves to the fact that it's just something humans do—but almost no horse likes it. Would you like to have your nose stroked? I am pretty sure that the main reason why I get along with most horses is that I stroke them on the neck, which they seem to enjoy, and I don't let my hands get near their muzzles unless I'm offering food.

Speaking of food, I wonder: Are prize animals kept alive, to compete at future fairs and to reproduce? Are the also-rans killed for food? Might I meet one of them at next year's fair, in the form of a Maid-Rite?

On J.D. Salinger

I never fully "got" J.D. Salinger, at least not to the point of according him the near-worship he inspired in some readers. Mainly, I'm just curious to find out what he's written in the nearly 50 years since he last wrote for publication.

It's highly unlikely that we'll see much of what he wrote. Conceivably, we won't see any of it. I can't imagine that Salinger repeated Mark Twain's mistake of failing to tell his executors which of his unpublished works, if any, were to be published, which kept back, and which destroyed. Mrs. Salinger, or whoever his literary executor might be, has probably been given absolutely pellucid instructions.

My prediction is that if there's any more Salinger to be published, it'll disappoint most readers. Probably a few people with a fanatical interest in the Glass family exist, and probably they can't wait to read whatever else Salinger wrote about that crew. I have a feeling, though, that once he'd exhausted his own interest in the Glasses (if indeed he ever did), he invented another large, peculiar family, and started writing novels and short stories about them. These, if they're published, will probably prove pale imitations of the Glass chronicles. They might be odder in style, crankier—but no more insightful or better-written.

Of course I hope I'm proven wrong. And I hope Salinger's instructions were not to destroy his entire unpublished *œuvre*. I never considered him a great writer, but certainly he was a very good one: interesting, intricate, and sometimes amazingly clever.

Unlike most Americans who read *The Catcher In The Rye*, I wasn't under 25 when I did so. I was 42. I'd made a point of not reading it, as a youngster, simply because everyone else was reading it. When I finally gave in, I wondered what the fuss was about. The book's style wasn't exceptionally good; I didn't find the protagonist very sympathetic; neither the action nor his thoughts told me anything I didn't know or explained anything that might have been puzzling me.

Possibly *Catcher* is considered a great book because so many readers read it when young: when they had not already read so many poor imitations of Salinger's style in high school and college writing classes. More importantly, they read it at an age when the book could reveal to them for the first time that other people had the same doubts, anxieties, and contemptuous views of adult society that they had. At 42, I'd already figured that out, and I'd encountered a lot of Salinger wannabees. I was no longer susceptible to astonishment by that book.

But if *Catcher* is overrated—and many people insist it isn't—Salinger still wrote other, better fiction. *Franny & Zooey* is considerably more complex and witty. Several of the *Nine Stories* are successful, to my mind, because they are about nothing. Others are successful because what they're about doesn't become apparent until the end. Most of them involve characters who are self-destructive, or self-hating, or just very insecure, and that makes for especially interesting reading when you're in your teens.

My favorite of the nine is "Uncle Wiggily In Connecticut," which was my first exposure to Salinger (I was 15 when I read it), and probably the most "adult" story in the book. It's probably the most straightforward of the nine, and the most classically constructed. It's plain to the reader, all the way through, what is happening with the several characters, and the protagonist's plight is particularly obvious: so much so that it's impossible to entirely dislike this character who, by most people's lights, should be eminently dislikable. Salinger uses the entire story to set up the last line—and when it comes, it takes the wind out of you like a perfect punch in the pit of the stomach.

Now that Salinger is dead, no doubt more people who have known him—or claim to have known him—will come forth with hair-curling revelations about his private life. Many of his little quirks—and his manipulative, sometimes almost sociopathic, behavior—are already well known. But I suspect we've only scratched the surface. Now unconstrained by libel laws (you can't libel the dead), horror stories will run wild and free. Old grudges will be brought out; those already revealed will be embellished. However, not too many people will care. Salinger's fans will dismiss the stories as jealous sniping, or, if they believe the stories, will immediately forgive the sins they expose. And nobody else will give a damn.

Joseph Dobrian

Boasting About Not Watching TV

My TV is almost never on. A couple of times a week I'll watch the news for 15 minutes while I have lunch, and that's about it. I'm just too busy to have the TV on. This makes me uncomfortable, because if there's one sort of person I don't want to be accused of being, it's the supercilious twit who asserts, "I never watch TV..." and then proves himself a liar by adding, "...but I just happened to see..."

What: not watching TV is a sign of coolness in the minds of such people? They think not watching TV will win them the Croix de Yuppie Scum, with oak leaf clusters?

Well, yes, that is what they think. This is a manifestation of an undying and unthinking tendency of mankind to blame the medium or the technology for any result that it produces that strikes a person as unsatisfactory. In this case, because quite a lot of unedifying or frivolous programming is available on TV, the machine is best not turned on at all, unless one takes it into one's head to "accidentally" watch something.

This sort of reasoning is similar to that used by people who assert that a complete ban on private ownership of guns will reduce crime—ignoring the undoubted usefulness of guns when not employed for nefarious purposes, as well as the statistics that suggest their beliefs are mistaken. In their minds, it's the technology itself that kills (in the case of guns), or turns the brain to mush (in the case of TV), and therefore the technology is undesirable by definition.

Granted, I've never heard anyone advocate a ban on TV ownership, but I certainly have heard people say that TV programming not considered sufficiently high-minded should be forbidden by law, or at least be shamed off the airwaves by an outraged public. I've also heard many people say that TV news, or politically oriented programming, should be tightly controlled to ensure that no "propaganda" is inflicted on the public—who presumably are too weak or stupid to resist the blandishments of those with whom the pro-censorship people might disagree.

There always seem, too, to be plenty of people who are eager to tell you what you *should* be interested in, instead of what's actually capturing your attention. People of that sort are to be found at all points of the political and cultural spectra (although people of the lower socioeconomic strata seem to be more tolerant of other people's tastes), and history would seem to know no era in which this sort of behavior wasn't current. Old people seem particularly inclined to complain about too much being made of people or events that they deem unimportant.

It wasn't like that in their day, nosiree: Can you imagine so many people becoming so fascinated with the death of Michael Jackson, for instance, if it had happened a couple of generations ago? Hell, why is anyone paying *any* attention to a guy like that, when there are wars, diplomatic crises, economic meltdowns, the environment, thieving Republicans, thieving Democrats, and all kinds of other much more important stuff on which we should focus?

Sorry: Rudolph Valentino and Marilyn Monroe got just as much attention when they kicked the bucket.

Very rare is the person who can resist telling you what *ought* to be interesting to you. Those who self-consciously don't watch TV often select their books (at least, those they read in public, or admit to reading) with a view to what other people will think of their selection. They choose their movies similarly. (For some reason, movies in general are placed on a much higher intellectual plane than TV shows, although there was a time not very long ago when movies were regarded with utter contempt in comparison to books.)

I used to buy this conventional wisdom, myself: looking down on those who discussed the story line of *Dallas* in public, for instance, when they could have been discussing epistemology. But you have to wonder who does more harm: those who take such puerile pleasures, or those who feel superior because they don't?

Who is to say whether it redounds more to your personal well-being to watch a soap opera than to read a book about foreign affairs?

Which person—the soap opera watcher or the high-minded book reader—is the happier? Which is the more likely to be inspired to meddle in the affairs of his fellow man and thereby (more usually) simply annoy us?

Should I condemn people who watch a lot of TV or who care about Michael Jackson? Not I! They allow me to go about my intellectually superior business, offering me no more censoriousness than perhaps a brief (amused) roll of the eyes. Would that we *élite* could grant them the same consideration! And would that all of us—patrician, plebeian, and helot alike—could get over the damn fool notion of blaming the product for the way some folks use it.

Where's the Conflict?

I got into a discussion the other day with a fellow editorial consultant about the importance of conflict in fiction, in novels particularly. Her position was that conflict pretty much had to be a matter of A wants B, but C stands in his way. If you don't have that, she suggested, you won't have a marketable novel. My own opinion was that plenty of good novels—classic novels, at any rate—have been written without that model of conflict. She countered, "Perhaps so, but they would not have been published today."

I then asked her whether she thought that that particular model of conflict were also necessary in a short story, and she replied that it was even more vital to the success of a short story than to the success of a novel. I disagreed, asserting that I'd read and admired many short stories that had very little actual conflict, or that at any rate relied less on conflict than on tension. Some very successful short stories rely merely on Angst. She replied, again, that while such stories might exist, they would probably not have seen the light of day if they'd been written in recent years.

She knows a lot more about the publishing industry than I do. But let's look back a few centuries. *Don Quixote*, generally regarded as the first long work of prose fiction (and thus the first real novel) written in any language, does not contain that sort of conflict. Don Quixote wants something, all right, but what's standing in his way is the fact that what he wants is nonexistent and unattainable. The story, it appears to me, is about perseverance in a delusion.

Consider Mark Twain's two best-known novels: *The Adventures of Tom Sawyer* and *The Adventures of Huckleberry Finn*. "Huck" does employ the standard conflict formula. But "Tom" doesn't. Tom Sawyer has no single great goal. He's scattered. The book is episodic; often he has no adversary other than his own foolishness; at other times he merely observes; there are a couple of chapters that just show him passing the time. Maybe that's why his adventures are less well remembered than Huck Finn's—and yet it was the success of "Tom" that allowed Twain to write "Huck."

Consider James Joyce's two supposed masterpieces: *Ulysses* and *Finnegan's Wake*. A lot of people claim to have read *Ulysses*. I've tried to, many and many a time. From what I can gather of it, the story is about Leopold Bloom's journey through one day of his life (and the actions of a great many supporting characters)—and the story is much more about the journey than about the quest (if any).

As for *Finnegan's Wake*, I simply refuse to believe that anyone has ever read enough of it to summarize it accurately. Those who write about it in their Ph.D. theses, I'm convinced, only get away with it because their professors can't verify anything that's written about it!

If indeed those two books are great novels, their greatness must be based on style and composition, rather than conflict. *Gone With The Wind*, written at about the same time as *Finnegan's Wake*, has certainly been read and loved by a great many more people. *Gone With The Wind* is nothing but conflict—written in a style that's easy to read but not what most people would call high art.

Which of those two is the better novel? Depends on your criteria and your taste. Which one of those two would stand a better chance of publication today? The answer to that would appear to prove my adversary's point with regard to the novel.

But what about short fiction? What, indeed, about James Joyce's short fiction? Consider what's probably his most famous short story, "The Dead." It contains a few minor conflicts but no overarching idea of A wants B and must overcome C. The resolution of the story is neither the success nor the failure of the protagonist, but a melancholy epiphany that's far more powerful than mere melodrama could have been.

"Quality," written by John Galsworthy at nearly the same time, doesn't contain much conflict. It's about a man who loves his work so much that it kills him—and it's clear that the man would not have had it any other way. The conflict is Man vs. Progress—and the outcome of that struggle is never in doubt.

My own all-time favorite short story is "Mr. Know-All," by Somerset Maugham. It has conflict aplenty, but not of the formulaic kind. What makes it a great story is the surprise at the end, when an obnoxious braggart proves that he can be a gentleman after all, when he protects a lady's reputation at the expense of his own.

Even some of Edgar Allan Poe's short stories are devoid of conflict. "The Masque of the Red Death" is a fable, famous more for the word-pictures the author paints than for the story itself. "The Cask of Amontillado" fascinates because of the horror described—not because there's any doubt of what's going to happen to Fortunato. "Ligeia" also gives the reader the creepy-crawlies with its style and imagery (some readers suspect that the story was intended as satire)—but there's no conflict to it.

Yet those stories, and others equally low on conflict, are still read and enjoyed today. Would they be read, let alone appreciated, if they were written today and submitted to a literary journal by an author with no great reputation? Or would he be told, "Take another pass at it, and put more conflict into it"? I've no idea.

Marilyn Holland

On the day Marilyn Harris Holland retired her son told her, "I remember you said you wished your mother and grandmothers had left you written memories of their lives. OK, Mom, now that you are retired it's your chance to do that for your granddaughters." This inspired Marilyn to write stories about her family and friends, about working abroad, world travel and, to the delight of our memoir group, everyday happenings with an historical perspective.

Cars I Have Known

From the time I was two years old until I was a senior in high school my family did not own a car.

It was an economic thing. With one child born in the late 1920s, three in the 1930s, another in the early 1940s, and as a single-income home, our family never had enough money to buy and maintain a car. Thinking about this now, I am amazed to realize that I never missed my parents' not having a car. For the first seven years of my life we lived in North Liberty, a small town where we could walk everywhere we went. For my father's commute to his job in Iowa City, and when we wanted to shop there, we had the CRANDIC Interurban Rail, which ran very frequently between the two places. After we moved to Iowa City we kids went places the way every other kid did: riding bikes or roller-skating. There was also the Iowa City bus service, which stopped less than a quarter of a block from our house and ran every 15 minutes, seven days a week, from five in the morning until midnight.

With a family of five children we didn't take vacations. Our idea of a great holiday was to have Dad stay home every day for his week off each year. When we wanted to visit relatives in Des Moines the Rock Island train would get us there in two hours, or my Grandpa and Grandma Swanson would take us in their car for a Sunday round trip. In the 1930s they had a Model A Ford (I'm not sure what year it was made). They would pick us up at 5 a.m. and all seven of us would ride comfortably. The front seat held Grandpa, Dad, and my older brother, Jack. The back seat was for Grandma, Mother, and the baby, Donna. Two small wooden chairs were placed sideways behind the front seat, and my brother Paul and I would ride on those.

Grandpa always kept his car immaculate so there were no liquid or sticky treats allowed. The top speed was about 30 miles an hour, so it was a four-hour trip. When we were on our way to Des Moines there was lots of talking and singing but the trip home was always very quiet, and we kids usually fell asleep.

When I started dating in high school, nearly all the boys had access to their parents' car. The exception was Terry McGee but he and I always enjoyed walking so it was no problem. One of my girlfriends lived outside Iowa City and had to have a car to drive to school. Her parents would only buy enough gas each week for her to get to and from school, and by Friday night her tank was always nearly empty. I remember many evenings when she would pick up three friends who would each chip in a dime to buy a gallon or two of gasoline for the evening's "riding around." That usually involved going to a high school sporting event or a movie followed by a stop at the Loughery's Drive-in on the Coralville Strip or the Root Beer Mug on Riverside Drive.

Another car I remember which gave us lots of fun belonged to my friend Don Minor. It was a 1919 Model T Ford touring car complete with side flaps for windows. The car had no fuel pump so gravity had to carry the gas from the fuel tank in the back to the engine in the front. The car never had more than a few gallons in it and to get up any steep incline we had to back up the hill so the gas would feed into the engine. That approach was not a common sight and we got lots of laughs on our Sunday afternoon rides when we would start up a hill, stall, coast back down, turn around, and back up the hill. There was always a cheer from the car occupants when we made it to the top.

When my brother Jack was a senior in high school he bought a 1928 Model A Ford. I think it must have been stored in a rat-infested barn for a long time since all the upholstery inside was destroyed. He thought the car was a real find and proceeded to reupholster the whole inside with brightly colored, striped awning fabric which was the cheapest cloth he could find. The Sunday afternoon that he finished the job we drove around Iowa City with the car's doors open to share its beauty with everyone else.

When I was a senior in high school I dated a boy who had a coupe with a rumble seat. We double dated a lot but I always regretted that Bob had to drive so I never got to ride in that rumble seat. Whoever was going with us would ride back there regardless of the weather. There was a tarpaulin and a heavy blanket on the floor of the rumble seat to be used by the riders to protect themselves from the weather if needed.

After graduating from high school and the university I moved to Des Moines to work. I had a place to stay near downtown where I worked, and when I came home to Iowa City once a month for a weekend, the Rock Island train was so convenient that it did not even cross my mind that I might like to have a car.

When I met Phil a year later he was in college and didn't have his own vehicle but had access to his parents' car and pick-up truck. Just before we were married he bought a 1947 gray Chevy coupe that had a very shallow back seat. It was all the space we needed. The seating arrangement came in very handy when he broke his leg six months after we were married and for over a year he had to wear a long leg cast on his six-foot-seven-inch frame. There was no room for him to get his leg in the front seat so a friend of ours removed the back of the front passenger seat. Phil sat in the back with his leg propped up on the front seat while I chauffeured him around Des Moines.

I remember the first brand new car that we bought, a 1956 black Ford four-door sedan. It had no chrome on it and absolutely no extras that might run up the price. At that time Phil was a traveling salesman and covered four states. Although he was on the road Monday through Friday, he never complained that he didn't even have a radio for entertainment or any air conditioning. He drove so much that in 1958 we had to buy another new car, and this time he did opt for the luxury of a radio.

In 1978 our daughter Janet began driving and we decided it was time to become a three-car family so she could shuttle herself and our son Jay to their multiple after-school activities. Phil found a 1962

Plymouth Valiant owned by an older lady who had driven it only 8,000 miles. She had never taken it out in the rain or snow and (according to her) only drove it to the doctor, the grocery store, and church. She said she wanted to sell it because her best friend had had an accident with her own car and the police had confiscated it and wouldn't give it back. We translated that to mean that her children wanted her to stop driving and when her friend had the accident, they used the police as the ruse to get her car away from her. Perhaps she felt that selling the car seemed a more honorable end to her driving days.

The Valiant was the perfect car for our kids. It had that Chrysler Corporation push-button transmission of the period, never seen before or since, and they loved to show that off to all their friends. It was light green and had a forward sloping hood that ended in a round chrome grill. Janet and Jay named it THE FISH. We did call to the kids' attention that it was the only 1962 light green Valiant in Iowa City so if it was misused, we would be sure to hear about it. It was a great car that lasted long enough for both of them to get through college with it.

Since our marriage we have had an assortment of new and used cars over the years, but my basic car philosophy has remained that cars are a necessary evil that must be put up with to get me from one place to another when it is too far to walk. As a matter of fact, by my own choice I never had my name on a car title. That all changed last spring.

Perhaps it's a sign of senility, but for the first time in my life I fell in love with a car. I don't need to get all poetic about it and I like to think I still have my feet on the ground, or is that "feet on the floorboards"? But you will notice a big smile on my face any time you see me driving my new blue Buick. It's just the right car for this kind of late-in-life affair. The model is called the Rendezvous, and yes, my own name is on the title.

Marilyn Holland

Country School Teacher

I was recently reading *Inventing The Truth*, by William Zinsser, and his quotation from Russell Baker struck me: "My prime interest was to celebrate people whom nobody had ever heard of." I knew someone just like that, largely unknown to the world at large, who had made a big difference in my own life.

Myrtle Work lived directly across the street from our family in North Liberty in the late 1930s. When identifying her, people would describe her as "an old maid." That meant she was single and probably past the age of getting married, which in those days was 25 to 30 years old. I think she may have been born a little before 1900. She was tall and didn't smile a lot but had a very kind face. I have no doubt that she was a firm teacher who had excellent control of her classroom.

She owned her own little cottage which had a living room and a kitchen downstairs while upstairs there were two small bedrooms and an area at the top of her staircase she called her "library." As I recall, she had no bathroom in her house but did have a pitcher pump in the kitchen to supply her with water. Her house was always immaculately clean, sparsely furnished, and bright with white ruffled curtains at all of the windows, hand-braided rugs on the floor, and quilts on both of the beds along with their white ruffled pillows. At that time in my life I saw the house as a very romantic place to live.

I was taught early on to respect her privacy but she frequently would invite me into her house when she saw me playing outdoors. She always made me feel so special and grown-up. She would invite me to sit at her dining table and read one of the children's books from her library. Sometimes she would give me a small glass of lemonade and a cookie to eat after reading a book. Reading and eating at the same time would definitely not have been an option because of the possibility of spilling on the book.

Yesterdays

Miss Work was a country schoolteacher. She lived in North Liberty and taught in a one-room school north of town near the cemetery. It was about three miles to the school from her house. She didn't own a car, and walked both ways every day except in the coldest part of winter when she would stay with a farm family near the school. This arrangement allowed her to avoid walking in heavy snow and extreme cold, and also to get to the school extra early in the morning so she could get the heating stove started and students would arrive to a warm room.

I almost never saw her leave for school because of the early hour she would begin her trek, carrying a paper shopping bag with everything she thought she would need that day. However, I frequently hung out on our porch about the time I expected her to return in the evening so I could say hello. In the winter when she did not come home in the evening, my father would keep the fire burning in the stove that heated her house.

Her school had grades one through eight, all meeting in one room. I believe she told me once that she had 14 or 15 pupils. She was responsible for keeping the school clean, and building the fire and keeping it going in the winter. The school had no plumbing inside, and she always kept a water bucket on a table in the back of the room for children to get drinking water. Ahead of her time regarding how diseases are passed from one child to another, she did not think it was right that all of the children should drink from the same dipper in the bucket (common practice in those days). Her meager pay did not allow her to buy individual glasses for each child, however. Nowadays of course if a student needs to bring something to school, a note sent to the parents usually accomplishes the goal. But at the height of the Depression, in rural Iowa, it would have been unthinkable to ask parents to send a drinking glass to school with each child.

Still, Miss Work found a solution. Cheese spreads in those days were sold in the grocery store in four-ounce glasses with colorful designs on them. She began eating those cheese spreads on bread as her noon lunch until she had collected enough glasses with different designs on them to provide each pupil with a personal glass. I remember her showing me the collection as it grew, and how careful she was to keep track of the patterns of the glasses so she didn't repeat them. She kept them neatly lined up on her kitchen windowsill, and it became more and more difficult for her to find new patterns in our small town grocery store in North Liberty. She persisted, however, and I think I was as excited as she was the day she finally had one glass for each student and took them all to school to present them to the children.

Today, I think about how boring her lunches must have been day after day, week after week and month after month. With her sense of frugality, I'm sure those sandwiches had only a very thin coating of cheese on the bread, and a four-ounce jar of spread would have been made to last an extra-long time.

The school had no budgets for anything beyond the basic costs of electricity, wood for the stove, and her pay. The fathers of the students also helped keep the woodpile supplied for her but she had to carry the logs inside as well as replenish the water bucket from the well each day. There were no supplementary funds, for example for books for the library, and those children were very fortunate that she was willing to buy such books from her small salary, selecting them carefully to ensure she had extra reading material available for each age level.

Even though I was never able to go to her school, she took the time to impress upon me the importance of reading. Whenever I finished reading a book in her house she would want to talk about it with me. She was a dedicated teacher 24 hours a day.

Miss Work continued at that same school until it was closed in the late 1940s, and about that time I lost track of her since we had moved away from North Liberty. Though I never formally sat in one of her classes, I still remember her as a great teacher. I've seen no monuments to her in North Liberty, but she was a wonderful friend for a child to have, and I celebrate her life.

John Hudson

John Hudson is a sociologist and writer. He is now concentrating on writing his memoirs and rewriting his previous academic work on creativity for a wider audience. As a sociologist, John has a special interest in the influence of groups and organizations on creativity. He has served on the faculty of several universities, conducted research and development projects, performed evaluation research, was co-owner of a real estate firm, and was president of the New England Sociological Association. John was a volunteer advocate for the arts after retiring, serving two terms on the Iowa Arts Council Board. John was a sailor for many years after learning to sail at the age of 11. His hobbies include travel, collecting books about historic railroads and square-rigged sailing ships, visiting art galleries and museums, and listening to classical music.

Steam and Steel

I eagerly pedaled my bicycle down the gently sloping hill toward the locomotive roundhouse. The semi-circular building sat solidly at one end of the Great Northern Railroad yard, named "Apple Yard" in honor of the famous apples grown in the Wenatchee valley of central Washington state where I lived. As I walked from the bright sunshine of my 15th summer into the dim interior, I could smell a wonderful mixture of oil, steam, and smoke, and hear the subtle sounds of steam locomotives resting. Faint hisses of steam issued unexpectedly from valves. From remote recesses within the steel beasts I could hear panting breath, almost as if they were alive. Warmth surrounded me from the banked fires within their fireboxes. There was something beautiful and awe-inspiring about these seemingly inanimate beings, these iron horses of the rails, whether quiescent or rushing across the terrain trailing cars of passengers or freight. These magnificent creatures drew me back time and again just to be in their presence.

Here and there men in oil-stained overalls were oiling critical parts of the engines, using oilcans with long spouts. Others were wiping down the piston rods or other moving parts with oily rags. Some mechanics were making minor repairs. A hostler was climbing up the ladder into the cab of a locomotive, preparing to take it out of the roundhouse.

Several of the men greeted me. I was not a stranger here; I had been visiting this mysterious and wonderful place for months, watching the action, asking questions, taking in the stimulating scene, the poignant sounds, the pungent smells. The men seemed to accept my presence as natural. I was careful to keep out of their way and to observe basic safety rules. I knew I was lucky to be allowed to hang around.

The simplest details fascinated me, like the tracks inside the roundhouse radiating like starbursts from the focus of the turntable outside. Each locomotive sat at an angle to its neighbor, and only one locomotive at a time could enter or leave the roundhouse by way of the turntable outside.

The locomotives, some for passenger trains, some for freight, were positioned on the various tracks, quiet steam hissing, issuing occasional light smoke from their smokestacks that wafted toward vents in the roundhouse roof. A locomotive's long black boiler recumbent above the arrangement of wheels, the headlight centered on the front of the boiler, the cowcatcher at the front with its coupler ready to guide the way, displayed an aesthetic that drew me back in rapt admiration again and again.

The tender was permanently coupled to the rear of the locomotive, carrying oil to feed the fire in the locomotive's firebox, and water to feed the boiler. The firebox heated the water in the boiler to steam. The steam surged to the cylinders, thrusting the pistons, pushing the piston rods, which connected to the drive rods and side rods, turning the drive wheels. Every part performed its function in the movement of these enormous engines.

The array of wheels and gear on the locomotives was intricate and a source of endless fascination to me. The huge wheels of the engines, some of which were taller than I, were the driving force for the locomotive. Forward of the drive wheels were smaller wheels under the cowcatcher, which helped to guide the locomotive around curves. Behind the drive wheels were smaller wheels which helped to support the firebox at the rear of the locomotive. The way of classifying types of steam locomotives was based on these wheel arrangements. The type of locomotive that I stood admiring in the Apple Yard roundhouse that day had four small wheels at the front under the cowcatcher, six large drive wheels under the boiler, and two smaller wheels under the firebox. This was called a 4-6-2 locomotive, or Pacific type. There were other designs, I knew, and my personal favorite was a 4-6-4, or Hudson type. Unfortunately for me, the Great Northern Railroad didn't have any Hudson locomotives.

The hostler in the Pacific climbed down from his cab and asked if I wanted to ride with him as he took the engine out to the water tank. Did I ever! This was something to tell my family and friends about. It was 1945, and the men who drove the locomotives were cultural heroes, like sports stars or rock stars today. Every kid who saw a train go by would wave to the engineer or the fireman. In our contemporary world it is difficult to imagine the lofty status these champions of steam and steel enjoyed when trains were everywhere and everyday. I felt a special sense of privilege about being allowed to ride the cab in a steam locomotive. This was going to be one of life's exalted moments.

The hostler made a last-minute inspection, climbed back up the ladder into the cab, and invited me to follow. I eagerly grasped the vertical sides of the ladder and up I went, my feet feeling each rung, finally stepping onto the steel floor of the cab. The roof of the cab extended overhead, covering not only the cab, but also the space between cab and tender. Windows on both sides of the cab were open above the seats for the engineer and fireman.

The hostler took the engineer's seat on the right; I sat upon the fireman's seat at the left. The hostler moved the reversing lever, opened the throttle, and the black steel creature moved slowly and majestically backward out of the roundhouse onto the turntable. Sounds of escaping steam followed us, together with slight clanking noises from the side rods, mingled with a few chugs from the smokestack. The hostler applied the brake, and the locomotive came to rest on the turntable.

The operator in the little shack on one side of the turntable moved his controls, and we slowly began turning. Looking through my side window straight ahead along the left side of the boiler, I could see its many rivets and tubing, the running board attached to its side with the long grab rod above. Atop the boiler sat the steam dome and the sand dome, with the bronze bell ready to toll its melodious warning,

79

and at the very front, the smokestack ejecting only a slight gray emission.

As I continued to look forward alongside the locomotive boiler, the moving turntable rotated the view in front of me. Several stalls of the roundhouse appeared past the front of the locomotive, some empty, some with locomotives quiet. An open space with a vista to the brown hills beyond was next. Then as the locomotive continued to rotate, the vast maze of tracks in the switching yard appeared. Myriad freight cars filled these tracks, waiting to be moved around and connected together in trains for distant destinations. A steam switch engine was moving several freight cars along one of the tracks, as a switchman stood by a switch, ready to direct the little switch engine with its cars to another track.

I looked out the hostler's window to the right, and I could see the repair shop for the electric locomotives, a space I was not allowed to enter, deemed too dangerous for a 15-year-old. These electric engines took the trains through the Cascade Mountain Range and the eight-and-a-half-mile Cascade Tunnel, one of the longest in the world. In the confined space of a tunnel that long, smoke buildup from a steam engine would be a health hazard to the engineer and fireman.

As the turntable continued to turn, the water tank on its long steel legs came into view directly ahead, its spout tipped up at a jaunty angle waiting for the thirsty locomotive. The turntable stopped, aligning its rails to the rails of the track to the water tower. The hostler moved his reversing lever once again, and we slowly moved forward off the turntable. As we approached the water tank, my gaze moved over the numerous dials, gauges, valves, levers, and handles covering the forward end of the locomotive cab.

There were more controls than I understood, although I realized their general purposes to control the amount of water and monitor the steam pressure in the boiler, adjust the oil delivered to the firebox to increase or decrease the fire heating the water in the boiler, make the locomotive go forward or in reverse, fast or slow, apply the brakes, ring the bell, blow the whistle, and all the other things needed to drive the locomotive.

The hostler carefully moved his throttle, stopping so the water cap on the tender was directly under the waterspout on the water tower. The hostler climbed onto the top of the tender, grabbed the pull rope on the water spout, pulled it down into the opening in the tender's water tank, and turned on the water. After the tank was full, he released the spout and it raised itself to its former angle. The opening was capped and the hostler returned to the cab. He moved the locomotive onto the ready track and applied the brake, and the Pacific slowly came to rest again with a sound of compressed air escaping. We climbed down from the cab and walked back together into the dimness of the roundhouse. The mingled steam and smoke inside molded the rays of sunlight streaming down through sooty windows into burnished bars of gold, caressing the glistening backs of the slumbering giants.

Fifty years later I stood on this same spot, remembering what had once been. This was a major division point on the Great Northern Railroad. Where once sprawled a massive rail yard, a roundhouse, repair shops, water tower, locomotives and rail cars, now there was only an enormous level expanse of gravel. Nothing remained of the bustling activity of 50 years ago. The main line of the Burlington Northern nearby was the only reminder of what used to be here. The scene was empty and silent, the sagebrush growing down the slope to the powerful Columbia River, the brown hills looming nearby, only the wind gently whispering goodbye forever.

From Qwerty to Dvorak

My high school advisor told me that I need not take the typing course, since I would never need to type. I had asked about it because, you know, wouldn't I need to know how to type when I got to college and had all those papers to hand in? Well, he was the advisor, not me, so I took his advice and didn't take the typing course.

When I got to college, just as I thought, I had all those papers to hand in. For a while I wrote them out in longhand, the old fashioned way. Tedious! Then for a while my girlfriend typed my papers for me. That lasted until I graduated and went off to graduate school. Then I was on my own.

August Dvorak was Professor of Education at the University of Washington in Seattle in 1952, the year I entered graduate study there. His office was down the hall from mine. Professor Dvorak had used time and motion studies in the 1930s to design a simplified type-writer keyboard that provided amazing results, with greater speed and more accuracy for the typist. The original typewriter keyboard had been designed before the invention of touch typing. On the early typewriters the type bars fell back by the force of gravity. Typing rapidly would cause the keys to sometimes hit one another or some-times stick together and jam the typewriter. Therefore the type bars for letters that normally appeared adjacent in text were placed far apart, to minimize jamming. In the keyboard design that resulted, the keys at the left end of the upper row spelled out "qwerty." The stand-ard keyboard has been known by that name ever since.

Professor Dvorak discovered a number of problems with the qwerty keyboard. Underlying all of them was the fact that a typist's fingers did a lot of jumping between the top row and the bottom row of keys, due to the fact that less than one-third of all typing was done on the middle row of the typewriter. This resulted in many typing mistakes. Fewer than 300 (uncommon) words could be typed on the middle row alone. To make matters worse, the left hand did more work than the right hand, and the weaker fingers did more work than the stronger fingers. Many common words were typed entirely by one hand. Everything considered, the qwerty keyboard was a mess!

```
Q  W  E  R  T  Y  U  I  OP  [  ]  \
   A  S  D  F  G  H  J  K  L  ;  '
   Z  X  C  V  B  N  M  ,  .  /
```
QWERTY KEYBOARD

```
'  ,  .  P  Y  F  G  C  R  L  /  =  \
   A  O  E  U  I  D  H  T  N  S  -
   ;  Q  J  K  X  B  M  W  V  Z
```
DVORAK KEYBOARD

As a result of these findings, Professor Dvorak designed a new typewriter keyboard to correct these flaws. Since most people are right-handed, he placed the letters so that the right hand does slightly more work than the left hand, and the stronger fingers do more work than the weaker fingers. He put all the vowels on the middle row under the left hand, and the most common consonants on the middle row under the right hand. As a result, on Professor Dvorak's keyboard 70 percent of typing can be done on the middle row, and over 3,000 (common) words can be typed on the middle row alone, providing more than a ten-fold improvement over the qwerty keyboard. Since vowels and consonants more or less alternate in English, a natural alternating rhythm between the hands occurs, making typing much easier. Because of the rhythm and the reduction of jumping between rows, the error rate of the typist was reduced by 90%. Dvorak demonstrated that typing on his keyboard was faster, easier, less fatiguing, and more accurate than the old qwerty keyboard.

Hearing about this wonderful keyboard, and about studies showing that learning the Dvorak method was relatively easy and fast, I decided it was time for me to learn to type. Professor Dvorak seemed delighted to find someone who wanted to learn his system. He offered to order a Dvorak typewriter for me at a discount. He knew Martin Tytell, who owned the well-known Tytell Typewriter Company in New York City. I also ordered additional keys with special mathematical and logic symbols for my Dvorak keyboard. I chose a portable, so I could always have my typewriter with me.

While I waited for my customized typewriter to arrive, Professor Dvorak loaned me one of his typewriters to practice on. I bought the typing textbook he had written so I could teach myself how to touch-type. I followed all the lessons, and by the time I finished, my new typewriter had arrived. It was accompanied by a most interesting bill of sale, which demonstrated Martin Tytell's sense of humor. The bill of sale reads as follows:

New Royal Portable Quiet Deluxe Model
44 bars ½ space ratchet
Dvorak keyboard plus special lunacy #3 sans
straightjacket keyboard a la mode with
whip cream and maple walnuts
He added to the bill a "special aggravation chge" of $2.00.

Years later, I was working in the office of the Commissioner of Mental Health for the Commonwealth of Massachusetts, writing a research proposal. The deadline was fast approaching. Rather than continue to write in longhand and have my secretary type the text, I decided to save time by bringing my portable Dvorak typewriter to the office to type some of the proposal myself. The sound of my typing was a rapid-fire and continuous staccato, and the bell of the carriage return sounded frequently. After a while my secretary and several of her colleagues came into my office to see what it was I was doing. They had heard me, a mere male, typing much faster than they. They were even more surprised when they did the proofreading to discover that my typed pages had almost no errors.

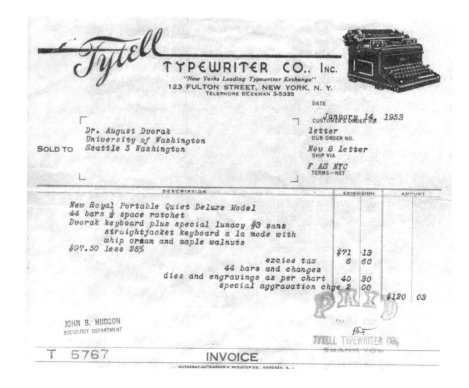

Fast-forward, this time to Cambridge, Massachusetts, and a political campaign for City Council. A group of us were finishing up the final draft of a platform statement for our candidate. It was getting late and we were all tired. I stopped to rest. One of the other people in the group volunteered to take over the typing for a while. As it happened, she was the only person in the room who did not know about my Dvorak keyboard. We all remained silent as she sat down in front of my typewriter and began to type. She stopped to check her work, looked at the nonsensical words on the paper, appeared flustered, and raised her head to stare at the wall across the room. She tore the paper from the typewriter, inserted a fresh sheet, and began again, but again her typing produced gobbledygook. She gave her head a slight shake, got up from her chair, and went outside to get some fresh air. When she returned and sat down in front of the typewriter, she studied the keyboard and asked, "Is there something wrong with this keyboard?" We exploded in laughter.

Now jump forward several more years. In 1983 I bought my first personal computer and retired my Dvorak typewriter after 30 years of service. I was able to buy a separate Key Tronic keyboard for my computer in the Dvorak layout. However, within a few years hardwired Dvorak keyboards effectively disappeared from the market. Fortunately, Microsoft Windows has a Dvorak keyboard configuration! You can access it by going into Windows and clicking on the appropriate commands, and voila! The Dvorak layout is enabled. Since I touch-type, I don't need to look at the keys.

This story was written using the Windows Dvorak utility with a qwerty keyboard connected to my personal computer. I appreciate my past associations with August Dvorak and Martin Tytell, so here's an acknowledgement for my "Dvorak keyboard plus special lunacy #3 sans straightjacket keyboard à la mode with whip cream and maple walnuts."

John Hudson

Beliefs of a Social Scientist

In growing up, I attended several different Sunday schools and churches. One consequence was that I did not develop a commitment to any one creed or set of religious beliefs. I spent my formative high school and undergraduate years in the Pacific Northwest. That provided me ample opportunity to immerse myself in the solitude of forests and alpine meadows. I spent many days hiking along mountain trails through lush meadows full of wild flowers, delighting in the colors of red Indian paintbrush, blue lupin, and yellow cinquefoil. Ahead of me, I could see the peak of Mt. Rainier looming above in the distance, with many glaciers flowing down its sides. I could hear the wind whispering through the forests of spruce and fir, and the rippling of water over stones in a nearby stream between moss-covered banks. I felt close to the beauty and the immensity of the cosmos in such times and places—a moving and spiritual experience.

During these same formative years, I was seeking a conceptual worldview that I could find intellectually and emotionally satisfying. I did lots of reading in science, especially astronomy, and I read the views of many scientists. As a graduate student, I read "The Religion of a Social Scientist," by Stuart C. Dodd, who interpreted many religious ideas into compatibility with social science. I discovered the Unitarian Church and its literature, which was both logically and intellectually consistent with my scientific training in mathematics, physics, and sociology. Reading in psychology, cultural anthropology, and existentialist philosophy followed. This diversity of experiences and ideas stimulated me to be creative in developing my own spiritual belief system.

As I matured, my preferred sources of truth or authority included personal experience, intuition, reason, science, and the natural and social worlds. Which of these comes to the fore depends on circumstances and the purposes that I seek.

I rely on personal experience and on intuition as early guides for investigation. Reason and logic are important in constructing ways of thinking about a project, so that the various parts fit together in a consistent way without contradictions or omissions.

Because I am a social scientist, I rely on the results of theoretical and empirical research. Central to my thinking is the idea that science is a *process*. Science is not a set of answers, as so many people believe. Science is a *process that gives us answers,* that are true as of a given time, and place, and circumstances. As we continue the scientific process, the answers may change, and we hope, always headed closer to the truth.

My idea of Ultimate Reality is that it is real and infinite. Our knowledge of it is imperfect, but our understanding of it is ever enlarging. What we know about reality becomes ever more accurate. I believe that time also is infinite, both into the past, and into the future.

I find the ultimate test of truth within the natural and social worlds. *Theory* is a causal map of the world—the physical world, the biological world, the social world, and the world of morality. The creation of causal maps is the scientific quest. We want to know the connections between events and actions, the links of cause and effect. The quest is more important than the answers, because the quest both produces the answers, and then continually revises the answers. Science is thus self-correcting. How you ask the questions is as important as the answers, because the questions *frame* the answers.

Social science tells us that our beliefs and attitudes include three dimensions: knowing, feeling, and evaluating. Any attitude or belief includes knowing, but it also involves our feelings about what we know. And most importantly, our evaluations or judgments are an important component of our beliefs. Knowing can be true or false, feeling can be positive or negative, judging can lead to good or bad evaluations. But for me, on my spiritual odyssey, I seek the positive of each dimension. In knowing, I seek truth. In feeling, I seek beauty.

In evaluating, I seek goodness. Truth, beauty, and goodness are my spiritual triad.

Our judgments influence our perceptions of both our own beliefs and those of others. Our judgments become a personal act of affirmation. Ultimately, our judgments lead us to action. But what is there to guide our actions? When taking action, the most basic principle is the admonition: *do no harm*. But what does this mean in daily life? How do we determine that what we are doing harms or benefits? How do we decide between good and evil?

The answer, for me, incorporates Abraham Maslow's theory of human motivation, with the existentialist idea that we create our own meaning within the background of our culture. I believe that *good* social arrangements are those that lead to the gratification of basic human needs, and *evil* social arrangements are those that lead to the deprivation of basic human needs.

According to Maslow's hierarchy, there are five levels of needs. The bottom four levels are deficit needs, that is, needs that periodically empty out and then must be replenished. The most basic level includes the physiological needs, such as the need for food, water, or shelter. When you get hungry, you need to stop and eat.

The second level of human needs is the need for security and safety. We seek predictability in our lives. Structure gives us predictability. If we are unable to assess the likely consequences of our decisions, we are not able to make rational choices, nor escape anxiety. Some degree of structure and predictability is a necessary condition for psychological comfort and stability.

The third level concerns our emotional needs, the need for love and affection. Much research has shown how personality suffers when love and affection are denied or manipulated. Cogent theory and research has shown that love must be unconditional for healthy personality development to occur in children. And we all feel how important love is for our healthy adult living.

The fourth level of human need is the need to achieve, and the resulting need for respect. When we excel at skills that are defined as important by those we respect, we gain their respect. When we internalize their respect, we develop self-respect.

When and if these four levels of deficit needs are reasonably well satisfied, they no longer motivate us—until they become depleted again. But when the four basic levels of deficit needs are satisfied, then a fifth level of need may motivate people—Maslow called this level self-actualization. Unlike the four lower levels, self-actualization is not a deficit need—it is a growth need. This means that we are motivated to use our creative talents and abilities to the utmost. The more we satisfy the need for self-actualization, the more it motivates us. The only reason we stop is when a lower need demands to be replenished. We can no longer ignore the need for sleep, or food, or safety, or the satisfaction of emotional needs.

Maslow has said that self-actualization becomes a sense of wholeness with the world. We become fulfilled, and we fulfill others. People are creative and oriented toward others, rather than self-centered. Self-actualization is part of the good life, part of a life well-lived. It seems to me that self-actualization is the ideal toward which we strive.

If Maslow is correct, as I believe he is, in asserting that everyone has these basic human needs in all cultures, then we have an *empirically objective basis* for judging whether social structures are functional or dysfunctional, good or evil. The basic human needs constitute a set of criteria by which social arrangements can be evaluated in terms of their functionality or pathology. This provides a basis for evaluating cultures and social structures without falling victim to cultural relativism.

I believe this is not to put forward our own value judgments, but rather to assert that these needs express what people everywhere want or need. This is not even to say that we define as *good* what people desire, but that people themselves define as *good* those things which gratify basic needs.

If we are willing to accept the correctness of the discussion so far, then such conclusions need not rest upon the observer's personal values or the values of any particular group or subculture. I believe that we are now in a position to assert as *a moral principle that social arrangements are evil, objectively speaking, to the degree that they lead to severe or sustained deprivation of basic human needs; and that social arrangements are good if they lead to the systematic gratification of these basic human needs.*

To paraphrase the anthropologist Robert Redfield, you don't mess with the sacred. But secular objects are always open to examination. The problem arises when someone questions an idea or practice that has always been considered sacred. By the mere act of *questioning*, you indicate that for you the idea or practice no longer has the quality of being sacred.

Summing Up

- For many people, religious beliefs are sacred and not to be questioned. It should be clear by now that I do not fit this mold. *The quest for answers is the essence of my life journey.* In the most general way, this is a quest for truth, beauty, and goodness.
- What authority do I claim for what I believe to be true? I believe personal experience and intuition are early guides for investigation. Reason and logic guide knowledge to fit together in a consistent way. Science illuminates reality by generating causal maps. The natural and social worlds are the ultimate test of truth, because they validate knowledge of cause and effect through the scientific method.
- My idea of Ultimate Reality is that it is real and infinite. Our knowledge of it is imperfect, but our understanding of it is ever enlarging. What we know about reality becomes ever more accurate. I believe that time also is infinite, both into the past, and into the future.

- I acknowledge that command of my destiny is limited by forces beyond my power, but I do control how I choose to respond to life events.
- I believe suffering is not meaningful if it is a random experience due to events beyond our knowledge or control. If suffering occurs because of our own acts, suffering can motivate us to change our behavior.
- I believe life after death is the memories that others have of us, and the lasting effects that we have brought about during our lifetime.
- I believe evil or sin is harm to others.
- And finally, I believe salvation lies in the fulfillment of basic human needs, and living in a world of truth, beauty, and goodness.

Sandra Hudson

Sandra Hudson finds playfulness in writing. She sets small challenges, such as writing a story in exactly 100 words, or entirely in a set meter, or using only clichés joined by conjunctions as she did while writing "When All Is Said and Done," a short story published in the anthology *Ruthlessly Kind*. In her first novel, *Strike Zone: The Games of Baseball & Money,* she played with blending genres when she transformed her business development manual into a sports novel for young teens. She is currently writing historical fiction and delights in the creativity of merging fact with fiction. In this anthology, her memoir "A Man of Contradictions" incorporates you, the reader, as a character in her chronical. As with her cooking, Sandra's writing is occasionally sliced and diced, with a bit of spice added.

Monocled Mogul

My childhood home, like many homes in the late 1930s and early 1940s, was divided into territories. The kitchen belonged to the womenfolk, the basement to my dad, the second floor to two of Mother's younger sisters, the first floor front bedroom was my parents', and the rear bedroom was mine. The living room, dining room, and bathroom were pretty much neutral territory where anyone could stake a claim.

The exception was Sunday evenings. On Sunday evenings at six o'clock sharp, the alarm clock on the stove would ring. Mother, Aunt Gwen, and Aunt Winnie would move out from their kitchen command post and invade the living room. There they would pull their easy chairs in close to the Philco radio to listen to Sunday evening radio shows and attend to their needlework.

That Philco radio stood as tall as I did. I didn't much like it, as it was my only serious competition for my parents' attention. When the Philco spoke, no one was allowed to interrupt. It always wore the same large golden grin on its face. When no one was looking I twitched its brown nose, and its long silver tongue whisked across its toothless grin. In the center of its forehead was a single demanding eye that glowed green every time it talked, sang, or played music. On Sunday nights "it" got to talk, while I had to button my lips.

The men could talk though. One would always say, "The old ladies are circling their wagons again." Make no never mind that there were no wagons and the oldest of the old ladies was my mother, who was just approaching the frontier of her mid-thirties. The men didn't much like the barricade the "old ladies" constructed. Those high-back chairs were very effective in fending off traditional male requests, such as, "Will you bring me this …?" or "Will you find me that …?" or "Will you fix me a piece of …?"

Within minutes of the "old ladies" barricading themselves around the Philco, the men usually invaded the kitchen, laid siege to the pantry, rifled the icebox, and transformed the family table into a gaming board. There they engaged in intense nickel games of strategy. Occasionally, a request volleyed forth from the kitchen, but it was always deflected without missing a stitch.

The hub of the "old ladies" circle was mine. That was a perfect place for a six-year-old who thought the world revolved around her. I wouldn't say I was spoiled exactly, but I most certainly was indulged, by both camps.

It was at the hub of this circle that I received my first sewing lessons. I remember one evening vividly. The "old ladies" each had a pile of brand new Quaker Oats gingham feed sacks next to their chairs. They would pick one up, study the machine stitching that ran along the bottom and one side, then quickly snip one of the strings with their scissors. With two long stretches of their arms they would completely unravel every last inch of stitching from the sack.

That process produced two long zigzag strings which were then tossed into my lap. From this pile of intertwined spaghetti, I was taught to create a giant ball of string. I learned to thread one end through a large coat button and tie it off with a square knot – right over left and then left over right, being careful not to create a "granny" knot. When I was confident it was perfect, I'd pass it up to one of the "old ladies" for review. From my perspective the review had nothing to do with quality control and everything to do with praise.

With the knot approved, the next step was to wind the string around the button, slowly rotating it, to create a ball. When the end of one string was reached, I'd attach another string to it with a thumb knot and continue winding until every last string had been incorporated into my giant string ball. I considered that to be such an accomplishment that after receiving praise from the "old ladies," I left the circle in search of further recognition.

Being a double agent of sorts, I was warmly greeted as I entered the male camp. They stopped their pinochle game to admire my ball of string. Harry even offered to buy it from me for a nickel. I eagerly accepted. It seemed like a real good deal to me since the cost of a double-dip ice cream cone was a nickel. I wasn't quite old enough to realize that getting rid of a nuisance factor was worth a whole lot more than a nickel to a man with a winning pinochle hand.

With the nickel in my pocket I scurried back to my place at the hub of the "old ladies" circle. By then, the gingham feed sacks had been folded and neatly piled next to Mother's chair. A pattern had been selected from a large cardboard carton that contained twice- and thrice-used hand-me-down patterns that had been ordered over the years from the Women's Section of *The Cedar Rapids Gazette*.

Only one decision remained: which buttons to use? Mother went to her closet. From the tippy-top shelf she retrieved a periwinkle blue Schraft's chocolate tin. Beautiful, large white peonies were painted on the lid. Inside were buttons—dozens upon dozens of buttons that my mother, and her mother and her mother's mother, had carefully removed from old garments. The Schraft's tin was a treasure trove of buttons: large, small, brilliant, dull. Buttons for hours and hours of sorting, counting, stringing, measuring, and labeling. Buttons for scavenger hunts. Buttons for game markers. Buttons for heroes' medals, coins of the realm, a queen's brooch. Buttons to imagine, imagine, imagine.

On this particular Sunday evening my Aunt Gwen selected a large shiny pearl coat button from the box and showed me how to wear it as a monocle. Once she was satisfied that I could keep the button in front of my eye, while at the same time repeating a tongue twister, she sent me on a mission. Holding the lid to the button box in front of me, in an alms position, I was dispatched to the kitchen with a special message.

I approached the table as coached and announced, "Monocled Moguls Make More Money." The men laughed. A donation of one penny was forthcoming from my father. I continued to stand there, the lid outstretched. My father then allowed as to how, if his mono-cled mogul expected to make more money, she would have to learn to play pinochle better than her old dad.

Harry chuckled and asked to see my button monocle. He placed it in his eye, stuck out his chest, and announced that his three large piles of nickels made him the undisputed monocle mogul of the evening. Thinking Harry had offered another trade, I scooped the three high piles of nickels into the lid of the button box and scampered back to the "old ladies" camp.

Harry let out a loud howl. The others roared with laughter. Mother smiled and announced that it was past my bedtime. I poured the nick-els in with the buttons, and believing that Schraft's tin to be worth a jillion nickels, begged to be the keeper of the box.

That night and many nights thereafter I went to sleep with that periwinkle blue button box tucked snugly under one arm. After all, who knew how many ice cream cones were in my future now that I knew – Monocled Moguls Make More Money.

A Man of Contradictions

Ted Chermak was a man of faith, but not of religion. He strove to be a self-sustaining man, yet wove about him a web of complex social networks. He was a man of inquiry, who seldom judged; an innovator and inventor, with little interest in implementation; a man of influence, who shunned power; a man of keen intelligence and a well-organized mind, who lived in clutter. In short, he was a man of contradictions.

It is easier to capture a bead of mercury than to catch the essence of my father. If you knew him, or even knew of him, it's almost certain you have a story or two to tell. Come, step back in time with me. You choose the year. Anytime between 1956, when he retired, and 1989, the year he died.

Why those years? Well, those are the years after he shed the last vestiges of the corporate life and moved 500 miles north to Nevis, Minnesota to become a dairy farmer. However, he discovered dairy farming left little time for the contemplation his personality required. He decided tree farming was more to his liking. Once planted, trees grow 20 years before they are harvested. Woodlands also offered endless opportunities to commune with nature. Just as he had transformed himself from corporation man to dairy farmer, he transformed his dairy farm into a tree farm, and from there... well, you'll see. Let's get started. It's a bit of a trip, but you must meet him on his home turf if you are to have even a glimmer of understanding of the man.

We leave County Road 13 a couple of miles south of Nevis, and cut west to enter the farmstead on a narrow gravel road. I see you admiring the beautifully scripted sign announcing "Nacirema." Ted has extraordinary penmanship, even when writing with a large paintbrush. What's Nacirema? You'll have to ask Ted about that.

How big is his spread? It's a section, give or take. About a mile square. Mostly woodlands, a couple of meadows, and some shoreline on Sixth Crow Wing Lake. There are also the remains of a prior owner's airfield. Ted planted three 40s as Norway plantations, but then got bored or distracted and left the remainder of the land to volunteer birch, scrub oak, white pine, poplar, and tamarack. He delights in watching those tamarack we just passed glow gold each autumn.

You're eager to meet him? In a sense, you already have. Everything you see here tells you about the man. You've entered his world. Slow down; you must notice the details. Without them, you could miss the substance of the man.

The cluster of buildings sits about a half a mile down, on the north side of the road. At first glance, it's a typical early twentieth-century homestead. A two-story Italianate farmhouse, a large white dairy barn, a red horse barn with a distinctive hex sign, a long narrow concrete block tool house and garage, a corrugated corn shed, and a weathered chicken coop. The buildings are sound, but all could do with a coat of paint.

Yes, the ranch-style extension on the west side of the Italianate farmhouse is an architectural contradiction. You might even say it's an eyesore, but it tells you something of the man. The new extension is functional. For Ted, function trumps appearance every time.

Don't bother to knock at the front door. Only possessions reside in the main house. They took up squatters rights slowly. At first, it was a wood-burning kit left on an end table, or an antique lumber implement stuffed under the sofa. Within a couple of years, rocking horses, saddles, an old Edison, curly-eyed maple furniture, brass beds, stained-glass lamps, a treadle sewing machine, mirrors, shoe boxes, hat boxes, cardboard boxes of all sizes and descriptions, along with orange and apple crates full of antiques and "junque," took over the two guest rooms upstairs, and began to infiltrate the margins of the living room, dining room, and the old kitchen.

A couple of years ago, on one particularly hot summer evening, Ted moved his bed onto the screened porch of the western addition. Before the summer was over so many auction items had accumulated in the master bedroom that it just seemed easier to winterize his sleeping porch than to move back into the main house. By the end of the next summer, the only open spaces in the original farmhouse were narrow aisles between towers of boxes.

That's not the half of it. The tool shed is filled to overflowing too. He's set it up as a shop for antique dealers from the East Coast. But not to worry, he still has ample storage remaining in his two barns, the chicken shed, and the corrugated corncrib.

You're seeming to show some hesitancy. I didn't mean to alarm you. Let me encourage you to take this side path. What's that? You're worried it's too early? Nonsense. Ted has been up before dawn all his life. He hasn't missed daybreak since I can remember. See, what did I tell you? He's spotted us.

Ted stands in the doorway. A gray-haired, heavyset man with remnants of muscle mass. He has one hand on the doorjamb and the other pushing wide the screen door in welcome. Age has shrunk him to just under six feet, but the stance and balance are still those of an athlete. Plastic rimmed glasses set low on his nose and his yellow and green specked hazel eyes glisten at the sight of you—someone new. He anticipates you bringing with you new ideas, new challenges, new opportunities. Meeting strangers always energizes him.

His plaid flannel shirt with the top two buttons open at the neck is unpressed, as are his soiled gray work pants, which ride his hips as precariously as a cowboy rides a rodeo bull. He's not wearing shoes; he never does indoors. His red-tipped Hudson's Bay socks shuffle along the floor as he directs us toward his inner sanctum. It makes no difference that he wasn't expecting us. Even if he knew we were coming, even if you had been royalty, he would have dressed the same, except in summer when his attire would have been a snagged sleeveless undershirt, rough-edged cut-offs, and a pair of leather slippers that served as his indoor sandals.

A large dog, perhaps a cross between a Husky and wolf, bounds around the corner of the house. You quicken your step to enter the open door. "That's enough, Sheba," Ted quiets the dog. He smiles and cautions you, "Watch your step, that fox trap can be nasty." You miss the fox trap, but stumble over a pair of snowshoes, throwing you off balance and into a rack of outerwear: sweaters, jackets, coats, rain gear, hunting vests, and snowmobile suits jammed together as if they had emerged from a compactor. Your arms flail, and a seining net falls to the floor. Ted sees your predicament, and without comment, bends, picks up the seine and tosses it in the general direction of a "summer" shelf without waiting to see where it lands. It hooks itself around a fishing pole handle and dangles across a half-deflated beach ball. You look anxiously toward the French door only a couple of feet away. A lace curtain partially obscures your view. It's uncertain what lies ahead, yet it appears to be less cluttered and claustrophobic than where you are.

Ted reaches past you and pushes open the French door. Without even knowing your name, he motions left toward the kitchen. "Help yourself to a cup of coffee and come take a load off your feet." You try to get a lay of the land. The new addition is a large open rectangular space. Everything is open to view. Rooms are delineated only by the placement of furniture or open-front pine cabinets. You quickly surmise that the man has no secrets, at least not behind closed doors.

The kitchen, which takes up about a third of the rectangle, is familiar and yet strange. There are two ranges: one a state of the art built-in, the other a cast iron wood cooking stove. There's a new full-sized upright freezer, and next to it a vintage Amana chest freezer. The new refrigerator still has its energy labels on it. You sense a pattern forming and you look for an old icebox. There isn't one. (Actually there are several vintage refrigerators and freezers still operating in the root cellar, and an antique icebox in the red barn). You spy an old microwave sitting on top of a tall tin-paneled pie cabinet. A large braided rug rests on the concrete floor.

I motion you toward the coffeepot, but you're distracted by the window view—an exceptional dormant butterfly garden and a multitude of bird feeders that are still covered by a night frost and glisten in the early morning light. Abutting the wall, under that long row of windows, is a large chrome-legged table. It's covered with envelopes, auction flyers, seed catalogs, magazines, newspapers, and a half-dozen dirty coffee cups. The ladies of the area will attest that the table has a white baked enamel top. They've seen it now and then when clearing dirty coffee cups. They know they can tidy up when and how they choose around Ted's place, as long as they never disturb the contents of that tabletop.

You turn toward me and your eye catches a large, red, ornate, 19th century commercial coffee grinder. It's a beautiful implement with a large turnwheel on the side; you can't resist cranking it. It moves effortlessly, and a quarter cup of fresh ground coffee falls onto the top of a 19th century white porcelain flour and grain cupboard. I notice your consternation and sweep the coffee grounds into a measuring cup while directing you toward the counter nearest the family room.

The entire counter is filled with clean cups awaiting your selection. There are no two alike. Some have quotations, others logos, and still others pictures. You take a moment to study them, sensing your decision may speak volumes. You pick one that seems appropriate without disclosing too much. It says "Iowaegin." You fill it from the restaurant-sized coffee maker, select a spoon from a large mug, help yourself to some sugar, and look about.

You notice a voluminous amount of reading material. A large magazine rack serves as a room divider. It's at least six feet high and eight or ten feet long. Magazines three and four deep fill every linear foot. Fishing, hunting, gardening, building, architecture, technology, history, literary reviews, newsmagazines, annual reports, and comics are all jumbled in together. You're right, college sophomores selling magazine subscriptions have an easy go of it when calling here.

Ten-inch-wide shelves encircle the room about 18 inches from the ceiling. They are lined with hardcover books creating a decorative border for the room that any leading decorator would envy. Paperbacks line bookshelves that frame the four doorways. Stacks of books, recent acquisitions, as well as those pulled from bookshelves in recent days, are piled haphazardly on the top of nearly every flat surface. The titles are eclectic: prose, poetry, technical books, mysteries, sci-fi, even joke books. You raise a questioning eyebrow. I told you before we started you'd have trouble gauging the man. It's just another of those scattered beads of mercury.

Surfaces that do not hold books are covered with art, crafts, puzzles, and games. Yet there is no evidence of a collection. They are just random items: some antique and some contemporary, some amateurish, others masterfully crafted, some functional, and others purely decorative. You look toward an antique organ, clearly a rare collector's item. The corner of a delicate tapestry which protects it barely peeks out from under the items stacked on top. On the floor next to the organ sits a sculpture of Iowa football coach Hayden Fry. It is made from tractor parts. Above that hangs an elegant piece of stained glass, next to the stained glass hangs a dried apple kitchen witch. There seems no rhyme or reason to arrangement, the room a conundrum, and I see you struggling to get your bearings.

Ted's organized mind permits him to live happily within what appears to be acres of clutter that most of us would find intolerable. Clutter for him is a time-saver. He can set something down, bury it under something else, or loan it, and weeks, months, even years later, know exactly where to find it.

Ted sits at the only truly clear place in the room, a large limed-gray oak 1950s dining table. This is his temple. He swirls his spoon around his coffee mug, creating a chiming sound, signaling that he's prepared to give you an audience. His eyes twinkle as he makes you the center of his attention. Yesterday your chair might have held a senator, a down-and-out alcoholic, a man of the cloth, a nursing mother, a farmer, a toddler, an old trapper, a snot-nosed eight-year-old, an independently wealthy investor, a high school athlete, a valedictorian or a dropout, a relative or someone who thinks of themselves as one. In short, the proverbial doctor, lawyer, or Indian chief have all had a seat at Ted's table. They value their time with this hilltop philosopher and folk hero of sorts. As far as I know Ted never entertained an astronaut, but you never know what one of those kids who scramble for a seat at the table might become.

I should warn you, once you bring your chair up to his table, you are his for life. It starts out innocently enough with a question. For the natives it's, "How's it going?" For a visitor like you, it's, "How was your trip?" The focus is always on the person in the chair. Ted's questions are genuine. He truly wants to hear your ideas, he looks for the merit in them, he plays with them, he expands upon them. Once he carries you with him into the realm of ideas you are bound to him, similar to the way mercury binds to create an amalgam. He is a master at helping you expand your personal universe. Ted midwives ideas, your ideas, coaxing them, guiding them into existence, and then he hands them back to you as your very own. That is his charisma.

In talking about your trip up, you find the opportunity to ask him about the Nacirema sign. He eyes you for a full 10 seconds and then he chuckles, "That's a long story, you sure you have time for it?" His body language puts you on the edge of your chair. He continues, "You strike me as someone who might know a bit about anthropology."

"A bit," you confirm.

"That's good, not necessary for me to define terms. Well, it's like this, the Nacirema are a North American tribe living in the territory between the Canadian Cree and the Yaqui, and Tarahumare of Mexico and the Carib and Arawak of the Antilles." He pauses and looks at you over the top of his glasses. "You're sure you want to hear about the Nacirema?" You nod. "Stop me whenever you've had enough…

These Nacirema are a vain tribe. They focus a lot of attention on their appearance. It's their dominant ethos. The literature says they indoctrinate their children in tribal rituals at such a young age, it's almost as if those rituals are imprinted."

"There was an old Nacirema who had moved to these parts to get some relief from the conventions of his tribe. He admitted that even living by himself, one of the first things he did to settle in was to construct a private shrine for his daily rituals. Just couldn't break the pattern."

"The old man admitted to bathing his face in a font of holy water each morning. Then dampening hog hairs, and sprinkling them with a magic powder, and moving them around his mouth in a ritual pattern. Can you imagine that?" Ted doesn't wait for a response. "Not only that, but this old guy also acknowledged that he frequently lacerated his face, then to quell the bleeding he'd apply small pieces of a special material that he normally would use to clean up, of all things, defecation."

Ted pauses just long enough to enjoy the look on your face and then he continues. "That's not the half of it. The Nacirema women are even more barbaric. Three, four, sometimes even five times, in a lunar month, the women join other females in a special dwelling, and put their hair inside small baking ovens for as long as thirty minutes." The story is interrupted by Sheba's barking.

A younger fellow in bright orange hunting gear gives a cursory knock at the door and without breaking his gait bursts into the room. He's greeted with, "How's it goin', Roy? Help yourself to a cup of coffee and take a load off your feet."

"Naw, see you got company, just came to see if I could borrow your cat for the morning."

"What's up?"

"Got the in-laws coming this afternoon and discovered some damn beavers have flooded my road to the cabin. I'd blast'em out, but I'd still have mud for a month. Best to make a short detour."

"You got some Nacirema livin' over your way, ain't ya Roy?"

Roy's eyes widen. "These two wantin' to meet a Nacirema?"

"Tell 'em a bit 'bout their powerful magic while I get shod up."

A story or two later Ted returns and addresses Roy. "Well, ya gonna sit there jaw-bone'n all day, or are you gonna get up off your duff and help me get that stubborn cat to purr."

You take a deep intake of air as the two men leave the room. "Wow, Ted's something else."

I chuckle. "English is his only language, but there's no question he's multi-lingual when he speaks it. You're an academic; he speaks to you like an academic. Roy there is comfortable in the backwoods. No matter how you speak, Ted speaks your language. He accepts you as he finds you: high tea, or down and dirty. Blue collar, white collar, teeny bop, baby babble, whatever, he'll be on your wavelength. Your language will be his language."

Ted pops back inside to grab a piece of scrap paper and one of his always-sharp pencils. He jots a note and pushes it over an eight-penny nail mounted on the door jam.

BEAVERS FLOODED ROY'S CABIN ROAD.
WE'RE MAKING A DETOUR.
COME LEND A HAND!!

Men, women, children, or elders, they all want to be a part of Ted's action plan, whatever that plan might be on any particular day. Ted attracts people like a honey pot attracts bear cubs. Common sense tells you that if you fancy honey pots, you better have a tolerance for stings; they come with the territory. That's true around Ted, too. His stinging remarks can leave a welt on your ego the size of a baseball. The problem is you'll have to admit he speaks the truth. Which proves the truth really can hurt. As soon as the swelling goes down, you'll find yourself drawn right back to the honey of his personality.

And so it was with cutting the detour around the beaver pond. Roy catches it for starting to clear an area before it had been scouted for wild flowers and endangered species. "Slug" gets stung for notching a large birch for the Kowalke kid instead of teaching him how to do it for himself. I notice you flinch when he chides me to stop my tree huggin' and get to work, reminding me I'm on a tree *"farm,"* not in a National Park.

Along around noon, Roy's wife comes to announce potluck is waiting at "Ted's place." You're surprised they would just take over Ted's place without asking. This weekend you'll learn that Ted's place is the de facto community center, vocational education center, free rent-all stop, lending library, family services center, non-denominational confessional, the gathering place before going out on Saturday night, and the only place to be after church on Sunday.

Ted has more dishes and flatware than most church kitchens, and he serves more coffee than the area's leading restaurant. He jokes about filing papers as a religious center. He figures people ask more questions about the meaning of life around his table than they ever do at church.

Over the potluck a couple of more Nacirema stories are shared. Then David asks to share a story. Ted quiets everyone down and makes sure the six-year-old has center stage. David giggles, blushes and begins, "Long time ago the Nacirema had this really 'portant chief, Not-gni-hsaw. He was real, real 'portant. He was taller and smarter than any other Nacirema, so that's why he was chief. He was also stronger." Ted plays the straight man, "Just how strong was he?" David nods and smiles a big smile. "So strong he could throw a piece of wampum 'cross a wide river." He stops and goes over to Ted. "I forget the river's name."

"Was it the Ma-to-mac?" Ted coaches.

David jumps back to center stage. "He threw the wampum 'cross the PA-to-mac. And when he was just a little older than me, he chopped down a really big cherry tree where the Spirit of Truth lived."

The look on your face is priceless. You let out a deep groan as you suddenly realize David is talking about George Washington and that "Nacirema" is just American spelled backwards. The room erupts in laughter. It quiets down a bit and then explodes again. It has the

108

rhythm of a roller coaster climbing and then making a wild descent. It's okay to blush, the community loves your spirit. Ted loves practical jokes, those he plays, as well as those that are played on him.

After lunch Ted excuses himself to take a nap. Neighbors can go or stay as they please as long as they're quiet. On his way to his sleeping porch he puts a hand on David's shoulder. "You're becoming a fine story teller, young man. When I get up from my nap I think I might make a few lead soldiers. I figure you're getting old enough to help if you want." Ted turns to you. "You're old enough too if you're interested."

Before we head back to Iowa, you not only learn to make lead soldiers, but also join a young farmer learning to butcher a pig, a teenage girl learning to fish, a bride learning to cook venison, and me as I learn to graft a tree. None of those things were planned. They just grew out of conversations around the limed-oak table.

Ted is the consummate do-it-yourselfer, of all things necessary and unnecessary. If he doesn't know how to do what you want to do, he'll study up on it and the two of you will do it together. He assumes you can do most anything. How well you'll do it is another matter. Failures are frequent, but that just creates an opportunity to do it again until you have a sufficient result. Then it's time to move on to a new challenge.

From just before sunset to dusk, Ted sits in good weather on the hill behind the dairy barn and gazes at the sky and the movement of the meadow grasses. The beginning and end to a day are his times to be alone. You are always welcome to sit silently beside him in your own aloneness.

After dark he'll turn on the stained-glass chandelier above his limed-oak table, pour a final cup of coffee, and settle in for an evening in his North Country salon. For Ted, knowledge is like love, something that can be given freely, and still retained in its totality.

David A. Jepsen

David Jepsen writes about growing up on an Iowa farm, learning in a one-room schoolhouse, and coming of age in a small town high school. David has enjoyed baseball all his life. He clings to the notion that baseball *is* a metaphor for life!

A Lesson from Losing

I scramble out of the old 1940 Hudson toting my Stan Hack glove and ash bat and race for the ball field. This is the day! After years of watching softball games in town, this is my chance to play in a *real* game between two country school teams—not a lawn game after the July 4 family picnic, not a "work-up" game or the rare boys-against-girls game at school recess, or one-on-one games with neighbor Larry in his sandy yard or mine. No, this is a game between two *real* teams of kids who live on farms within separate two-mile square areas. There can be no last-minute paid pitchers or "ringers" smuggled from another county as so often disrupted friendly competition in adult town team softball. Miss Flanigan, our new teacher, arranged for our school, Pittsford #1, to play the game at Bennezette # 5, the school two miles north. Today her speech and pace are more rapid than usual.

I rehearsed this game in my imagination many times and contrived reasons why we cannot lose. For starters, Miss Flanigan is a *real* softball player—I watched her play last summer on the Bristow women's team. Of course, the game wasn't quite as exciting as the men's games but it was real softball, played on fresh-mown grass flooded by lights, with an official new white ball and complete with "Hey, baby!" chatter. And now Miss Flanigan is teaching us how to play. Why, she even added two extra outdoor recesses this week so we could practice for the game. I confess that I am not nearly so eager to learn within the walls of our one-room schoolhouse—things like the names of seven continents, spelling multi-syllable words, multiplying two-digit numbers, and what clues help discover how that fascinating civil war mystery book turns out.

A second reason is that we have power hitters. Bob Schneiderman, a tall eighth-grader well-muscled from long hours of farm labor, can drive the punkest softballs onto the gravel road and walk out his home runs. He has done it every time we could persuade him to play with us. The other boys are not so powerful but at least they make contact and are fast enough to beat out hits.

Third, we have speed. Bernard and Larry are fast runners. But Colleen is, hands down, the fastest of all the kids in our school and she is only in the sixth grade! But Colleen isn't much interested in ball games and only Miss Flanigan can persuade her to practice with us.

Finally, we have the right equipment. Today, those of us who own them are wearing "tennis shoes" instead of "work shoes"—they are *so* much lighter! Bernard and I have our own ball gloves and bats; Miss Flanigan has loaned her gloves to Larry and Charles. The school board bought new bats and balls this year. We have the stuff we need to play well.

The September skies are cloudy and the air is cool. The Bennezette # 5 ball field is, really, a mown weed patch with four bare dirt patches arranged in a diamond with another patch in the middle for the pitcher. The square wooden home plate lies loose on the hard clay only a few feet in front of a chicken wire screen backstop. Burlap bags filled with straw are thrown on the other three bare spots. The outfield stretches to the gravel road but Big Bob will have no problem hitting it there, especially since Miss Flanigan found an official new white ball for this game.

The Bennezette lineup includes no kid as big as Bob but they do have a couple more boys than we do. When they all take the field for the first inning there aren't too many places to hit the ball but I am confident Bob will find a place: over their heads! Miss Flanigan's defensive strategy is to play our biggest and best players in the field to stop balls from going to the road and to ask Colleen to pitch because she can run down weakly hit balls. The Bennezette strategy is simple: send the best player out to pitch. The pitcher is pale, tall, and willowy, dressed in a loose-fitting shirt, jeans, and work shoes. As we soon learned, she throws the ball hard, hits the ball far and runs faster than anyone on the field—including Colleen and probably

Miss Flanigan, too. But she looks as old as Miss Flanigan and later we are told that she is 16 and working to finish the eighth grade this year.

About an hour later, Miss Flanigan calls us together and we pile back in the cars. I am disappointed and a bit humiliated. Miss Flanigan's lower lip is quivering, a sure sign that she is upset. I struck out and, after Miss Flanigan asked their pitcher to slow her pitches, hit a weak ground ball. The Stan Hack glove was only a decoration on my hand at third base. Big Bob hit one long ball but he ran no further than second base. Colleen was tenacious in her efforts but there was little she could do to stop the merry-go-round of Bennezette runners. The Bennezette pitcher batted three times and each time she rounded all the bases running "like a girl" with arms stiff at her side. In all my fantasies, I had not reckoned with a player like her. Neither had I allowed that any other player could possibly look forward to this game as much as I did. But there it was.

I learned a lot in fourth grade: the smallest continent is *not* Antarctica and there is a "t" in the first syllable; starting with the last pages of a mystery will spoil the read; don't trust memory on 14 times 14; when writing, always choose a pencil with a good eraser; and...

Talent trounces Gender.

The Boys

A gently sloping sand hill with a gravel road cut through the center divided the farm to the south, owned by my father, from the farm to the north, owned by the Frisbie brothers, Roy and Ray. Father called them "the Frisbie boys" as in "I see the Frisbie boys mowed their alfalfa today." When I was growing up, the "boys" were in their late 40s, bachelors who lived with their mother in a large 19th century farmhouse about a quarter mile off the road. Even though less than a mile separated our homes, I would not see the boys for weeks or months at a time. Still they were our most memorable neighbors.

Our family's respect for the Frisbie boys stemmed from an event that occurred when I was four years old. At the height of a January blizzard, my sister was born in the living room of our farm home. A local nurse assisted with the delivery but she could not help the baby and mother with the life-threatening complications that followed. So a call was made to Dr. Roder and he immediately started the six-mile trip into a blinding snowstorm. The doctor was only able to drive within two miles of our farm before the car stalled in snowdrifts. Four farmhouses fronted on the road between doc's car and our home and, because those neighbors were all on our telephone party line, they knew all about my sister's and my mother's condition. So Harry Reed, Forrest Wickham, Henry Cassman, and the Frisbie boys grabbed grain scoops and walked through blowing snow to move the doctor and his car closer to his patients. Roy and Ray walked the greatest distance, more than a mile and a half, from their home to the nearly-buried car.

The five neighbors took turns clearing the road, shovelful by shovelful, for more than a mile. Then tall drifts on the west slope of the sand hill were too much and the doctor abandoned his car. He grabbed his black bag and stood beside Father who drove his reliable Farmall F-20 tractor through snow banks to our home. I don't know what medicines and comfort the doctor brought, but both mother and baby recovered within a few weeks. Our family was forever grateful to those neighbor men for giving help under extraordinary conditions. And "the boys" from the other side of the sand hill received the lion's share of our gratitude.

Ray Frisbie, the younger brother, filled his bib overalls with a straight, tall profile. When his straw hat was removed, as it always was in front of my mother, there was a distinct white forehead above black, bushy eyebrows and jet-black hair combed straight back. I recall only one time when I saw Ray in anything but the bibs and that was at a neighbor's funeral. Funerals were the only occasions when "the boys" attended any church service. When the time comes to cast Ray's part for the movies, George Clooney would fit his likeness very well. Ray could carry on comfortable conversation not only with farmer peers, like Dad, but also with my mother and Grandpa Ole, both college graduates, and usually with good humor. One of Ray's sayings was "If it ain't one thing, it's six" which he offered whenever bad weather, machinery breakdowns, or livestock diseases impeded a farmer's work. Indeed, I often wondered why such a polite, interesting, and good-looking man never married nor left the sand hill to "see the world."

When I was 14, my younger brother, a neighbor friend, and I were biking on the gravel road that cut through the sand hill. The family dog, Smokey, was chasing whirling bike wheels the same way he would chase rotating car tires—a habit we could not break him of even when we doused him with pitchers of water thrown out of a moving car. An oncoming car slowed to pass us and Smokey turned his attention towards bigger game. He set out as fast as he could go then slipped on the round gravel and slid under the moving car. We heard a thump-thump-thump and then Smokey's limp body emerged when the dust cleared. The car stopped immediately. Ray Frisbie jumped out and ran to tend to the dog. Ray was clearly shaken while I was thinking Smokey had finally met his match.

Ray couldn't revive Smokey so he gently placed the dog on the back seat and drove to our farmyard. We boys peddled home hurriedly and arrived shortly after Ray deposited Smokey on the lawn. Mother was listening to Ray's profuse apologies and offers to replace the dog. But she, too, didn't think Ray was blameworthy given Smokey's habitual high-risk car chasing. They were talking this over for a few minutes when Smokey began to stir, and Ray breathed a sigh of relief to see these signs of life. A few days later Smokey was back chasing cars.

Roy, the older brother by three years, was also tall but his profile looked like the gopher mounds on the sand hill, pushed out and rounded in the middle. His ruddy complexion reflected three decades of daily exposure to the elements and enveloped large features, including a big nose and a wide mouth. His eyes became wide slits when he threw his head back and roared in laughter as he often did. He must have weighed 275 pounds and would often joke about his weight: "If my ass were five pounds lighter, I never would have made it through that mud hole," he bellowed as he drove the little tractor pulling a load of hay through our farm yard. Listening from the kitchen window, Mother winced. I couldn't help but laugh at the joke and the sight. Here was the rotund farmer sitting over the flattened coil spring supporting the tractor seat, just chugging along at a walking pace.

As a little boy, I recall the amazing sight and sound of a huge steam-powered tractor pulling a long threshing machine and a wagon filled with wood down the road past our home. I got a long look because the entourage took over 20 minutes to travel one mile. Today you only see such machines in museums and at threshing day events. Iron wheels taller than Roy drove the machine. The steam engine puffed loud enough to be heard for a half mile down the road and smoke from the firebox left a trail in the hot summer air. Roy was standing in the cab and driving. Occasionally, he tossed wood into the firebox and poured water into the boiler or gave a corrective tug on the big iron steering wheel.

A few years later when I pitched hay in the haymow alongside Roy, he kept me laughing with off-color jokes and stories. His ribald language was much more clever than that of older boys at school. On very hot summer days, Roy would come to work in nothing but bib overalls and shoes…no shirt, no socks, no underwear. "Too damn hot for clothes," he grunted.

Just before I entered high school, Roy surprised neighbors and local town folk when he announced his marriage to Laura, the town postmistress, and that he was taking up residence in town. Roy did a full day's work on the farm and then drove to town for supper with Laura. Each morning after a fresh rain or snow, we could see car tracks on the road leading toward the sand hill. Laura was short, plump, and red-haired with a smooth, freckled complexion. She taught our Sunday school class when I was in high school and was instrumental in cultivating my interest in religion. She was one of a handful of townspeople who earned my respect for her thoughtfulness and steady, firm manner. Nevertheless, the contrast between Laura's grasp of Bible verses and Roy's use of the same words in curses was difficult to reconcile.

Roy was an outspoken New Deal, capital D Democrat, one of few who boasted about it in a county where Republican candidates for local offices were usually unopposed. If my father or other neighbors ever talked politics, it was generally grumbling about bureaucrats or Harry Truman. But Roy was an unapologetic booster for FDR's programs and Truman's policies.

My grandfather Ole Davidson, a retired civil engineer, lived with our family during my high school years, when he was in his late 70s. He spent most of his time reading—often re-reading and underlining his Bible in red pencil—and had no callers. Consequently, he felt no compunction to shave or dress up or put in his false teeth on a regular basis. He would shuffle down the stairs in his slippers to dine with us at noon and for supper.

Grandpa must have met Roy and Ray at a noon meal during haying and was drawn to the Frisbie boys. Perhaps it was the stories around the dinner table or the sheer volume at which they were told. Whatever his fascination, Mother recognized it and invited "the boys" for supper one summer evening. They arrived dressed in clean shirts and overalls, were greeted by Father and followed Mother's instructions to find a seat on our screened porch. Soon Grandpa joined them, clean-shaven, mouth full of teeth, and wearing pressed pants and shirt and polished shoes.

What a trio! Since graduating from Iowa Agricultural College in 1897, Grandpa had worked building railroads and hydroelectric dams in many places around the Midwest, such as Bagnell Dam in the Ozarks. Except for occasional visits home, his work kept him away from wife and children. After Grandma died and the Depression slowed building projects, he managed a CCC camp in Oskaloosa, Iowa. During the Second World War he worked for Stone and Webster Engineering Company building rail lines leading into Oak Ridge, Tennessee but did not know what was going on there until after the war.

Roy and Ray trusted radio and newspapers to inform them about the world beyond our neighborhood. They each had completed less than seven years of formal schooling, succumbing to the lure of the farm at about age 15, perhaps through no choice of their own as their father was incapacitated. I don't believe they ever purchased new machinery or new cars, preferring to run their equipment to a "natural" end and then park it in the grove.

After serving preliminary iced tea, Mother retired to the kitchen to prepare a meat-and-potatoes feast while the main feature commenced on the porch. The three men took turns telling stories, making jokes and arguing politics. Father and I were reduced to spectators. I recall the peals of laughter—long, loud laughter that echoed off the barn's mansard roof. It was as gleeful as any evening I remember on the farm. I'll never know what common ground they found; was it progressive politics, salty humor, loud talk, exaggerated stories, or their hermit-like life?

Manitoba Moments

Canadians, and Manitobans in particular, pridefully describe their communities as "cultural mosaics" rather than "cultural melting pots." At least that is what they told visiting Iowans in the summer of 1975 when our family lived, worked, and played in the Winnipeg area for a seven-week summer. All summer long, ethnic groups such as Icelanders, Kiev Russians, Croatians, Scots, Irish, French, and so on, celebrated their heritage at weekend festivals. Community members served ethnic foods, such as the Icelandic prune pastries we sampled one weekend. At another festival, we felt the crescendoing emotion as Kiev kids finished a traditional deep knee bend dance and a teary-eyed crowd leaped to its feet, cheering and clapping wildly. We paused to view a map of Croatia and were given a short lecture punctuated by strong emotion about how they were simply visitors in Canada and would return to their homeland soon.

One such ethnic celebration attracted us in late July to Morris, Manitoba for a full-day festival. I recall seeing a wide-based Dutch windmill squatting prominently on the festival grounds as I steered the Plymouth sedan into the parking area. My wife, two daughters (ages five and three), and I tumbled out and walked toward the frying food aromas and the rhythmic sounds of folk music. The expansive deep blue sky contained not a single cloud to protect us from the sun's burning rays and steamy heat. No clouds, that is, until midmorning when a little lone dark gray cloud peeked conspicuously over the western horizon. After about 30 minutes, I spotted the same cloud—now much larger but still alone, still dark—still moving toward us at a rapid pace. People around me took notice of the lonesome cloud but we all continued to enjoy the celebration, watching gaily attired dancers, listening to "oompah, oompah" music, sampling mellow cheeses and drinking cool fresh milk. Then, all at once, the cloud unloaded big splatting raindrops that bounced off the grass, far apart at first but wide and juicy. Then drops found our heads and we scurried for cover inside the windmill. The rain increased in intensity accompanied with bright flashes that preceded loud claps of thunder.

The windmill was crammed with celebrators like olives squeezed in a jar. Just as the crowding was getting uncomfortable, especially for the three-year-old I was holding, the rain stopped and the sun shone bright as ever. And the festival took up where it left off as though a maestro had cued the small crowd to resume playing after a rest in the score.

This storm was not at all like Iowa thunderstorms I had experienced from boyhood on. Instead of cloudbanks on the horizon, I saw one lone cloud. Instead of warnings from gradual darkness and rumbling thunder, the sun shone brightly most of the time and the thunder waited courteously until after the super-sized raindrops made their appearance.

As the Plymouth carried us north toward home that afternoon, the eastern skies radiated a deep, dark blue, more like what we see in Iowa *before* a rainstorm. A dazzling rainbow stretching from the northeast horizon to the southeast horizon gradually appeared, dim at first and then brighter and brighter until the colors shone vividly against the darkened sky. Then we noticed a much taller, multicolored arc spanning the sky above and semicircling the first rainbow. Finally, like a small nesting doll, a third rainbow peaked from under the first. Three distinct rainbows—nature's mosaic—beamed at us simultaneously as we cruised along between Manitoba wheat fields.

Gandy Dancing

A mid-1950s Iowa summer morning and the sun pounds down on eight men bent over work with picks and shovels. Mixed smells of creosote and sweet clover linger with no breeze to move them. Visible waves rise from the steel railroad track and rock roadway cut through a draw. This was my workplace for two summers between college terms. The job was railroad section hand, also called gandy dancer. The job paid well, provided regular if tiring 40-hour weeks, and introduced me to skills my muscles soon forgot and characters not easily forgotten.

My first day working for the Chicago Great Western (CGW) railroad began early one June morning at the Hampton depot. A fellow section hand named Ob, short for Obadiah, had given me a ride for the 18-mile trip from his town. His son Johnny, a remarkably frail kid, had finished high school one year ahead of me and immediately enlisted in the Air Force. Like Johnny, Ob was short and skinny, didn't talk much, and smiled easily. We agreed to share rides for the summer. One morning I arrived early at Ob's house, knocked on the door, and Mrs. Ob invited me to wait in the front room. What I saw has stayed with me the rest of my life. The floor was simply a series of unfinished 2 x 8 planks—no rug, no linoleum, just bare planks. There were spaces between the boards and visible through those spaces were the tops of weeds! Implausible as it seems now, I am certain that's what I saw; a room that needed sweeping—and weeding!

Ob was frequently the object of anger from our foreman, Carl, who showed little patience when Ob didn't get tasks done quickly enough. Ob said nothing, grinned meekly, and went back to work. One day Carl found a shovel with a broken handle and immediately confronted Ob. After bawling him out, Carl ordered Ob to take the shovel home and replace the handle himself. The next morning Ob climbed into my car with a grin and placed between us a shovel with a new handle.

On a typical morning, Ob, Carl, and I waited at the depot while about 50 yards down the track the assistant foreman, Pancho, and four other crew members lifted a small motorized rail car onto the tracks. This car was called a "putt-putt," after the sound made by its two-cylinder engine. They coupled it to a short tool car, loaded with shovels, picks, jacks, long crowbars, etc., and pushed it down the tracks to the depot. The crew placed their lunch pails and a large water cooler onto the tool car and took their seats. Lowest in seniority, I sat on the end of the tool car, watching the depot gradually disappear.

Our crew was responsible for maintaining about 35 miles of railroad, checking track and roadbed, and then making repairs. As we rode the rails, Carl sat in front on one side of the putt-putt and Pancho on the other, each scrutinizing one rail for signs of deterioration. The crew's most common tasks were tamping ties when water or wear had loosened gravel underneath, straightening rails that slipped out of gauge, and replacing broken ties or missing spikes. As the rookie, I carried 50-pound steel jacks, two at a time, from tool car to work site, then jammed the jacks under the rail and pumped the jack handle, a five-foot-long steel crowbar that also functioned as a lever when shoved under ties. When the rail and ties were lifted to the appropriate height—as determined by when Carl yelled "Whoa!"—workers used shovels to tamp ballast made of gravel and crushed rock under the lifted tie.

Most days, three or four trains moved freight over our section of track. Carl knew the times when trains were going to pass, so we could stop our work and clear the tracks a few minutes before a whistle was heard. One afternoon, we looked up from tamping ties to see a locomotive headlight bearing down on us from around the curve. Carl raced toward the train signaling the engineer to slow down while Pancho yelled orders in Spanish. We yanked the jacks out, threw tools in the ditch and scrambled to a safe spot on the rise near the fence. As the locomotive slowly rolled past us, the engineer wagged his finger.

Some days, Carl would ride the putt-putt alone to examine the full 35-mile section. He left the tool car, the crew, and Pancho with instructions to supervise a specific work project. Pancho always worked at a fast pace and expected the rest of us to do the same. Poor Ob got no rest when Pancho was boss. Pancho seldom spoke and when he did it was in broken English. Usually he would show me how to do a task and seemed to take special delight in doing so. As the summer progressed, he called me by name, "Day-bees," usually when he wanted me to work faster. Even today, I call myself "Day-bees" when correcting mistakes or accelerating my pace.

The work crew usually ate lunch under a shade tree or in a depot. One day, Pancho offered me a "sweet" pickled pepper fresh from his wife's kitchen. I bit off a small bite and ran for the water cooler amid a chorus of laughter.

Carl was unquestionably the boss. He was a short, well-muscled man in his late 30s dressed in solid blue bib overalls, blue work shirt, and straw hat—he refused to wear the typical striped denim railroader's cap. First thing in the morning he would always appear clean-shaven, smelling of after-shave, with eyes that sparkled when he greeted me. About the time the work gang pushed the putt-putt to the depot, his cheeriness dissolved into a riveted attention to tasks at hand. Each morning, he emerged from the depot with work orders from his boss, the division superintendent, that he received via telegraph or telephone. On my second day on the job, I was tamping ties using a shovel grabbed off the tool car. Carl came up to me, demonstrated the correct technique and then, pointing to his initials carved on the handle, commented "Nice shovel you have here." The crew looked up in anticipation, but Carl moved on and I found another shovel.

124

Later in the summer when our crew was laying new rails—we laid rail one full Saturday thus earning double pay—Carl called me aside to check his calculations about the number of rails per mile. I was glad for the break—and apparently my response was satisfactory, as he asked me again, and later we talked about solving mathematical problems associated with his job. I sensed that he didn't mind having the college kid around. Decades later, a cousin—who, it turned out, attended the same church as Carl—told me that Carl thought highly of my work.

That first summer job went smoothly. After eight weeks I was laid off because by contract any railroader who started a ninth week must join the union and be given first call the next time the crew was enlarged.

So how did the name gandy dancer get attached to this work? Railroaders don't know but a little research revealed two plausible explanations. Apparently "Gandy Company" was stamped on the iron tools such as long crowbars and jacks used in 19th century railroad maintenance, but no one has found any record that such a company existed. And "dancing" is derived from the workers' rhythmic sway when carrying rails (with tongs) and when applying their collective strength to crowbars in unison in order to straighten track. African-American railroad workers sang or chanted verses to cue synchronized rhythmic pulling. Mid-50s Chicago Great Western workers, however, were satisfied to pull in unison to Carl's call of "One, two, three, pull!"

Gandy Dancing, Part II

The following summer I applied for a section hand position with the Chicago and Northwestern (CNW) railroad. A section crew worked out of Dumont, only six miles from home, and I was in luck, as they needed another hand.

I joined a crew of three men: Adolph, the foreman, and two sec-tion hands: a short, slender, middle-aged man who boasted that he was from Frost, Minnesota, "the only town where there's Frost on the depot year round," and Rupert—perhaps in his mid-twenties—who had worked for the railroad a few years and took it upon himself to orient me to the job and union rules. For example, he insisted that I join the union and compel the CNW to terminate me after eight weeks.

Rupert told the story about how Adolph moved to Dumont 20 years ago to work for the railroad and, seeking companionship, placed a mail order for a wife. A few weeks later, a woman arrived at the depot and Adolph immediately took her to the justice of the peace to make the bond official. They now had several children. Adolph's appearance was distinctive; for example, his salt-and-pepper hair hung unfashionably long and unkempt and many mornings he arrived with a day or two's growth of whiskers. His wire-rimmed glasses with thick lenses fogged over when he worked up a sweat. He sported conventional striped bib overalls, blue work shirt, and railroader's cap. But what stood out—and workers snickered about it behind his back—was the long hairs hanging from his nose. Rupert said it was an especially sorry sight in the winter.

Later in the summer our local crew was joined by a special work crew that bunked in an old caboose on a sidetrack near the Dumont depot. Their appearance in town occasioned a lockdown; the only other times houses were locked was when carnival troupes came to town or when gypsy bands camped nearby. This crew lived up to ad-vanced billing. About six men tumbled wearily out of the caboose each morning usually dressed in the same clothes as the day before, lifted their own putt-putt and two tool cars onto the tracks, filled their water coolers, and scooted out of town. The days that our crew worked next to the special crew, I was on edge. I felt sure that one large fellow had his eye on me from the time he first saw me. One day when I was moving jacks around a curve in the track and out of

Adolph's sight, he started to ride me pretty good. But Adolph sensed what was happening and appeared in a few minutes. A little reflection about the work I was assigned during those days would probably reveal other instances when Adolph or Rupert stayed close enough to intervene if needed.

Each day, we took breaks for morning coffee and much-needed drinks of water as well as a lunch break at noon. One noon we were visited by an old railroad hobo named Scoop Shovel Scotty, so named because he could play a "tune" by bouncing a scoop shovel on the bar room floor and earn a few coins. I later read that Scotty had been voted "King of the Hoboes" at the annual Britt, Iowa, Hobo Festival not once but *eight* times, the first in 1936. I was told that Scotty would arrive early at the festival and prepare mulligan stew for the voters, his fellow hoboes. The same news story noted diminished competition because hoboes were becoming extinct in the 1950s. Actually Rupert and Mr. Frost, Minnesota did most of the talking that noon, as Scotty would nod and grin but uttered few words. Despite temperatures in the 90s, Scotty was dressed in overalls, long-sleeved flannel shirt, and heavy socks, but I don't recall seeing his bindle or shovel that day. His face was weather-beaten and his entire left ear was missing, exposing the ear canal. I was told the obvious: that the ear had frozen off.

Rupert made it a point to tell me that hoboes are not beggars or bums; they worked for their food and lodging, such as it was. "Hoboes will work, tramps won't, bums can't." Scotty made regular stops around Dumont, visiting back porches where a warm meal would appear and friendly businessmen who would offer a half-day job cleaning a garage or vacant lot.

I admit I once imagined romance in railroading. As a young boy, I listened to a distant wailing train whistle on sultry summer evenings. As our old Hudson waited at a railroad crossing, I practiced counting railroad cars. And, of course, whenever I caught their attention, I waved at engineers. One particularly hot afternoon that summer, the "local" train—a short one that stopped at every town and was composed of an engine and a caboose with eight to 10 cars between—stopped where we were working. Since the section crew was finished working for the day, I accepted an invitation to ride the caboose into the Dumont depot. I climbed the back steps and surveyed the inside of the caboose, the brakeman's workstation. Nothing special. When the train started, I bounced along sitting on a plain board seat in the all-metal car with no open windows and, like a bad dating experience, lost all sense of romance.

Postscript

Fifty years later I watched a section gang replace a railroad tie on the Boston-to-Washington Amtrak line running near our summer cottage in Connecticut. The work gang was about the same number as our 1950s crew. Instead of jacks they used a backhoe-like machine to lift the rail. Then the tie—molded concrete rather than creosoted wood—was removed and replaced in about the same time our CGW gang would have taken. The 21st century Amtrak gang stood and watched. Such is progress.

Mildred Lavin

Mildred Lavin's personal essays and poetry have entertained the members of multiple writers' groups for nearly two decades. She in turn receives pleasure in listening to the stories of those whose backgrounds are different from her own experience of being a "first generation" American. As a writer, Mildred provides an honest look at life based upon her 52 years of marriage, the raising of three children, an academic career in continuing education, and on the cutting edge of women's equality, her nearly two decades as a widow, and the everyday experiences of aging. No matter how serious the topic might be, Mildred provides a counterpoint with a bit of light humor. She frequently writes about her good fortune to live in Iowa City, "the very best part of our world."

A Habit Learned Early

Now that I've lived long, I take some time to look back, to think about some of the years gone by. I find it interesting to think about who I am, have been, and continue to be—still with some old habits. Makes me wonder why they persist, even through a consistently changing life. And yet, why do I hang on tightly to some old, old habits? Not that I'm regretful or negative about them. No, it's just that I wonder about their perseverance through my long years. After all, by now I should have enough insight to make adjustments to newer, more contemporary lifestyles. And truly, I do. So, I ask, why do some of my old-time behaviors stick with me—forever?

Here's one old habit I've just figured out for myself. It has to do with my never-failing and prompt *bed-making*. I realize I *just can't* leave a bed unmade. When I thought about that possibly compulsive addiction, I realized it has a history behind it going back to my childhood. Let me explain.

By my age four, the family had rented a small apartment in Logan Square, Chicago, up on the third floor in a red-brick building on Emmet Street. I liked it up there, where I could look down from our back porch to see the neighbor kids playing hide-and-seek.

One item there I cannot forget was my parents' bed. It was called an "in-a-door" or Murphy bed that folded up into its rear wall in the living room, with two doors closed on it to conceal springs and feet. My Mama and Daddy had given the apartment's one bedroom to my brother and me. Of course, we went to sleep hours before they did.

When we went to school, after a nourishing breakfast ending with that horrible spoon of cod liver oil, I never thought of our unmade beds. But after school, our bedroom was ever so neat. Those bedspreads of royal blue satin—they shone! We were careful not to mess anything in that room—never played in there. Only in a corner of the dining room and at the small kitchen table did my brother and I have a space to use crayons or play games. A bedroom was for sleeping. And being neat! Our mother had standards.

When I was 11, our parents decided their son and daughter should not be sharing a room: soon I would become "mature." We left Emmet St., moved farther north to Dawson Ave., again on a third floor, but this time with a bedroom for Mama and Daddy. And in two years there, also room for a crib: we now had baby Joanie. Yes, she was a surprise addition to our family.

My memories tell me the beds, wherever we slept, were always properly made as soon as Mama got to them. Never left open, except to air momentarily. When we moved again, we went farther north to St. Louis Ave. where we rented a small bungalow. Enjoyed a back yard with grass and flowering shrubs. I slept on a narrow daybed in the dining room, brother in a closed porch, my parents in one of the two bedrooms. Grandfather, Mama's dad, lived with us then and he had the other bedroom. Beds were always neatly covered: Someone might come to visit; it would be a *shandeh* (shame, in Yiddish) not to have them presentable.

And then, still another move to a house on Lawndale Ave. We Hanzels rented the apartment on the second floor. Little sister and I shared a small bedroom. I liked to come home from Von Steuben High School to a quiet place for reading in that bedroom. Only, of course, if little Joanie was taking her afternoon nap.

High school years over, I went to one of Chicago's junior college night schools to start on a college degree. Days were spent keypunching at a downtown War Department building. My bed was sorely needed for my sleep, and I had no concern to see to its neatness, as I recall. My mother took care of everything at home.

By age 20½ I left that apartment to marry my loyal, steady boyfriend. I left my seven-year-old sister to my old bedroom. We newlyweds redecorated it; now it had dark blue walls, the bedspreads of bright red corduroy.

That year, 1945, apartments were under "rent control." We were lucky to find our Chase Ave. first apartment—furnished. Only a few blocks from Evanston, on the north end of Chicago, it had one room with a tiny kitchenette/dinette, for $50.00 per month!

And now we were the sleepers on a Murphy bed. It settled right down in the living room for the night. My husband and I straightened the bed coverings and cheerfully replaced our bed into its closet each morning.

Our first-born had his crib in what had been the dinette. Before he was two, we moved into a five-room apartment on Seward St. in Evanston: a second child was on the way. Our bedroom, by that time, had proper furnishings. I made sure the bed was neatly made as soon as possible. It shouldn't be a *shandeh* if someone came to visit. Or was that just for my eyes?

From here we moved to our first custom-built house, in Glenview, just west of much fancier Wilmette. Our third child, a daughter, had her early years there, away from the city, in a small town that had recently become a Chicago suburb. And she had her own bedroom. There were chenille and woven bedspreads in appropriate colors for all our beds. Our kids were taught to "make their own beds." This was a family tradition.

Leaving Illinois to be graduate students at the University of Iowa, we rented a duplex apartment in Iowa City, on High Street. It was more than adequate; it included *three* small bedrooms, enough to sleep family when they visited.

Daughter Amy, after graduating from Southeast Junior High School, could walk to City High. Both our sons, by then, were gone from our home. After achieving our graduate degrees, and obtaining employment at the U of I, we knew we'd be Iowans from then on.

Our first house was on Willow St. and then in two years, we built on acreage along what is now Rapid Creek Road. Our next house rose from a cornfield then on Amherst St. and Lower West Branch road, in the east end of town. All had sufficient bedrooms, and during the days, had neatly covered beds. Oh, yes, guaranteed.

Do you assume I am judgmental about the many unmade beds I've observed over the years? Heck, no! Those folks enjoy the casual, inviting look—and why not? They should enjoy what pleases them. Their unmade bed calls to them, "You're invited: just pop right in and snuggle up with a good book." No doubt their mothers approved.

Today, it's almost 12 years since I became widowed. Many things have changed in my life. Yet, I still find myself attending promptly to my bed-making chore. Yes, even for a temporary hotel bed. It's a steady habit in my lifestyle. And no wonder: my mother taught me well. And for so many years, my husband appreciated orderliness throughout our homes.

No, this bed-making is not my compulsive addiction. It's nothing to fret about at all. I know it's OK for me—especially now that I've taken the necessary time to consider its varied history. Each time I make my bed, this little habit ties me to all those places and times, and reminds me of the satisfactions of a life well lived.

Becoming a *Mensch*

My friend Victor Camillo recently gifted me with a book that lists the necessary guidelines for being a true *mensch.* That's German for "person," but when Eastern European Jews adopted the word into Yiddish they gave it much stronger meaning. For them it was a high achievement—almost "noble"—to be considered a *mensch.* The word for them included attributes of kindness, generosity, compassion, humility, justice, respect for self and others, and even more. The book relates these attributes for being a true m*ensch* to teachings in the Hebrew Talmud, the book of Jewish teaching (beyond those in the Bible) put together by scholars over the centuries that Jews lived in the Diaspora.

Even into the modern era, when a youngster was heading for foolishness (teasing his sister, not respectful of teachers) an angry parent would shout to the kid, "Be a *mensch*!" So you can understand why I, raised by non-orthodox Jewish parents, would value a book explaining the teachings of the Talmud as these relate to being a *mensch.*

So much to strive for! In this book, the term *mensch* is both male and female—a modern adjustment. I read on the cover and on the internet about the book's author, Dr. Ronald Pies, and was much impressed. He is a professor of psychiatry at two medical schools: SUNY and Tufts. He has authored many books. His list of research articles in the book's bibliography would take me a year to peruse.

How has Dr. Pies' book affected my thinking about living my long life? I never thought it was easy to be truly a *mensch.* Our parents did make efforts to teach their children to live the *menschlike* philosophy. With their encouragement I tried to practice these ethical principles, though consciously trying for such high ideals didn't always come easy.

One doesn't have to be Jewish to be "like a *mensch.*" In 1969, my husband and I first came on a visit to Iowa City from Chicago to participate in interviews as possible candidates for the Ph.D. degree from the University's College of Education. We hoped they would take on two Master's degree graduates who happened to be married. That shouldn't matter one bit, we thought. Still, it was not a certainty. We hoped to make good personal impressions in addition to the academic records they had already received.

After a comfy overnight in a quiet motel, we decided we should take time to stop for a light breakfast on our way to the Jefferson Building in the "downtown" of this Iowa City.

We were told the Jefferson was once a hotel, but now it housed the office of the college where we were soon to appear. On the way, we noted how un-crowded this downtown was. We liked that.

Now we spotted an eatery called *Hamburg Inn #1*, on Iowa Avenue. Seating ourselves, I checked my lipstick (had the mirror in my purse). I must look well-groomed for my interview!

A young waitress came to our table. Before I could tell her my order I noticed that a button was just about to fall off my jacket. "Oh!" I moaned as I held that button in my hand, my eyes swelling. I was dressed in a two-piece suit I had purchased especially for this important event. How could this happen now, an hour before our appointment?

Our waitress noted my distress. She told me, most sincerely, "Don't you worry honey. I'll get you a needle and thread. You'll be fine."

Sure enough we saw her quickly returning from the back room with the needed items. My emotional thanks to her were most sincere. I remember thinking, "This would never happen in Chicago!"

The button attached, our scrambled eggs finished, and coffee happily imbibed, we set out for our interviews. As we left *Hamburg Inn* my husband remarked to me, "Now there's a *mensch* for you."

Grinning with happiness, I responded, "I hope we get to live and work here."

We did, of course, and 42 years later I'm still here, feeling like a *mensch* for the good luck and good decisions we made.

Fixings

Why was it that they never let me fix things when I was a girl? Dad showed my only brother how to use hand tools and fix things when he was still just a kid. I remember looking at my hands: Were they any different from my brother's hands? We were so close in age that our hands were actually the same size. We both took piano lessons and played with just about the same skill at our recitals. But hand tools for fixings were only for males. I never questioned this sex stereotyping, at least not until decades later.

Even as a little kid I noticed that my mother never gave even simple cooking lessons to my brother. She surely did with me, whether I wanted to cook or not. Yes, I did understand that kitchens were strictly of female concern. In that small Chicago apartment, I stood on a footstool to assist my mother at the kitchen sink. She cautioned me about the dangerous knives I would handle, cutting the mushrooms, scraping the carrots, slicing the cucumbers. I had to be careful or I could cut a finger. Looking back, I realize we certainly used all kinds of equipment in the kitchen, some of it dangerous, but never considered those sharp, effective items as tools.

In public school, manual arts or "shop" was the course for boys and home economics (that was cooking) was only for girls. Something mysterious was going on here.

When anything needed fixing, Dad went right to it. Mother's role was to inform him of the need for repair. Dad approached a repair task seriously. Cooking didn't seem to merit the same respect compared to those important chores that required pliers, wire, measurements, sandpaper, and drills.

I think I would have been amazed and pleased if I had been invited to observe the challenging needed repairs. I blame myself for not seeing earlier this faulty logic of assigning interests and occupations by gender. I could have watched the fixings, learned some of the essentials, but my girlfriends and I never thought about what we were being denied. We sought to read a good book or go out to play jump rope. Early on, I settled for not learning to live a fuller, hammer-and-nail-filled life.

Came marriage, and it was my husband who was the appointed one to fix, and to be keeper of the fixing tools. But he was a man who said he wanted a "partner/wife." To my surprise, he wanted me to know how to work with the hand tools, as he did. I didn't have to admit my zero experience with tools. He knew. His expertise was far superior to Dad's and brother's. The tools in his hands simply sang—never a mistake, never a wound from mishandling. He loved fixing stuff and building things and I was terribly proud of him. And he taught me well—everything but the power saws.

Some women friends I made in my later life admitted to no such disadvantaged pasts when it came to fixing things. They were from rural backgrounds. Some claimed to be just as good at fixing things with tools, large and small, as their brothers. Some of them appreciated the advantages of their equality in fix-it roles. Others told me they couldn't wait to get away from all the heavy work. They happily took up life in the city, where landlords did whatever fixing was needed.

My biggest luck was to have a rare husband who never took on macho characteristics. He encouraged me in all aspects of learning. I learned to use steel wool, and to fix squeaks with a bit of oil strategically placed. So simple. In our home in rural Iowa, I gardened with rakes and hoes, and broke into the earth with a heavy rototiller, though I used that machine only when he was right there with me.

Coming to Iowa, already in my middle years, I had more to learn about other fixings. Here in Iowa I heard the term "fix a meal," as in "What should I fix for supper?" First time I heard it I thought, what's wrong that needs fixing? No, I learned, that was just "preparing or making a meal" as we big city folks called it.

We just didn't know the roles that fixing played in the more rural parts. I heard about pet animals getting fixed: this needed some explaining.

Then there was intention, as in "I'm fixing to take a nap now." "Are you fixing to argue with me?" These were all new to me.

First time I heard "I'll fix his clock" I asked, "What's wrong with it?" But when they told me "She's got herself in a fine fix now," shaking their heads negatively, looking gloomy, I understood that one without further explanation.

Today, I'm alone in my house. It needs fixing here and there. Nothing major requiring the professionals as yet. In my kitchen there's a deep drawer filled with hand tools, nails, sandpapers, glues, and tapes. I do enjoy correcting the small wearings and tearings as they occur. I can even fix a decent meal for company. Actually, a delicious one. I think my parents would be proud. I know my old partner would think I've got it just about right. From him, I can even hear applause.

Mango Lesson

In my good, long life, I had never eaten of the mango: that plump fruit from south of the border, its multicolored skin so temptingly smooth. It was finally time. It happened during a Chicago visit with my old friend, Anita. Sharing high school memories, we are still best girlfriends. While grocery shopping together, we stood at a display of these mango beauties. Wasn't I buying the wonderful mango, she asked me? No, I admitted. I'm a failure on this matter. Don't have the necessary skill to bring it to the edible stage.

Enthusiastically she began to sell me on the delights of this delicious fruit, introduced to *Norteamericanos* in recent years, flown up to us in cargo planes. I had noticed these Latino fresh fruits, even admired them, so neatly stacked with their cousins, the papayas, the guavas, alongside vast displays of our domestic standards.

On a vacation some years ago, I remember seeing mangos in that small Caribbean island, Cozumel. There, a short Mayan street vender offered this fresh treat, peeled and cut into petal shapes around the hidden pit. I didn't even recognize it as mango.

Shopping back home now, Anita was coaxing me not to be an old fogey. "Oh, come on," she says, "You've just got to try it—for a new taste thrill. Don't be stubborn. That's not like you." Anita can talk to me that way.

Believe me, I do indulge in foods from cultures other than my own. Still, I approached mango eating with less enthusiasm than my friend thought reasonable. Way back, as high school seniors, we two were adventurous teenagers. Young women that we were, we had the courage, or the romantic notion, to study the playing of the harp. At home, we helped our mothers with preparations for baking apple pies, peach and rhubarb pies. We knew nothing of the mango.

Today, in my 70s, I'm adventurous again. I buy two perfect mangos to take back to Iowa with me. Dear friend that she is, Anita offers to teach me how to prepare a fine mango—how to peel and cut it.

Apparently, there is a knack to doing this properly. At Anita's home, we go directly into the kitchen for my mango lesson.

I watch attentively. After she washes it thoroughly (Anita's too smart to skip that part), she scores the perfect orb with vertical cuts about two inches apart. I see she tries, with some effort, to take the skin off these sections, which are solidly stuck onto the pit. No easy peeling here. After struggling with the deeply dented mango, she moves quickly from the counter. Now, you bend over the sink to eat some—bite into it, let the juice drip. Wipe your face. We look at each other and start to giggle.

Seriously now, her knife slashes away and she shows me the oversize pit. I had no idea that it was the largest part of a mango. I think, this foreign fruit is a charlatan. I'm offered a chunk of mango cut away from the massive hard interior. Nice flavor, lovely texture. Thinking it takes some smarts to wrestle with a mango, I compliment my friend on her achievement.

Anita is picking at her teeth, looking for the toothpicks—and now she runs to the bathroom for dental floss. Seems there are fibrous threads near the pit. If you try to eat mango pulp off the pit you'll have to floss for sure. Anita sucks her teeth and frowns. It's not a giggle anymore. Suddenly she's hysterical, the wild laughter kind. I, too, simply cannot stop laughing till there are tears. Now we're grabbing each other's waists as we hum a Latin rhythm and swing into a mango-tango. We're kids again.

Sobering up, we sit for a breather. Anita reports on her daughter's advice about mangos. That pit, she tells me, is a *bonus*. If you split it open, you'll find a light colored seed nestled within. Handle it carefully! It's only an infant now. Wrap it gently in a wet, paper towel. Soon it will sprout. Then you'll plant it in a flowerpot and, voila!—there's a new mango tree aborning. Yes, that's a bonus all right, if you've a yen for a mango tree. Still, I must give hearty thanks to Anita; she saved me from being a "head in the sand" old senior.

Yesterdays

To myself, I think, I'll choose a good, red apple, a sweet, just- ripe pear, an easy-to-peel tangerine. And seedless grapes are so good. Give me a dependable young banana, never a big pit to add non-edible weight to the grocer's scale. For now, I tell Anita, "Someday, when I'm feeling strong, I promise I'll work on a mango."

Mildred Lavin

Memoir

Me? Write my memoir?
I suppose it's time.
Still, that's hard, holding up memories
Like mirrors, looking for truth in them.
Life hands us so much smoke,
I don't know what's not distortion—delusions.

I begin to write—soon I think I'm lying.
Can it be my life's past was that good, that lucky?
Am I exaggerating?
So easy to forget the sad and bad stuff,
The tough parts, disappointments, embarrassments.
And why not?

There's still time to get it right, for your kids and theirs.
You think you owe it to them.
Or maybe they'll know some things from you—
They couldn't otherwise!

Shall I pursue the work of writing an honest memoir?
Is that even possible?
I may give it a try. But later.
Am I being elusive, dishonest?
Heaven forbid. I'm simply giving a cheer,
I'm still here!

With so much gone now,
Why look back too hard,
Except to bring out the best?
Hang on to that,

Yesterdays

Those wonderfully pleasant stories in your head,
The secret triumphs, the glorious moments—
I'll draw out my memories,
I'll create my truths from them!

Mildred Lavin

Some Words You Don't Ever Forget

There are some words you hear only once and you cannot forget them. Even when you've lived long they stay with you. The experiences they bring back continue to make you smile—or cringe. You wonder at yourself, feeling again the lift or the disappointment those words gave you. I mean the pain of embarrassment, of indignity, nonsense, or sweetness. I want to tell you about just a few such memorable words that still stick with me.

I was only five or so when words gave me a memorable trauma. Picture me at my uncle's wedding where in the midst of the happy family I say of the bride, "Her face looks like a horse." I had heard my mother say that privately. Why didn't my mother get slapped? I can still feel the sting on my cheek.

By eight years old, I was allowed to check out books from our neighborhood public library. This was a treat for me. But one cold winter day, that mean old librarian scolded me. "Wipe your nose little girl!" she says loudly, and in a library! I carried the shame for years. I hear her words and make sure my purse never lacks the essential tissues.

I had become a young woman at 12, almost 13. Mother helped me buy brown wrapped boxes of Kotex at the drugstore. She saw that I was properly prepared for the momentous event, having read Kotex's famous pamphlet, "Marjorie May's 12th Birthday." I must have had some need to show off that I was so grown up. At school I approach an admired hall-monitor girl and asked her, "Which brand of sanitary napkins do you buy—Modess or Kotex?" She shoots a pained look at me with a loud "Shssh!"

Memorable words don't have to be painful. At 15, I'm walking in our Chicago neighborhood with my aunt, Anna Beck, just recently escaped from Nazi Germany. Aunt Anna is married to Mother's cousin, Arthur. My new aunt's English is halting, but I love to hear it. She shares her most important secret with me. Wants me to re- member these words: "*Love* is the most important thing in life." Though I'm so young, I feel sure that I'll keep those words of heart- felt advice. And I do. They've stayed with me over the long years.

Now I'm a know-it-all 17. I'm at war with my mother. My older brother watches me crying and shouting angrily. He tells me in a se- rious tone, "If your boyfriend Marv sees you like that you'll lose him for sure." Those words, though totally faulty, stuck with me. And I never lost him, not for 52 married years. Though I admit to some quiet crying in our early years together. I was accused of being "thin skinned." How thin? He tells me: "one cell thick."

I'm 18 and we're going steady. This evening, I am to meet my sweetheart at the downtown Blackstone Hotel lobby. Of course, after a day-long job at a War Department office, I must duck into the ladies room to refresh my face at the mirror. Must have overdone the black eyebrow pencil. On dashing out, heart aflutter to see my beau—he's laughing! What? His unforgettable words: "My God, you look like Groucho Marx. Get back in there!" Will I ever live that one down?

One of the many "bosses" I worked for was Dr. Louis D'Amico, director of research and development at my college. That year I was allowed time off the job to attend a last course for my Master's De- gree. A lasting quote from this boss came when he realized that I was better at conference planning than at typing. Looking over my typed work one day, he noted, in a mumble, "I thought you would get better at this." Would I ever forget that callous comment? I should have— but see, it's still with me.

It wasn't until my late 40s that I finally got to travel overseas. For years, I had longed to visit my dad's Israeli family—my cousins. Pi- oneers in British Palestine, those Israelis are known for their frank- ness. They don't intend rudeness; they just haven't adopted the cus- tom of sugarcoating their words. My cousin Chaya studies my figure critically as she throws her shoulders back, pulls in her distended abdomen and says, "Dun't get fat—your Mudder was fat." An exaggeration—but those Polish Jews would never get over their jealousies of the German/Austrian ones whose assumed uppityness was an affront. I forgive Chaya, and remember her so-kind words, too.

Now I'm thinking again of my early years. I can still hear my mother's voice, her accented English. Folks couldn't tell where she was from. A blend of Viennese, French, and Romanian had them guessing. Some of Mother's colorful language is still a source of humor for me. Especially when upset, she would revert to native German-Yiddish expressions. *"Vie a schtein im gurten"* (like a stone in the garden) she would accuse my father when he wouldn't agree to go along with some fun doings. In a happy mood, I hear mother's voice imitating the Viennese slang of the early 1900s. *"Kshossen hamst auf die Schmertz"* (the cannon was fired on the Schmertz mountain). This was said to an almost deaf person who continually asked, "What was that?" We kids got that Schmertz mountain comment when we inquired into grownup matters not intended for our ears.

After bragging to my spouse about the considerable money I saved with a phenomenal bargain, he'd come up with his clever humor. With an outstretched hand, palm up, he wanted to *see* the money I saved. His oft-heard words: "You're still laughing at that one?"

Only a few years ago, I experienced a favorite set of words that won't leave my memory. A friend wrote a sympathy note to me after my husband's memorial service. She shared favorite memories of Marv—his spontaneous humor—and her special thought that remains with me. She wrote, "He looked at you as though he were still your bridegroom." Yes, those cherished words will not escape my old brain. Such a memory stays. It is balm for my heart. Some words can do that—if you don't let them go.

Jeanne Liston

Direct, honest, bold. That is how our group would characterize Jeanne Smith Liston's writing. She draws upon her experiences as a daughter, sister, nurse, mother, grandmother, and friend, and she finds within her personal experiences a "seed of truth" with which readers may identify.

Denise

I admitted Denise to the Gyn/Oncology unit at Loyola Medical Center. She was scheduled for exploratory surgery the next morning so her standard admission orders included a complete blood count, chest x-ray, urinalysis, and enemas until clear. While getting her vital signs I found out that she had been diagnosed with uterine cancer the previous year and had received over 20 radiation treatments at another hospital, but still had her uterus and ovaries.

Denise told me she was in her early thirties and a single parent of three small children. She was about 5'6" tall and quite thin except for a protruding abdomen. She had lanky brown hair that hung to her shoulders and generally had the look of a person that life had not been kind to. She told me she had a boyfriend but did not talk much about her personal life, and I never saw any visitors during her entire stay in the hospital.

Later that evening I went into her room to begin the enemas. I gathered my equipment and got the solution ready. I had Denise roll over onto her side and lubricated the enema tip. I attempted to insert the tip into her rectum but was only able to get it in about an inch and a half. I continued trying to maneuver the tube for a short time, but it was obvious it was not going to go in. I left Denise and went out to the nurse's desk and paged the resident on call and told him what had happened. He said "Just do what you can." In essence all I could accomplish was rinsing her rectum. I had never had this happen with a patient but knew it was not a good sign for Denise.

When I came to work the next evening I found out that Denise had been taken for emergency surgery during the night for a bowel obstruction and had been admitted to the intensive care unit. Loyola had a policy of not admitting cancer patients to intensive care, but had made an exception for Denise because of her young age. About a week later she was transferred back to our unit. Her first night on the floor I accompanied her surgeon into her room to attempt to open a colostomy using a cautery machine. We had some difficulty with the machine and the surgeon finally stopped the procedure without accomplishing his goal. When he had performed her surgery, he had brought a loop of bowel out onto her abdomen but had not finished the colostomy procedure because of her critical condition. Besides the loop of bowel, Denise's flat abdomen had a long sutured incision running from just below her ribs to her pubic bone. She also had a row of four retention sutures. These consisted of button looking disks lined up in a row about two inches on either side of her incision. Suture connected each of the four disks to the corresponding disk on the other side. These kind of sutures were usually reserved for morbidly obese patients.

Since I only worked part-time, I did not see Denise for about five days. My next evening on duty, I was assigned to care for her again. Despite the advantages of continuity of care for Denise, the part-time nurses would be assigned to her to give the full-time nurses a break. Caring for her was very time-consuming and traumatic. All of the nurses were about her age. She was not a difficult or demanding woman but watching what was happening to her body was very unnerving. Her abdominal incision did not heal and gradually opened. Her skin, fat, and abdominal covering gradually seemed to rot away despite everything we did. We spent hours coating her skin with medicated ointments in an attempt to stop the progression.

Denise never appeared to be in pain and would watch us as we cared for her incision. She would visit with us but never asked any of us nurses about her condition or her prognosis. The last evening I cared for her, she said she would like to have some stewed tomatoes. Since these were not on her diet, I called the resident and asked if it was alright. He told me, "Give her anything she wants." About five minutes after eating the tomatoes, I could see them bubbling up in the gaping hole in her abdomen. I rolled her over on her side to pour the liquid contents out of her incision, and again put the ointment on the skin surrounding the wound.

I was off the next couple of days. When I came back to work, I was told she had died. The nurses told me that her electrolytes had continued to get out of balance so that the last day or so she was not aware of her surroundings. That would have been a blessing. I never knew why she was given radiation treatments instead of, or before, having a hysterectomy. Any other patient I cared for over the years had had the surgery first and then the radiation. The problems with the skin were a result of her being over-radiated. I suspect nothing anyone did was going to save her life, but no one should die the way she did.

I thought about Denise a lot and for years her condition and death haunted me. I'm sure many of the other nurses felt the same way. She was our age and we knew something like this could happen to any of us. I always wondered how she could stand to watch us care for her gaping wound and what she was thinking during those times. I hadn't been able to look at my own finger being amputated, and yet she was watching her belly rot. Did she think the doctors were going to be able to fix it? Did she think she was going to get better and go home and care for her children? Or did she know what her fate was going to be? Had she accepted her death before she even came in the hospital? I'll never know.

And if I was back there again, I wouldn't ask her. To ask her prying questions like that would have been cruel and inappropriate. If she had wanted to talk, we were there for her, but it was up to her to initiate the conversation. Many of the young oncology nurses I worked with at Loyola were frustrated when the doctors did not tell patients they were going to die. In my opinion it was the nurses that had the need to talk about the patient's death, not the patient. Most patients knew they were dying; they did not need to be told. Conversations about one's death are usually extremely private and often only occur between the patient and their loved ones.

In my year working that oncology floor, I only had one patient talk to me about her imminent death, and that was to share with me the arrangements she had made for her young children. She also was a young woman in her thirties who had started out with vulvular cancer and had had extensive disfiguring surgery several months before being readmitted with metastasis to the lungs. I had cared for her during both admissions and I felt she had wanted to share that with me. I took her for a CAT scan of her lungs the night before she died and was able to see that she had almost no lung function left. Toward the end, she could no longer talk. She sat up in her bed with her forearms leaning across a pillow on her overbed table. All of her strength was needed just to breathe. I remember looking into her eyes while she gasped for her last breaths. Each breath became farther and farther apart until they finally stopped. I can only hope that what I have read about the dying process is true, and that the changes in body chemistry initiate a feeling of comfort that I was unable to visually perceive.

During that year I watched a lot of patients die, but I had had personal experience with death, so I don't believe it was quite as traumatic for me as for many of the other nurses. Denise was the exception.

Jeanne Liston

Essential Tremor

I have the proud distinction of having failed the Palmer Method of handwriting in elementary school and I even failed printing in nursing school. I drove my teachers crazy with my horrible handwriting, and I have to admit I can't always read my own writing. Thank God for Microsoft Word!

In my late teens and early 20s I became aware that the problem with my handwriting was due to a tremor. My tremor is referred to as an essential or familial tremor that is thought to be inherited through an autosomal dominant pattern of inheritance. I remember my mother having a tremor as she aged, but mine started when I was young and has continued to worsen. My mother's younger brother had a very severe tremor which culminated in his committing suicide in his late 60s. I always wondered if he had any fears of just wounding himself when he held the shaky gun to his head.

Unlike the Parkinson's disease tremor, which occurs when voluntary muscles are at rest, my tremors occur when I try to do something with my hands. Since any kind of physical or mental stress makes the tremor worse, I've had some interesting and embarrassing experiences over the years. I suspect my tremor has had more influence over the path my life has taken than I am even conscious of. As a student nurse, my operating room rotation was a nightmare! Surgical gloves come with five fingers, not the four and a half fingers that I have on my right hand, which was a problem in itself, and shaky hands are not considered an asset in the OR, even if you're not the one doing the microsurgery.

My emergency room rotation was just more of the same. Lots of high-stress and hands-on work with gloves and sterile fields, which I knew were not going be my career path. I couldn't wait to finish with both of them.

Although my fine motor skills have never been good, they continue to deteriorate as I get older. I constantly drop things, not just once, but sometimes repeatedly. I've started counting the number of repeated drops and when I get past three, I frequently let loose with a string of profanity. This seems to help and doesn't seem to bother my dog. I do have to be careful though that I don't do the profanity thing when someone else is around, especially my grandchildren. My daughter does not approve.

Dropping things on the floor is bad enough, especially fragile things, but dropping food is even worse. I can barely get through a meal without dropping at least one morsel of food. A napkin on *my* lap is absolutely no help at all when I miss my mouth. A double mastectomy would alleviate that, but I think that's a little extreme.

Buttons have become the bane of my existence and I absolutely hate them! I almost have to count on extra time to get dressed if I'm wearing something with buttons. My fingers slip and slide all over the material and the buttons fight me all the way. Sometimes I have to just stop and take a deep breath and do something else before going back to the buttons. Blouses do need to be buttoned though as public nudity is illegal, so eventually I have to try again before finally venturing out of the house.

Jewelry is almost a lost cause. I'm allergic to nickel so I can't wear costume jewelry anyway, so when I get a necklace or bracelet on, it's going to be on for a while. I'll be the one playing pickleball with the jangling bracelets. After the trauma I go through to get that lobster claw clasp to work, you can bet I won't be taking it off again until my social calendar is clear. Earrings are almost as bad. Those teeny, tiny backs for stud earrings are impossible for me to manage so I never purchase them.

I gave up on sewing some years back. Spending an afternoon trying to thread the needle on the sewing machine has lost its appeal for me. I can still sew on one of those pesky buttons if I have plenty of time and the hole in the needle is big enough, but I have to be extremely careful with material that will show blood spots.

Does everyone else have to be stripped down to brush their teeth? How many people get toothpaste on their nose? It's a frequent occurrence with me. You'd think with the size of my mouth it would be impossible to miss, but usually at least once a day I will find myself with a big smear of frothy toothpaste on the end of my nose or my chin. Whitening toothpastes are very popular with the public but they work because they have bleach in them. Bleach does not enhance dark, solid color clothing.

Unfortunately we don't get to choose our genetics, so I will just have to put up with the trembling and hope it doesn't get too much worse in the time I have left. On the bright side, a few times my shaky hands have actually been an asset at the poker table. Players who don't know me will notice the shakiness, think I have a big hand, and fold on a bluff. That is truly sweet, although it usually only works once or twice. For the most part though, my tremor is just an embarrassment and an aggravation that I either have to live with or use the shaky gun solution.

Physicians

Physicians are the self-ordained Gods of the healthcare world. As a student nurse in the 1960s, it was immediately clear as soon as I began taking care of patients that the physicians were in charge. They were in charge of their patients and they were in charge of the hospital. They didn't own the hospital, but they had tremendous influence over hospital administration. If a nurse ever crossed them, or for some reason they did not like you, you would be gone. I've known physicians that prided themselves on getting nurses fired.

As soon as a physician approached the nurse's desk, you immediately stood. No matter what you were doing you stopped it and deferred to him. They were all "him" then: all physicians were male. As soon as he arrived at the desk, the charge nurse would get to her feet, gather up the charts of his patients, and follow him from room to room as he made rounds. Frequently the charge nurse would even write his verbal orders in the chart for him to sign. The term "handmaiden" commonly used to describe the nurse was not inappropriate. All power flowed through the doctor and we were subservient. Physicians only talked to student nurses if there was no one else around. We were at the very bottom of the pecking order, they knew it, and we knew it.

If you were caring for a patient when he entered the room, you just stopped and waited while he talked to the patient or the charge nurse if the patient could not communicate. You were the one caring for the patient, but he never asked you about the patient, nor did he read the nurse's notes which you labored over. It was always said in jest, but was actually true, that the only people who read the nurse's notes were the lawyers.

In my first position after graduating from nursing school in 1963, I had a physician ask my opinion about a patient. I was speechless, literally struck dumb. I had never been asked for my opinion about any-thing as a nurse, much less by a physician. I don't remember what I finally said to him, but 47 years later I still clearly remember the incident.

One time as a student nurse I was assisting a physician in the operating room to remove a sebaceous cyst. A sebaceous cyst is a simple cyst that forms at the base of a hair follicle. It was one of the first cases I ever assisted during my surgical rotation, and I was helping a general practitioner who had a reputation for being very difficult. Back in the 1960s general practitioners would occasionally schedule simple procedures to be done in the operating room. I suspect their motivations for doing this were complex, but the leading reason would be money. They could charge more for their services if the procedure were done in the operating room.

The patient was a young man about 18 years old, my age at the time. He was wide awake for this procedure, which was being done under local anesthetic. Before the doctor arrived, I had scrubbed the patient's forehead and begun to drape him for the procedure. When the physician arrived, I held his gown for him and helped him to glove. We finished applying the sterile drapes and the physician began the procedure. It was my role to hand him the few instruments and suture that would be needed. A few minutes after we began, the patient began complaining about being too warm. I reached down and removed some of the drapes covering his chest. The physician went absolutely ballistic, screaming at me that I had contaminated his sterile field. He ranted and raved at me for several minutes, first telling me to get out of the room and then demanding that I come back in and re-drape the patient. After the procedure was over and I was taking the patient back to his room, he said to me, "Boy, I was glad I was me and not you."

This type of behavior was not unusual. What was unusual was doing it in the presence of a conscious patient. I've known physicians to throw instruments, break telephones and other equipment, and just generally have meltdowns in the work place. Those that behave this way would claim they just lost "control." Ironically, they have enough control that it is almost unheard-of for them to do it in front of the patient.

Many physicians are verbally abusive. In my last nursing position I worked with a physician who was frequently verbally abusive. One day we were at a clinic in Mason City and he saw on the schedule that the last patient of the day was listed as a new patient. He called me into an exam room and reamed me out for this perceived problem. When he actually saw the child he found out that this patient was not new to him. He had seen the child before at the university. He never said a word. Physicians never apologize to nurses.

I never worked with him again. Nurses almost never have the power to remove themselves from abusive physicians, but by that time in my career I was in a position where I could get out of going to clinics with him and I did.

Over the years of my nursing career I worked with many physicians. Occasionally I worked with some who were considerate and good partners, but more often than not they were arrogant and condescending. On one occasion as an RN I was sitting in the back of a nurse's station charting. A physician came in and asked me to move. Reflexively, I got up and moved only to discover he just wanted my chair so he could continue a conversation with a colleague. This type of disrespect was common.

In 1976 I took a position at a brand new hospital in Downers Grove, Illinois. All of the staff were registered nurses. There were no nurses' desks. Charts were kept outside the patient rooms and all care was provided by the nurse. The doctors hated it. Their biggest complaint was they could not find the nurses because they were in the patient rooms.

With the current healthcare debate, one of the things not being discussed is the amount of money that doctors make. Most but not all doctors work very hard and have a tremendous investment in their education. It is not unusual for them to finish school with huge debts for financial aid. But how many of us can pay off financial aid in a couple of years? It is not unusual for a physician to charge $40-50,000 for a complex procedure that is done in an operating room. The hospital provides all of the supplies, equipment, and staff; the physician provides his shoes, shorts, and brain. I worked with one physician who groused about the fact that medical school did not teach you how to invest your money.

As I think about the relationship between nurses and physicians, the biggest problem I see is the lack of respect that most physicians have for nurses. They do not see or appreciate that the nurse's role in patient care is just as important as theirs. It is the nurse who spends the time with the patient, provides the hands-on care, and does the teaching. The average physician spends about five minutes a day with the patient. If the physician orders the wrong medication for a patient, he can be held accountable for it, but the nurse is also held accountable if she gives the wrong medication that he ordered. We are not paid enough for this kind of responsibility.

It is not possible to examine the nurse/physician relationship without equating it to the women's movement. Most physicians traditionally were men and most nurses were women. The few men that become nurses are usually easily promoted up through the ranks to the top positions. Unlike male teachers, male nurses are still a small minority so they have not had the same equalizing influence in our profession. Just in terms of gender alone it has never been a level playing field. Men have always had more power and make more money. As more and more women enter medicine we may see a change in this, but we are not there yet.

Michael L. McNulty

Mike McNulty shares an understated dry humor when he writes about his childhood and coming-of-age years in the coal mining area of the "Mon Valley" in western Pennsylvania, or attending California State College. The fact that California State College is located in Pennsylvania, and not in the state of California, may have awakened the spark of passion for his lifelong career as a geographer. In addition to serving as a faculty member in the University of Iowa Department of Geography, and Associate Provost and Dean of International Programs, Mike has visited 20 countries to conduct research, teach, or participate in technical assistance projects with the U.S. Agency for International Development. Those experiences enriched his teaching, research publications, and now his memoirs.

The Fire Chief

My father was the Chief of the Ellsworth Volunteer Fire Department, which meant I got to watch a lot of parades. The Pennsylvania summer, with its long afternoons and lingering sunsets, was the perfect marching season. Weeklong carnivals and Friday night parades were held in every town of any size all up and down the Monongahela River valley and the surrounding countryside.

The Fireman's Parade was a great excuse for the volunteer firemen in the valley to fire up the massive engines of their fire trucks, drive over to neighboring towns, and show off their gleaming trucks and screaming sirens to the folks in surrounding communities. Every community took great pride in these machines with their shiny chrome valves, black coiled hoses, and thick block letters that boldly identified the town they represented. Charleroi, Monongahela, Monessen, Donora, Belle Vernon, Ellsworth, Bentleyville, Cokeburg, Roscoe, Stockdale, Richeyville, and California, all had their annual carnivals and parades.

Ellsworth was my town and my dad was the Fire Chief!

Daddy had driven my mother, Nonnie, and me down to Belle Vernon for the parade. He parked the car, kissed us 'good-bye', and went off to join the men of the Ellsworth Volunteer Fire Department. My mother and I found a place on the curb along the street that afforded us a fine view of the parade route.

We waited in excited anticipation for the start of the parade.

"When is Daddy coming?"

"It won't be long, Michael."

The atmosphere was charged: crowded sidewalks, balloons, carnival rides and other attractions down on the ball-field, and the crowd's anticipation of the Fireman's Parade.

A siren sounds, signaling the start of the parade. All eyes are turned up the street and people crane their necks and stand on tiptoes to get a glimpse of the first marchers in the parade.

161

"Here they come!" The shout goes up.

Led by the Grand Marshal, surrounded by local beauty queens in an open Chevrolet convertible waving and smiling to the crowds, the various units of the parade file by—each town represented by a volunteer fire department and many accompanied by their high school marching bands.

The people of the Mon Valley take great pride in these representatives of their communities—as they do their football teams during the fall. Fierce rivalries and competition between towns were the norm for the Valley.

As we sat on the curb, I watched with great interest as the units swept by: fire engines, marching bands, men and women of the local community organizations and, of course, the Shriners.

The drivers of the fire trucks raced their engines, sounded huge chrome air-horns, flashed emergency lights, and howled sirens as they passed through the crowded streets. The drivers would speed-up suddenly, then back off the gas, causing the massive truck engines to emit a deep-throated rattle and backfire loudly, sending the crowd swaying back on the curb. Those throbbing engines echoed the pounding of my heart as I felt the power of those trucks course through my body.

The engine companies and marching bands paraded by, one community at a time, sending up great cheers and applause from the crowd and eliciting great whoops, shouts, and whistles from the people along the way. Individual knots of people applauded wildly when the men of their community rode by.

My mother and I watched and watched as the units passed by: Charleroi, Monesson, Belle Vernon, then, Ellsworth!

"There's Daddy!"

My father rides by in the cab of Ellsworth Fire Engine No.1: a fine-looking man, black curly hair, handsome face, waving and smiling to the crowd.

"Hey, Reggie!" Someone shouts nearby.

Daddy turns, looks straight at me, flashes a special smile, and gives a wave intended only for me, and then the parade moves on.

My mother and I watch as unit after unit marches by.

Rumpety-dumity-dum…

Ba-ba-ba ba aba ba BOOM!

Bumpty..Rumpity…Bumpty..Rumpity dum!!

Ba! Ba! Ba! BUM! …RUMPTY-TUM-TE TUMPTY-TUM!

RUMPTY-TUM!!! DA…DA Dum!

DADA DUM! PaPaPa PUM!

RUMPTY-TUM!!! RUMPTY-TUM!!!

RUMPTY-TUMPITY-TUM…. RUMPTY-TUM…

RUMPTY-TUMPITY…RUMPTY…TUMPITY DUM!

Rumpety-dumity-dum…Ba-ba-ba ba aba ba BOOM!

Bumpty..rumpity dum!!

Ba…BOOM!

As the last band fades, here come the Shriners in their bright red fezzes and gaudy jackets, proclaiming the El-Kadir Temple of Donora, careening wildly around on the pavement, weaving patterns on the street with their midget scooters, and signaling the end of the parade.

"When is Daddy coming?"

"It won't be long, Michael."

The crowds begin to disperse, drifting toward the carnival grounds down at the ballpark, some squeezing into bars lining the streets, and others returning home, as the long dusk finally gives way to evening.

"Where's Daddy?"

"I don't know, Honey."

"Is he coming back?"

"I'm sure he will. We'll just wait here."

The streets are nearly empty. My mother recognizes a man walking by and asks, "Have you seen Reg?"

"Hi, Non! Yea, I saw him up at the Eagles Club right after the parade."

Yesterdays

Later, another two fellows walk by and my mother asks if they have seen my dad.

"Reggie? No, I ain't seen him. Hey, Chunty, you seen Reggie?"

"Yea, I seen him in O'Brian's a half-hour ago with some guys from Cokeburg."

"Whatsamatter? He got lost?"

"No, I'm sure he'll be here soon."

Finally, one of the men of the Ellsworth Fire Department came by and said, "Hey, Non. Maybe you and Michael better ride back home with us."

So we did.

I was happy and excited.

I got to ride up on the front seat in the massive cab of Ellsworth Fire Engine No. 1.

Even though it was dark and nobody lined the sides of the winding road as we drove back to Ellsworth, I pretended to wave to the crowds as the loud sounds of the engine echoed back from the steep wooded slopes of the valley.

My mother sat very quietly. She seemed tired. She didn't wave.

McRoots: The Girl with the Curl

Meeting Darlene—Doc's Class

I met Darlene in Doc Bontrager's class on general psychology at California State College in western Pennsylvania. Doc's class was perhaps the most interesting, stimulating, and terrifying experience I have ever had in a classroom. Doc was an extraordinary man. He shook the students up intellectually, and emotionally, and his comments were often taken personally, even when he was striving for a larger lesson. He shook me out of the intellectual doldrums of high school. But, more on that later. The other life-altering experience in Doc's class was meeting Darlene Marionette Marshall, the girl I was to marry shortly after our graduation from California.

Darlene sat in the row next to the one I occupied but several seats closer to the front of the room. From my vantage point nearer the back of the room, I could look down the aisle and have a grand view of Darlene. Darlene was a relatively short young woman with beautiful long brunette hair that fell over her shoulders, cascaded down her back, and ended just below her waist, thus drawing attention to a very shapely, ah, bottom. I always tried to hang back at the end of class to follow Darlene out of the classroom and down the hall. I didn't make any overt effort to meet her, not being quite sure how I might initiate a conversation. I had mentioned my interest, and my reluctance, to my friend, Mike Davis—everyone called him "Hubla." He acted as my intermediary, walking straight up to Darlene and telling her his friend would like to meet her. What a concept! So, after this introduction, Darlene and I talked briefly, and in the course of that first, brief, conversation I asked if she ever attended the Saturday night dances at Stockdale, a small mill town north of California on the Monongahela River. She said she did— and I said I hoped I might see her on Saturday. She said, "Fine!" She and her girlfriend might attend.

Stockdale Dance

I, Boozie, and several other friends showed up at Stockdale on Saturday night and joined a growing band of guys standing around the perimeter of the very large hardwood dance floor of the Stockdale Fire Hall. Most of the towns in the valley had large fire halls that served as community gathering places for weddings and other festive occasions—and of course bingo, the national sport in western Pennsylvania. The dance floor was largely populated by couples consisting of two girls dancing with one another while the boys stood around the perimeter, checking out the girls. Once it became clear who was looking at whom, a number of mixed couples began to appear on the floor. The fast dances—jitterbugs, rock 'n' roll, and the like—got out the most dancers, with the girls still outnumbering the boys. Most guys were more interested in "slow dancing" than rock 'n' rolling. For one thing, you actually had to know a little more about dancing to do a decent jitterbug, as opposed to a slow dance. And, most important, the slow dance brought you in much closer contact with the girl you were dancing with. Especially the way a lot of couples tended to dance in the valley: slow, really slow. Often, the couple did little more than hold on tight to one another and sway to the slow beat of the song. "In the still of the night! I held you, held you tight, in the still of the na..ha..hite." A couple could get through most of the record without ever taking more than a few dance steps.

Now, on the appointed night I had planned to meet Darlene, I could not see her anywhere in the crowd. I made several slow walks around the perimeter of the dance floor, trying to act cool and not let on that I was looking for anyone in particular; just sort of checking out the scene. Darlene was nowhere to be seen. As the night wore on, I decided Darlene must not be coming and so, I asked another girl—with a single, long, long curl down her back—if she would like to dance. Several dances later, having learned that she was from Monesson, I asked if she would like a ride home—which she agreed to. Just after that, I spotted Darlene standing with a group of girls along the edge of the dance floor. I went over to her, said, 'Hi!! I thought you weren't coming. I looked all over for you earlier."

"We were a little late getting here," she said. We talked a bit more, and then I told her I hoped I would see her again next week.

The following week, Darlene and friends appeared early. We met up and began to dance: one, then another, then another dance. Finally, when I was really comfortable with her, I asked Darlene if I could drive her home. "So, where's the girl with the curl?" she asked, coolly. But, she agreed I could drive her home, and told her friends she would not need a ride home with them, and we left the dance hall.

The Drive to Allison

Darlene told me that her home was in Allison "not too far from Brownsville," so we set off in that direction. I knew my way to Brownsville with no problem, and we had a nice talk along the way —how did we like Doc Bontrager's class, what were we each majoring in, what did we like to do for fun, what kind of music did we like, etc. Once we got to Brownsville, Darlene said I should follow Route 40 (the "National Pike") toward Uniontown for a few miles, then we would find the turning to Allison, where she lived. Once we had turned off Route 40 the road to Allison turned out to be a narrow winding road that meandered along, clinging to the hillsides and then plunging rather unexpectedly into the creek valley bottoms and across narrow bridges constructed as WPA projects during the Depression era. Not only did the terrain appear more rugged and the valleys more desolate than many that I had seen before, but as we continued along the road, the landscape grew darker and darker— until finally, I swear, I thought we had passed beyond the edge of the lighted world. But, just as I despaired of seeing another light, and started wondering what I had gotten myself into, the few lights of Allison appeared on the next ridge.

Yesterdays

Meeting Bucky

Driving into Allison, Darlene directed me to her home. It was a small house sitting on the right side of the road, on a sloping lot above the road. She asked me to park near the steps leading up to the front porch—which was unlighted, as was the rest of the house. I got out of the car, went around and opened her door, then escorted her up to the house. Still no sign of life appeared, until we reached the porch. As we walked up the last step, a form—that's all I could see, a form—arose from the porch swing to my right and a massive-torsoed, bare-chested man stood looking directly at Darlene.

"Where have you been?" he asked.

"I went to the dance in Stockdale," Darlene responded.

"How did you get there?"

"With my girlfriends…"

"That's how you should have come home!"

By this time, he had opened the front door, ushered Darlene through, and now forcefully slammed the front door without ever looking at or addressing me. I stood there on the dark porch and felt as if I didn't exist. It's a wonder I ever went back.

Michael L. McNulty

Graduation Day – 1962

I really hadn't wanted to attend college. I was surprised when I was actually accepted by the admissions office at California State Teachers College in California, Pennsylvania. I had planned to enter the army, but was persuaded by my mother, Nonnie, to attend college for at least one semester. So, I did. I enrolled in the summer session and attended several classes that literally turned my life around.

I enjoyed the college experience very much, in contrast to my high school experience. In high school I had done everything I could think of to just get by, and often ended up barely squeaking through—and was often thrown out of classes as a "disruptive influence." I graduated 38th out of a class of 52 seniors at Bentleyville High School in 1959.

Now, here I was, three years later, standing along with several hundred other soon-to-be graduates of California State Teachers College. Moreover, I was to be honored at the graduation ceremony by being recognized as the first honors graduate of the college.

I had taken extra credit during each semester and in the summer sessions so that I was earning my degree in only two and a half years of college. My family was very pleased and proud of my accomplishments—especially my mother, Non, who had been responsible for me entering college in the first place. So were my professors: pleased with the work that I had done in coursework and with the independent study that was the basis of my honors degree. With the encouragement of my professors in geography, I had applied for and been accepted into the graduate program in geography at Northwestern University. Moreover, I was also the recipient of a three-year NDEA TITLE IV (National Defense Education Act) Fellowship by the African Studies program at Northwestern. Now, here I was basking in the warmth and fellowship of my classmates and fellow graduates, being offered congratulations on my graduate fellowship and the recognition to be conferred that day as the first honors graduate of the college.

I must say I was very pleased and excited with the recognition and celebrity that would be bestowed on me at the graduation ceremony. I may even have been tempted to feel a little proud of my accomplishments and perhaps too ready to accept the praises of others on that day. But, as fate would have it, I was to be taught a lesson in humility, a lesson that has stayed with me to this day. Whenever I get to feeling a little too satisfied with myself, or tempted to believe that what I am doing is really great and, perhaps, even worthy of the praise or admiration of others, I recall that lesson.

Try to imagine the excitement and anticipation of the graduates and their family and friends milling about the lawn outside of the auditorium. Now, try to imagine that scene as the camera swoops up and away from the assembled crowd and you are treated to a bird's-eye view of the mass of graduates in their flowing gowns and jauntily angled mortar-board hats with tassels. And, as the graduates lined up and prepared to march into the auditorium, a solitary bird flying high above the scene, chose that particular moment to deposit a rather large white dropping on the right shoulder of my black academic gown.

To this day, when I start feeling a little too pleased with myself or sense that I'm getting a little too self-congratulatory, I look up over my shoulder and look for that bird.

Michael L. McNulty

Humpty and Me

Humpty and I go back a long way. So far back that I can't remember the pre-Humpty days. I don't know if Guinness keeps records of such things, but Humpty might well qualify for a world record. I mean, how many 64-year-old cotton-stuffed, hand-crocheted, green-and-white eggs have you seen? Now, don't get me wrong. Humpty's not the same old egg he used to be; he's been through a lot, you know! At 64, Humpty has shrunk to perhaps half his original size—but then, he's not the only one to get smaller as he's grown older. And, his now compacted cotton innards and frayed crocheted exterior reflect a life-time of travel separated by long periods of sitting around on my bed and other furniture waiting patiently as I went about my life. Humpty currently sits atop a chest-of-drawers in the bedroom—keeping an eye on the door to the hallway and commanding a fine view of the room—but with his back securely against the wall. We don't want any accidents; besides, I suspect that all the King's horses and all the King's men are long dead and wouldn't be of much help even if they aren't.

Like I said, Humpty and I go back a long way. He was a gift to me from my Aunt Evelyn for my second birthday. So, Humpty has been a part of my life for 64 years! During all of those years, there were few times when we were separated. Even when I traveled, Humpty went with me. Aunt Ev was my father's sister and the eldest of all the children (she was my father's half-sister, really, because Grandma had been married to a man named Alcott and had borne him a daughter, Evelyn, before he died in an influenza epidemic at the beginning of the 20th century). My Grandfather, Anthony J. McNulty, met and married the young widow and Evelyn became the first of the "McNulty" children.

My Aunt Evelyn and her husband, Albert Carchio—whom every-one called "Fritz"—had no children and often invited me to stay with them for days or even weeks during the summer. Ev and Fritz lived in Duquesne, one of the many small mill towns that lie on both sides of the Monongahela River in southwestern Pennsylvania. All of the towns along the river, and many away from the river, were connected by intra-urban and inter-urban lines— the "trolley" lines. These lines connected the mill towns and coal mining centers with Pittsburgh (the regional industrial center), and with one another. Spurs of the trolley lines also ran up the creek valleys that led to the small coal mining communities that owed their existence to the steel mills, blast furnaces, rolling mills, and other industries that lined the river valleys that spread out in all directions from Pittsburgh, the regional hub.

At an early age, Humpty and I began riding the streetcar. My mother, Nonnie, would see us off at the trolley stop in Charleroi. We were living at the time with her father, Leonard Brand, my grandfather: "Bop," as I called him. The trolley conductor looked after me and Humpty during the trip to Duquesne, a journey of some 16 miles as the crow flies, almost due north of Charleroi, but actually longer than that since the trolley tracks hugged the edge of the river valley and followed the serpentine curves of the Monongahela River. Along the way to Duquesne, after leaving Charleroi, we passed through the towns of Monongahela, Donora, West Elizabeth, Clairton, West Mifflin, and Dravosburg. Across the river, the towns and mills of Monesson, Elizabeth, Glassport, and McKeesport provided a panorama of belching smokestacks, black metal sheds, buildings, cranes, dumps, railway cars, and other fascinating structures too exciting and interesting to be ugly. And between our side of the river and the other bank lay the Monongahela itself: a wide, slow-flowing, murky brown mass of water, laced with industrial waste and municipal sewage, cut now and then by the progress of coal barges pushed along by squat sturdy riverboats and tugs. Barges moving downstream—that is, north, toward Pittsburgh—rode low in the water, piles of rich black coal visible above the edge of the barge. Those barges heading south rode high in the water, empty now of the coal that fuels the steel furnaces and electrical generation plants of western Pennsylvania. They pushed against the current on their way south toward the mining towns scattered along the river valley all the way to West Virginia. Then, after collecting new loads of that rich bituminous coal so highly prized by the steel industry, they would begin the journey to Pittsburgh again.

Humpty and I sat next to the trolley window, peering out. The scenes along the river never ceased to thrill and fascinate me. Humpty, on the other hand, seemed pretty much unimpressed by all this. His expression never changed: eyes rolled up toward the top of his head in a look that seemed to say, "Oh well, here we go again!"

But I would sit up straight, face pressed close to the window, fascinated at the scenes that rolled past us—sometimes very slowly, so slowly you could see everything in great detail. At other times the landscape whizzed by at breakneck speed accompanied by a shaking and vibrating of the streetcar so violent that it was impossible to keep a clear, focused vision. At times, things rushed by so quickly I couldn't focus on them and I got sick to my stomach every time I tried. At those times, Humpty and I sat on the seat looking straight ahead, locked in a tight embrace, until the world slowed down and came back into focus.

When we finally got to the trolley stop in Duquesne, Aunt Evelyn would be waiting for us with a wide smile, a huge hug, and big welcome. As we walked away from the trolley tracks, Humpty and I waved and said, "Bye-Bye" to the conductor, and I held tightly on to Aunt Ev's hand because my legs felt like they were still vibrating with the motion of the streetcar.

When I was young, Humpty played a visible and high profile role in my life. As I got older, he took a more subdued and "back seat" role—especially through my teenage years. Teenage friends could be a bit cruel at times, especially if they had something really important to pick on—something they knew would embarrass the life out of you. I used to get very upset when my smart-alecky buddies would grab Humpty and start tossing him around my room like a football.

During those years, I had to put up with a lot of teasing, and I worried to death that one of my buddies would rat on me and tell the whole school about Humpty and me. Humpty remained stoic through all of this period, content to sit on the pillow on my bed and watch me reading at my desk.

In addition to those early trips with me to Duquesne, Humpty also enjoyed some other exciting travel, including a trip to West Africa. That's right, West Africa: a journey that took him to Nigeria and Ghana on a 10-month visit while I conducted field research for my Ph.D. dissertation after three years of graduate work at Northwestern University. Darlene and I discussed it, and we considered leaving Humpty with Nonnie and Dad, but that just didn't seem right. Packing Humpty away and storing him with our other belongings was out of the question. So, when we left on a journey that took us through New York, London, Paris, Rome, Lagos, Ibadan, and then to Accra, Humpty went along for the ride.

Darlene, Humpty, and I also had another passenger on this trip with us. Darlene was pregnant with our first child when we left for Ghana. At the time, not knowing the sex of the fetus, Darlene and I referred to our unborn child as "Poochie." So, it was Darlene, Humpty, Poochie, and I who made the journey. As it turned out, Poochie provided a very convenient "cover" for Humpty. It was much easier than explaining to curious immigration and security officers that Humpty actually belonged to the "top-level-researcher" leading this party!

There were a number of interesting elements to that journey and to the nearly year-long adventure that it turned into, but perhaps Humpty's most memorable incident occurred in Nigeria. We had arrived in Nigeria from Rome to spend two weeks with my Nigerian mentor, Professor Akin Mabogunje, and his wife Titi, a lawyer. Akin and Titi were very generous in inviting us to Ibadan and introducing us to many of their colleagues, friends, and relatives—starting our stay in West Africa off on a wonderful footing. Akin and his colleagues at the University of Ibadan were also very helpful in preparing me for the dissertation research I was about to undertake once I arrived in Ghana.

Humpty's big moment came when we were being driven from Lagos to Ibadan a day or two after arriving in Nigeria. The Western Region of Nigeria at that time—the summer of 1965—was the scene of turmoil, conflict, and bitter disputes among various political groups and ethnic communities. The presence of the police and military was felt everywhere, and nowhere more visibly than at the numerous security check-points along the major highways. We had gotten started from Lagos later than we had anticipated, owing to the horrendous traffic jams in the city and surrounding suburbs. Thus we arrived at the first checkpoint on the highway as darkness was approaching. Especially when traveling at night, these security checkpoints could be quite menacing, especially for one not accustomed to encountering heavily armed men who stop your car and proceed to question you in a most menacing fashion. A uniformed soldier, carrying an automatic rifle loosely in his hand, approached our driver's window, leaned in to peer first at the driver and me in the front seat and then at Titi and Darlene in the back seat.

"To where?"

"Ibadan."

"Why now?!" Not meaning the *time*, but the *purpose* of our travel.

"These friends from America are visiting us at the University of Ibadan, and we are just from the airport."

"What de for boot?" (That is, "What do you have in the trunk?")

"Our friends' luggage and handbags."

Pointing his rifle toward the boot: "Open 'em; open de boot."

So, the driver, me and Titi got out of the car and walked around to the boot. The driver opened the boot revealing our suitcases, hand bags, the spare tire, and a petrol tin. The soldier, pointing to one of our bags said sharply, "What de?"

"Our clothes and personal belongings."

"Open dis one-o!"

So, I proceeded to unlock and open the suitcase. Peering suspiciously into the boot, the soldier leaned forward to examine the contents of the bag. Humpty stared up at him with that "Oh well, here we go again" look, his eyes rolled back in his head.

The soldier bolted back, eyes wide, and shouted, "Shut 'am – Go! GO! You can GO!"

Waving impatiently to the driver, the soldier turned back toward his colleagues at the roadblock. They waved us through.

I can only imagine what that soldier must have thought when he saw Humpty Dumpty staring up at him from the suitcase. My personal fetish or "JuJu" of some sort, most likely. At any rate, nothing to mess around with. THANKS!! Humpty!

Don Ross

Don T. Ross is a man of numbers. After graduating from the University of Iowa he stayed on as an accountant in the University Business Office serving as the University Cashier for 35 years. Among his retirement hobbies is memoir writing. Initially, Don wrote for his wife Nancy, and their three children and five grandchildren. To his surprise, he has discovered many others enjoy his memories about growing up on a central Iowa farm and attending small-town schools, and his stories of family, friends, and interesting characters that have crossed his life's path. Retirement has also given Don the time to spend summers at Lake Belle Taine in Nevis, Minnesota, as well as opportunities for world travel, and therefore additional memoirs.

Crow Funeral

Have you ever been to a crow funeral? Growing up on our farm near the little town of Clemons in central Iowa, I had more than one occasion to observe one of those amazing events.

Our house and chicken yard were on one side of the road with the main farm buildings on the other. A large catalpa grove surrounded the house and chicken yards. Catalpa trees grow very tall and very slender when they are planted in such a large grove, and they are truly wonderful to view in the springtime when they bloom with huge clusters of large flowers. These flowers are so fragrant that the scent permeates the entire farm. After the flowering the trees grow very long, skinny beans that birds like to eat, especially large birds like the crows.

Our catalpas provided a popular nesting places for the crows, which would come early in the spring to build their nests. We usually did not bother them during their stay in the grove unless they decided they had a right to dine on our baby chickens. When this happened, drastic measures had to be taken.

My dad would get out his shotgun and shells and go into the grove. There he would wait until the parent crows began to return from their foraging. One by one as they returned to their nests, he would take careful aim and shoot, killing the parent crows as well as the young in the nest. He would continue this for some time. It was always a wonder to me that the shooting did not scare the other crows away. Startled by the gunshot, they might take off and fly around the grove for a short period, but then they returned to their nests. After much shooting and making sure as many of the crows were dead as he could get, Dad would at last return to the house with his shotgun.

Then it was time to wait for the funeral. And I do mean funeral. As evening approached, the sky would begin to darken with flights of crows. I don't know where these extended families lived, but they seemed to be coming from all directions to our catalpa grove. They would sit in the treetops and start cawing. This noise would go on all evening, as more and more crows appeared, and the wake would continue all night. By sunrise the next morning, our grove would be literally black with crows, and the noise would become almost unbearable. There would be few crows flying now, only the stragglers that would every now and then appear on the horizon and come in to find any last empty space on our catalpa branches.

By evening, our ears would be ringing with their raucous songs and we would be anxiously waiting for sunset. Dusk brought the end of the "crow funeral" and the departure of all the crows. The next morning the place appeared deserted. There would be only a couple of crows that remained in the grove, but they would not have any young, nor would they bother our baby chickens.

It wasn't necessary for us to do the slaughter of the crows every year, so the crow funeral was not an annual event. But anytime in my life since, when I hear the cawing of crows, the memory and the wonder of those remarkable crow funerals once again fills my mind.

A Spring to Remember
(Graduation Time and a Family Vacation)

The spring of 1999 turned out to be a momentous time in the lives of our family. It started with the graduation of our daughter Jennifer's boyfriend, Brian Kirschling, who was receiving his Doctor of Optometry from the Illinois College of Optometry. As class president and emcee of the senior banquet two nights before graduation, Brian used his final speech closing the evening's festivities as the opportunity to kneel before Jennifer. He proposed marriage in front of all his classmates and the faculty of the school. She, of course, accepted.

The day of graduation arrived with Brian's parents, his Kirschling grandparents, Munganest uncle and aunt (Brian's mother's brother), and the Rosses in attendance. The excitement of the celebration was compounded when the motel where we were staying had to be completely evacuated. It seems some high school seniors had pulled the fire alarm.

Brian's graduation behind us, the next order of business for Brian, Jenny, Nancy, and me was to make final arrangements for our trip to San Diego, where our son Matthew was graduating from Grosemont College with certification as a cardiovascular technician. The entire Ross family was to make the trip, and of course this now included Brian (almost family).

Nancy and I arrived first in California, since the certification ceremony was at a special banquet two nights prior to Matt's actual graduation. Matt introduced us to new friend Amy, who was also receiving her certification, though she was not getting a degree from Grosemont. Amy's mother and aunt and uncle also attended the banquet. We had lunch with Amy and her mother, Susan, the next day before Susan left for home.

We had arranged for a time-share exchange for two six-person units at San Clemente, just a few miles north of Grosemont and San Diego. Matt, Nancy, and I used Matt's car to get to San Clemente and check into the condo. Matt agreed to meet his brother Andy and his wife Carolyn in San Diego the next day, while Jenny and Brian, flying into Los Angeles, would pick up a rental car we had arranged for them.

Being "very proper" parents, we planned for one married couple (Andy and Carolyn) to stay in one condo unit for six with the single guys (our son Matt and the "almost family" Brian). The other married couple (Nancy and I) stayed in the second unit with the single gal, our almost married daughter Jenny. We also had room with us for Amy if she chose to attend, but she declined.

The day after everyone arrived was graduation evening. We spent most of the day at the beach with the exception of Andy and Carolyn, who rented a boat to sail on the Pacific. Sailor Andy's delight was perhaps not quite as enthusiastically shared by the seasick Carolyn.

The evening of graduation was clear, the temperature just right. For the ceremony on the lawn of the campus we sat in the back row of chairs. The processional came down the stairs just behind us with Matt on our side. It couldn't have been any better. After the ceremony we went to a delightful dinner club where Matt had made reservations for all of us. Amy joined us for dinner but did not accompany us to San Clemente for the night.

We had another two days before Andy, Carolyn, and Jenny needed to get back to work, and Brian to report to the VA Hospital in Cleveland, to begin his residency in the Ophthalmology Department. Beach activity, sightseeing, and eating occupied us for those two days. There were also several board games being played and a lot of high jinks going on with the younger set, such as burying each other in the sand on the beach, shutting Jenny in the wall of the Murphy bed, and many others.

When the kids left we checked out of the condos and moved to Matt's home in San Diego to spend a day before our return home. Amy joined us for dinner and some sight-seeing on our final day. It was during this last day that Matt informed us that wherever he got a job, Amy would be going with him. Eventually he accepted a position in the cardiovascular lab in the Presbyterian/St. Luke's Hospital in Denver, Colorado. If he couldn't stay in San Diego he was pleased to be in Denver, close to the ski slopes.

At last, a little out-of-breath emotionally, we found ourselves home again in Iowa City. We didn't have much time to catch our breath, however. It was already time to start making plans and arrangements for Jenny's December wedding.

The Beginning

My third year of employment was beginning. I can say "Life was good," and I do mean *good*, including my exciting work in the Business Office that put me in daily contact with students, faculty, and staff throughout the University of Iowa.

I had also found a new church home. I was attending the First Presbyterian Church at the corner of Market and Clinton (now known as Old Brick) where a good friend was a soloist for the choir. I had become acquainted with the senior pastor and was enjoying his sermons very much. Late summer of 1963 the church hired a new assistant pastor, Robb Gwaltney, a young man my age, single, and an exciting person to know. We became friends, visited often, and drank a *lot* of coffee together.

One day Robb told me he thought there was a great need for a new kind of group in town, for those who were not students, to bring together young adults who were in Iowa City as gainfully employed persons. After a lot of discussion we decided that he should move ahead with plans to form such a group.

Robb made contact with all of the other religious organizations in town since he felt the group needed to be nondenominational or ecumenical in nature. They all agreed to make announcements from their pulpits when a get-together was planned, and to urge attendance of their young adults. He also contacted some of the University departments and was given permission to post notices on their bulletin boards.

Robb chose October 19, 1963, as the day for the beginning. He would be host at his residence with snacks and drink for all who came. This was a little risky since he had no idea how many would attend. When the big night finally arrived his small apartment was crowded, but not overflowing. The odds were in the guys' favor with 18 women and only 4 men present. The lucky guys were Robb, myself, my friend Larry from work, and another of my friends, Dan.

Needless to say, the women were highly disappointed that the numbers were not more evenly divided.

We spent most of the evening discussing what the group should and could do to further the cause of our "type," meaning young adults gainfully employed (and, being truthful to ourselves and everyone else, seeking a mate, preferably lifetime). We decided that everyone there would receive a list of names, addresses, and telephone numbers of those present. Though anyone could call anyone else for individual get-togethers, we would begin meeting together as a group at the First Presbyterian Church on Sunday evenings for meals to be prepared by members. Further plans would be made on those Sunday nights for future group outings.

During the following week we obtained listings of the grad student population from the University. Though this was at variance with the original plan to exclude students, we needed more men, and we used telephones and the mail to notify all of these people about our organization.

During our first weekly group meeting after the beginning gathering, Robb suggested a weekend retreat to get to know one another better. He was able to obtain the facilities at Stronghold Castle in Oregon, Illinois. This Castle was originally the home of a Chicago newspaperman and was given to the Presbyterian Churches of Illinois for retreats and conferences. Mailings again went out to the group, reservations came in, and car pools were set up.

After only two weeks of operation our group descended upon Stronghold Castle with 20-plus persons, and this time, happily for the women in attendance, the gender division was equal.

Our weekend was a delight, including homemade doughnuts and cider after a hayrack ride late one night. The meals were superb and our accommodations were a thrill, including secret passageways throughout the castle, accessed behind a hidden door in the library. You had to know which book to remove from the library shelf for the door to open.

This weekend retreat was the beginning of "pairing off" of couples. Some were shyer than others about making approaches to the opposite sex, but the retreat was a step forward. At the end of the weekend we returned to Iowa City as a united group, sure of our survival, though some of the original members would leave over time, while new members also joined.

Game playing soon became a pastime with the group, with bridge a favorite for many. Most of our members had no homework to be done for school, so our evenings were mostly free. Soon there was a game night or bridge happening every night of the week. Some nights a small group would get together for dinner or a movie on the weekend.

December came along with its Christmas parties. My friend Larry came to me at work one day and asked if I had asked anyone to the Business Office Christmas Party planned for the Lark Restaurant in Tiffin. Our group included two women teachers who shared an apartment, one teaching elementary music and the other the first grade. Members often referred to them as "the schoolteachers" because they were always together.

I told him I hadn't yet asked anyone to join me for the party, but I was considering asking one of the schoolteachers. Larry looked shocked. "Which schoolteacher?" he demanded. He had the same intention, it seems. When I told him the brunette he laughed. He had had his eye on the blonde, he admitted. We both asked and they both accepted.

Larry and I were the two bachelors of the Business Office and everyone was anxious to see if our dates passed muster. Larry was not one to be known for being early and I am still known to be "previous" in going places, so we were late arriving. Everyone else was already there and seated at their respective places. The room was in a lower level with an open stairway down to it. It made us all a little nervous, for we had to make our entry into the room and down the stairs with 92 pairs of eyes watching. As we came in the room became quiet, and then some smart aleck started clapping.

The evening was a huge success in more ways than one. It was the icebreaker Larry and I needed to begin spending many evenings with the schoolteachers, getting to know them better and really getting to know more about ourselves, too.

The group had many holiday parties in December and January. The long winter nights were filled with games, bridge, movies, dinners, and just dating. With the advent of spring we made many excursions to outlying areas for sightseeing and adventure.

Easter time arrived and I invited my schoolteacher, Nancy, to visit my parents' farm since her family lived in Kansas and she wouldn't be going there. She consented, much to my delight and that of my parents. A big dinner was prepared so that my entire family could become acquainted with her. We made many return trips to the farm during the springtime.

When Memorial Day 1964 arrived, it was moving time for Nancy's parents. They were going to be stopping over in Lincoln, Nebraska, at Nancy's sister's home, and they wanted us to come visit. Off to Nebraska we went, to meet the whole Daasch clan, a task that took us for visits to different members. After stops in Grand Island, Lincoln, and Omaha, we finally returned to Iowa City, and that is when everything really became *wild*!

As soon as we got back, Nancy and I decided that we were just delaying the inevitable. Somehow we chose August 1, 1964 to be as good a time as any to get married. Our decision came as a surprise to many of the Young Adult group. Most of them thought that Nancy and I were dating just as a favor so that Larry and Margaret (his schoolteacher) would have someone to double date with. Almost everyone thought they were the serious couple and that Nancy and I were "just having fun." Surprise! We were serious and having fun.

Of all the people involved in our relationship our parents on both sides were the least surprised by our decision, and by the speed with which we intended to execute it. Since it was already June we had a job ahead of us, with less than three months to get the church lined up, the minister, the organist, the soloist, the invitations designed, ordered, and mailed, etc.

We found an apartment close to the school where Nancy taught and furnished it quickly with neat furniture and fixings. We were excited to discover that our tastes were more similar than we had anticipated.

Since we were the first of the Young Adults group to make the big leap, many organized parties for us. Robb agreed to do the honors as pastor to tie the knot.

The big August day arrived, *really* arrived, with all that August days in Iowa can bring. Our scheduled time was 3 p.m. on Saturday, and by 2:30 that day the bank thermometer read 103 degrees. Of course, Old Brick did not have air-conditioning, and our cake and punch reception in the dining hall of the church would bake the cake a second time, and all of us with it. Robb called about 11 a.m. and suggested that we move the tables outside and have the reception under the trees so we could have some breeze. All went well thanks to his suggestion.

Our marriage started the ball rolling. Within two weeks there were four more marriages announced from the group, and within the next year there were numerous more, including Larry and Margaret.

Years have passed and we have grown older but those memories linger of good times with our Iowa City Young Adults Group, and we have stayed in contact with many. Larry and Margaret have a son two weeks younger than our first adopted son, and a daughter four months older than our second adopted son. They couldn't keep up with us after that, however, for we also have an adopted daughter five years younger than our second son. We have kept in touch with other Iowa City Young Adult members, especially Robb, now in Louisville, Kentucky. He did us the honor of returning to Iowa City in December, 1999 to perform the marriage ceremony of our daughter and son-in-law. The priest who had married our son-in-law's parents assisted him.

We had a reunion this past November with about 20 of the original group, but faced a problem with what to call ourselves, since none of us are exactly young adults anymore. So with our reunion we declared ourselves "Yesterday's Iowa City Young Adults," and the one thing the years did not change was the pleasure we found in one another's company.

What About Me?

Some time ago I read to my memoir group from the book *Mississippi Sissy*, a memoir of painful experiences in childhood by Kevin Sessums. Since then I've discussed and thought a lot about the experiences he describes, and realized he and I have much in common, though Mr. Sessums is gay and I am not. I began my elementary school days at the age of six. We had no kindergarten so we all just plowed into first grade. I was very thin, wore glasses, and was not at all athletic. These all branded me as "the sissy" of the class. My male classmates as well as the boys in the upper grades constantly harassed me. Our school's eight grades occupied four classrooms, with two classes in each room. No matter which grade I was in it seemed I heard the same calls: *"Hey skinny"*; *"Hey four-eyes"*; *"Hey sissy"*; or *"There goes the teacher's pet."* And there was worse. It was always "pick on Ross" at school and on the school bus ride home.

At our recent 50-year class reunion, the husband of one of my classmates did not recognize me. When I told him who I was he laughed and said, "It can't be the same one that I always stole his baseball cap and threw it out of the bus window?" I replied yes.

"I remember that well now," he said. "You know, every time I did that I had to get off the bus to pick up and return your cap, and then they made me walk the rest of the way home!" I almost had the feeling he was expecting me to apologize to him for the inconvenience.

Our recess periods were the worst. We were expected to play softball in the lower grades and baseball, touch football, or soccer in the junior high grades. We had to be outside unless it was raining, when we went to the school gym and played basketball. Lots of kids always said recess was their favorite time in school, but I only wanted to be back in class or doing my homework. I longed for learning. My family couldn't afford to buy books, but I read anything I could find in the school library along with books that I could beg from friends and relatives. I even got a library card from the library in Marshalltown

25 miles from home, where we went on rainy Saturdays in the spring, summer, and fall, and more frequently in the winter.

I was for many years the tallest in my class, but completely non-athletic. I was so thin that people regularly questioned my parents about whether or not I was ill. When I reached high school some of the nastiest names that I've not mentioned here were dropped, but "Skinny" held on. As for height, other fellas didn't get taller than me until 10th grade, and then only six of them did. One of the shorter ones, now aged 71, still hasn't gotten over the fact that he never did pass me in growth.

In high school a new nickname also popped up among some of my classmates' parents, who referred to me as "The Professor." One father of a friend even suggested to the athletics coach that I should be awarded a letter for the help on homework that I was always giving to the athletes, keeping them eligible to play.

My class was small: only nine boys and six girls. As I look back, I reflect on an interesting phenomenon in that group. I had "friends" among them on an individual basis or at Sunday school and church. Some of these friends would come to my home or invite me to their home to play. But whenever we were together with other guys from school, they would revert to teasing and harassment.

The nickname "The Professor" stuck for many years after high school probably because I was one of only two of the nine guys in our class to continue with a college education. The rest of the nicknames are now gone—including "Skinny" as anyone can tell just by looking at me. I am 50 pounds heavier than when I got married at age 28, and 25 pounds lighter than I was six months after I quit smoking.

Many people look forward to class reunions. My former school, which is now incorporated into a larger district, still holds an alumni banquet every year for all graduates of Clemons High School. The membership is gradually falling as each class gets older. I did go to some of the first gatherings soon after I graduated, but found I just didn't fit in. I have since returned for these reunions only three times during my married life. The first time was the 100th anniversary of the founding of the town of Clemons, the second was my 40th reunion, and the last was my recent 50th reunion. I will not be attending any more.

The 40th and 50th reunions were comfortable and friendly enough, but our interests are so different that we have little to discuss. After reporting about our families, what we do now in our retirements, and our health, all talk returns to the "good old school days," and the funny stories and laughter begin. It's like nothing has changed after 50 years: what seems funny to a lot of them remains a painful remembrance for me. I don't need that.

So to Clemons Alumni Banquet and the Class of 1954 I say: *Farewell to you, I left you and conquered new fields and see no reason to return.*

Gordon Strayer

Forty years in the office of News, Information, and University Relations at the University of Iowa gave Gordon Strayer an authoritative perspective on the dynamics of his alma mater, which he expresses with a unique humor and fondness. In *Yesterdays*, you will appreciate his skills as a participant observer and enjoy his wit and wisdom as he recounts serving in the Army of the United States during War II. Gordon was born to American citizens farming in western Canada. He is a product of high schools on both sides of the 49th parallel, and several U.S. colleges and universities. Iowa City became home for Gordon and his dynamic wife Faye when he used the GI Bill to earn his M.A. in Journalism and Public Relations at The University of Iowa. Gordon is the author of *Snippets: A Memoir*.

A Memorable Trial

During the fall of 1945, my last months in the Army of the United States after the end of World War II in Europe, I had a brief if unspectacular career as a staff sergeant serving as a one-man Regimental Courts and Boards Section, administering military justice while stationed in Sens, about 100 kilometers southeast of Paris. My job required me to draw up charges and specifications against soldiers accused of one or more violations of the Articles of War, to set dates for trials, to attend and record those trials, and to publish their outcomes.

One of my most interesting cases during that period involved a technical sergeant, one Wilbur Johnson (not the real name), accused of various impolite, not to say antisocial, actions.

It was alleged that after several hours of drinking with friends one Saturday night and well into Sunday morning, Johnson had been charged by the Military Police with publicly urinating on the street, violently resisting arrest by the MPs and threatening their physical safety, and uttering profane and insulting remarks about the MP commander, one Captain Bender (not the real name). Such serious charges could cost the sergeant his stripes, loss of pay, imprisonment for up to a year, and a dishonorable discharge.

But Sergeant Johnson struck it lucky on his day in court. His appointed defense counsel, the newest (of course) second lieutenant in the regiment, was one Lieutenant Walker (not his real name), fresh out of law school and taking his responsibility very seriously. When we took our places in the more than century-old French courthouse, the *Palais de Justice,* the trial judge advocate, or prosecutor, was prepared with a small handful of MP witnesses waiting and eager to take the stand to testify as to the sergeant's despicable behavior. And Lieutenant Walker had brought at least a dozen other soldiers from Johnson's company, whose purpose in being at the hearing the rest of us all hoped to hear soon.

The prosecution made its case quickly, its few witnesses testifying to every point in the charges and specifications on which Sergeant Johnson was being tried.

"Yes sir, he did urinate very publicly on a street still crowded with people."

"Yes sir, he took a fighting stance when the MPs came to put him under arrest, and he proceeded to strike at those MPs."

"Yes sir, they succeeded in subduing the sergeant, but not without some heavy blows being struck."

"And yes sir, Sergeant Johnson did indeed speak abusively to Captain Bender. What did he say? Well, sir, it was pretty profane."

"What did he say? Sir, it really was profane, and I'd rather not say here in court."

"But yes sir, I can repeat it word for word if I am ordered to do so."

"All right, sir: he called Captain Bender a 'chicken-shit son of a bitch.'"

"No, sir, that was all he said—but he said it maybe six or eight times, looking right at the captain when he said it."

"No, sir, there was no doubt but that he meant Captain Bender and none of the other MPs, sir."

Then it was young Lieutenant Walker's turn to mount his defense of Sergeant Johnson. When he asked the sergeant's company commander about the performance of one of his senior non-commissioned officers, he was advised that Johnson had been "one of the most effective sergeants ever to serve under my command."

"No, sir, I really can't imagine his saying anything like that with reference to a commissioned officer, and I truly find it hard to believe that he could have talked that way."

His defense counsel then trotted forth, one after the other, five or six other enlisted men from Sergeant Johnson's company, each of whom responded almost identically to Walker's questions.

"Sir, I have known and served with Sergeant Johnson ever since our company was formed back in the States. No, sir, I have *never* heard Sergeant Johnson speak disrespectfully of an officer.

"But haven't I maybe heard him speak in disgust about some order we thought foolish or downright wrong? Oh *no*, sir. Sergeant Johnson just doesn't talk that way, sir."

After the fifth or sixth of these sound-alike testimonies, the president of the five-member court-martial asked Lieutenant Walker if the same general testimony would be forthcoming from the other half-dozen soldiers brought in as defense witnesses. When Walker replied in the affirmative, the president of the court asked the prosecution to agree to waive further testimony of this nature, and the trial judge advocate happily agreed to do so.

Then, on request of his counsel, Sergeant Johnson stood, approached the bar of justice and was sworn, then placed his hands on the bar, which looked much like a porch railing, and waited for his counsel's question. Walker asked him if it was true, as had been alleged, that he had urinated in a public place, and he mumbled that "Yes, sir, that is true."

Whereupon Lieutenant Walker turned to face the court and asked, "Since when, members of this Court—since when has it been against the law to piss on the streets in France?"

The president pounded his gavel and responded with apparent heat, "Please, Lieutenant Walker—we are in a court of law, here in this historic old *Palais de Justice.* I order you to watch your language!" Walker looked—or rather, tried to look—chagrined, and replied, "I do sincerely beg the Court's pardon, and I will re-phrase my question. Since when, members of the Court, has it been against the law to urinate on the street in France?"

The prosecutor jumped into the act at that point, asking the court's permission to advise the defense that, legal niceties and local customs notwithstanding, such an act in the presence of passersby of all ages and sex was simply not the act of a genteel person, and most certainly unworthy of a non-commissioned officer of the Army of the United States. Sergeant Johnson bowed his head in apparent shame and made no comment.

Then Lieutenant Walker said it was time to get to the heart of the complaint, and he asked, in a loud and clear voice, "Sergeant Johnson, it has been alleged that you referred to Captain John Bender, of the Military Police Detachment of Sens, as a, and I quote, 'chicken-shit son of a bitch.' Did you in fact call Captain Bender such a vile name?"

Sergeant Johnson drew himself up at the bar, looked squarely at the five members of the court, and replied, "No sir, I did not."

"Well, Sergeant, you obviously said something that led other people there to believe that you had called the captain a chicken-shit son of a bitch. Just exactly what did you say?" asked the sergeant's defense counsel.

"Sir, what I actually said—and I know I shouldn't have said it, you don't have to tell me that, sir—what I actually said, was 'I'll be a son of a bitch—such chicken shit!' And that's exactly what I said, sir."

"May it please the Court, the defense rests," said Lieutenant Walker, and sat down. The president looked inquiringly at the trial judge advocate, who simply extended his arms and hands out toward the court, palms up, meanwhile shaking his head, and stayed in his seat. Whereupon the president ordered the courtroom to be cleared, and ordered me to guard the door when the others had left. I strained to hear what was being said as the court then huddled for its deliberations on Sergeant Johnson's guilt or innocence.

In ten minutes or less, the president of the court called to me to open the courtroom door and summon the others to come back in and be seated. Then the president said, "The defendant and his counsel will rise and face the Court," Sergeant Johnson and Lieutenant Walker stood side by side at the bar of justice, awaiting the verdict.

"Sergeant Johnson," the lieutenant colonel presiding over the court said, "this court-martial finds you guilty of all charges, and sentences you to forfeit one month of pay and allowances, subject to the usual `review by higher authority. This case is now closed, and we are adjourned."

Having delivered the verdict and sentence, the five members of the court all rose to their feet and left from the front of the room, while the defendant, prosecuting and defense counsels, and I left by the rear door.

From the few words I could hear during the court's deliberations, and from observing their efforts to contain their amusement throughout Lieutenant Walker's questioning of those soldiers who simply could not imagine Sergeant Johnson's ever having made such crude remarks about the MP captain, I knew the verdict reflected the court's own belief: that Captain Bender had been quite accurately described by the sergeant in his alcohol-inspired reading of that MP's character.

I had heard enough around headquarters to know that Bender was pretty generally disliked as a petty bully by many if not all of the other officers, and downright despised by most of them. Of course the sergeant had to be disciplined, but to be let off without any demotion in grade, sizeable reduction in pay status, or imprisonment was as light a sentence as could have been handed to him.

As for Sergeant Johnson, I am sure it was well worth losing a month's pay for the opportunity to read out his opinion of the captain in front of his own MPs, to repeat that opinion again several times in open court, and to look forward to its posting a few days later on every company bulletin board throughout the regimental area when I published the proceedings—including the sergeant's alleged description of Captain Bender—and the verdict for all to read.

I hastened back to my office to begin that task with enthusiasm.

Death of a President

The date was April 12, 1945, when word reached our base camp in France, as it did to American servicemen in every theater of World War II, through Armed Forces Radio Network newscasts.

"This news just in! President Franklin Delano Roosevelt died today of a massive cerebral hemorrhage at his Southern White House in Warm Springs, Georgia. The President …"

That was as much as I heard from the tiny and tinny radio in our eight-man "hut," my ears and brain both having essentially shut down after the newscaster's first sentence. There was total silence for a minute or more throughout the double row of canvas huts. Then voices erupted.

"What the hell?" "They musta got it wrong!" "How could that be?" "Listen, guys, that's probably just Axis Sally with more Kraut propaganda!"

But subsequent newscasts left no doubt that our Commander-in-Chief was indeed dead.

That fact did not bring universal grief to all our colleagues in uniform. Some of the older men among us muttered to the effect that they'd be damned if *they* felt sorry—after all, hadn't the so-and-so with the phony accent got us into war in the first place? Or they said he had made a mockery of hard work, with his WPA and PWA projects making it possible for lazy men to lean on their shovels most of the day and still get paid good money out of taxpayers' pockets. Or, they said, now maybe this will keep that homely wife of his out of the coal mines.

But to what clearly seemed a majority of the hundred or so fellow members of the 327th Glider Infantry Regiment, 101st Airborne Division of the Army of the United States, Roosevelt's death dealt a blow to the *solar plexus.* After all, FDR was the only president many of us "youngsters" could really remember. Barely five months earlier he had had my very first vote for any U.S. President, cast back in Camp

Crowder, Missouri, in complete defiance of the officer who had re-marked, while notarizing my absentee ballot envelope, "1 hope you're not voting for that sonofabitch Roosevelt."

Our base camp, located perhaps 50 kilometers east of Rheims and the so-called "Little Red Schoolhouse" where the armistice would be signed a month later, was strangely quiet the next several days. Even the intermittent poker games evoked little noise, either of rejoicing or complaint, from players or spectators. We went about our business, forgoing the usual bitching and wisecracking.

Came the day of Roosevelt's funeral, advance details of which we had perused in our daily *Stars and Stripes* newspapers, work was suspended throughout the camp late that afternoon. Men gathered in small, hushed groups out in the clearing between the rows of huts to listen to the broadcast of the services. A gentle snow was falling in big, wet flakes out of a depressingly gray sky, but there was no wind and the temperature was friendly to bare-headed men as we stood outdoors, most of us in our "fatigues" but a few actually in dress uniform. The camp's few officers were not in evidence, presumably gathered in a hut to listen in more comfort.

Except for the voices and music coming to us through the radio, silence prevailed as the service began and progressed, but men, in-cluding our handful of tough warriors who had survived the Battle of the Bulge scarcely 100 days earlier, bowed and shook their heads sadly, and tears were clearly in evidence on the faces of many of those same and other grown men.

None of us had known FDR, of course, nor had any more than a radio and newsreel acquaintance with our Commander-in-Chief. But he had been very real to us, and his death, right at that point, while we were thousands of miles from the U.S., and especially with vic-tory in Europe so clearly in sight, seemed every bit as cruel as the artillery fire we were sure we could still hear occasionally when the wind blew from the east.

Tarnished Brass – Or, A Timely Reminder

Once settled in the seat I was lucky enough to have to myself in the Atlantic Coast Line railroad car, I had time to take my first good look at the schedule to determine just where and when I'd be changing trains in order to reach my destination of a little prairie town in western Canada three miles from our family farm.

I had just left Fort Bragg, North Carolina, to start my 45-day, post-overseas furlough. I was headed back to Saskatchewan in February, 1946 to visit a friend of the female persuasion for a few days. After that I would return to the U.S. and, several days and railroads later, arrive at Fort Lauderdale, Florida, where I would spend the last month of my furlough with my parents and youngest brother, who were in Lauderdale caring for my ailing widowed grandmother.

I had vaguely known that my route home would take me through Washington, D.C., where I would change to a Chicago-bound train, but I hadn't realized that there would be a layover of several hours in Washington. This was actually good news, since I had never been in our national capital, and there would be sufficient time to see at least something of that city.

In Washington's teeming Union Station I quickly found a rental locker for my two small pieces of luggage, and caught a cab to the Capitol building, where I had just begun to wander around when I happened upon some history in the making: the final day of the Congressional hearing into the surprise attack on Pearl Harbor, four years and two months earlier.

Whether the fact that I was in uniform had anything to do with it I'll never know, but I was immediately admitted to the Senate hearing room, while many other people appeared to be waiting for that very thing in the hallway outside the room.

In the course of the next 90 or so minutes both the Army's Lieutenant General Walter Short and the Navy's Admiral Husband E. Kimmel were called to the witness stand, obviously not for the first

202

time, there to be tossed a succession of tough questions by the senators before whom they were appearing. I immediately identified Senator Homer Ferguson of Michigan, he of the white bushy hair and eyebrows, who bored relentlessly into the question of how our military and naval forces could have allowed themselves to be so vulnerable that terrible December 7.

While I cannot begin to remember specific questions or answers, or which senator asked, or which general or admiral answered, I can never forget one aspect of their embarrassing interrogations as long as I live: the invariable use of "sir" by those two high-ranking officers whenever they responded to a senator's question. It was "Yes, sir!" or "No, sir!" when answering a yes-or-no question, and "Well, sir, this is what happened..." or "No, sir, we had not anticipated that..." when the question was more detailed.

Sitting there in my staff sergeant's uniform, and listening to that "big brass"—those high ranking officers—"sirring" their senator inquisitors, just as I had been answering, or initiating every question to, a succession of lieutenants, captains, majors, lieutenant colonels, colonels, and the very occasional general for the past several years, I had a happy thought. And I could only smile to myself thinking how good it was to be reminded that no matter how high in rank our military people might rise, they must *always* answer to a civilian, and show sincere respect as they did so.

The Day My Parachute Didn't Open

The sun was bright, that September morning of 1945, and the early fall air was warm but still a little brisk in the shade, and wind-speed on the ground appeared to be even lower than it must have been far above us, where the few fluffy cumulus clouds floated lazily in a medium-blue sky. The field where we climbed out of the Army trucks, perhaps 125 kilometers southeast of Paris, was grass-covered and level, while the fields immediately around it were newly plowed for fall. Spires of a cathedral and several lesser structures in the city of Auxerre were clearly visible, about a kilometer to the east of where we waited for the Army C-50 cargo plane to arrive.

In short, it was a perfect day to jump out of an airplane and float to earth under a parachute, while pretty much counting on making a relatively soft landing in a plowed field.

That was why I had agreed so readily to fall in with the paratroopers in my 101st Airborne Infantry outfit in hopes to try my hand—along with the rest of my bones—at what would be my very first parachute jump. The troopers had been bugging me that I was "only a glider-rider" rather than a jumper, purporting to view me as much less of a man because I was serving—temporarily, to be sure—in a glider infantry outfit rather than a parachute regiment.

It was early fall of 1945. Fighting had ended in both Europe and, within the past month, the Pacific, and my unit was quartered in the city of Sens, about 100 kilometers southeast of Paris, as we awaited shipment home. Technically, we were part of the American forces that would serve at scattered points in Europe over the next several years, but we were not officially occupying Sens or anyplace else. We were just there until space could be found on troopships to take us back to the U.S.

Of course we had to continue some sort of military exercises, presumably to keep us on the ready in case trouble erupted elsewhere in Europe, Outer Mongolia, or perhaps even the Falkland Islands that would many years later be perceived by Great Britain's and America's leaders Thatcher and Reagan to be a fearsome threat to world peace. While there were airstrips close enough that might have been used for launching military gliders, the topography was unsuitable for landing those big, cumbersome, canvas and plywood birds, and we glider troops were no longer subjected to being trucked to a distant airstrip for several takeoffs and landings every month, as had been the case while we occupied Berchtesgaden, Bavaria during the previous summer.

Paratroopers, however, had to jump periodically, always bragging upon their return about the bravery they had just displayed in bailing out of a plane three-fifths of a mile above the earth, and the great skill they had employed in guiding their parachutes to a landing that resulted in no broken bones. Their bragging was bad enough, and being razzed about the comparative levels of skill and bravery between jumpers and glider-riders had become pretty old stuff for us glider troops.

In any case, I had been at least mildly curious for some months about how it would feel to parachute from sky to earth. That curiosity stemmed from my flight instruction days in Illinois several years earlier, during which we student pilots, and our instructors, always wore parachutes. Those were days when I told myself that if I ever got into serious trouble in one of those single-engine training planes, I would have not the least hesitation about bailing out, since I had infinitely more confidence in my parachute than I had in my own flying ability.

So on this day I had joined up without authorization to ride to the jump site along with a couple dozen fellow GIs, several of whom were very helpful about showing me how to get into my parachute harness, even buckling me tightly into it. I took my place in the middle of a 10- or 12-man "stick" of men all "chuted-up" and with chinstraps buckled extra-tight so our helmets would be sure to stay on our heads as we tumbled through the air.

Fellow members of my stick kidded me only in very low voices. They didn't want to give away the secret of my amateur status to any commissioned or non-commissioned officer authorized to ground me for attempting to deceive them. As the C-50 plane that would take us up for the jump landed, turned 180 degrees and taxied toward us, we formed several lines of a dozen men each, and it looked like my chance for a jump had finally arrived.

Just then a young lieutenant approached the sergeant at the head of the line I was in. I heard the officer say, "Sergeant, I've got to make five jumps today, to complete my qualifications as a parachute infantry officer. They're not repacking any 'chutes here today after people jump in them, so I've got to round up five 'chutes that nobody is using. So far I've got four, and I'm looking for the fifth 'chute. Sergeant, are all of these men in this stick qualified jumpers?" The sergeant, who was completely unknown to most of us, saluted and replied, "Yes, sir, as far as I know."

"I'll just have a little old look-see for myself, Sergeant," said the lieutenant, and he started down the line, peering sharply at each man's chest to make sure it bore a set of silver parachutist wings. He nodded his head each time he stopped, inspected a man, and moved on down the line.

I had been keeping my head turned aside, to avoid eye contact. As he looked at my pitifully few ribbons and badges—and especially, at my own silver *glider* infantry wings—he stopped in front of me and barked, "What's your name, soldier?"

"Strayer, sir," I replied with a salute.

"Sergeant Strayer, are *you* a qualified jumper?" My brain immediately messaged that I could get into serious trouble for lying to an officer—well, at least if he caught me lying—but I thought it safe to risk a little hedging, so I looked him in the eye, saluted smartly and replied, "Not yet, sir!"

206

The lieutenant's face broke into a big smile as he held out both hands and said, "Step out of this line, Sergeant Strayer, unbuckle and gimme that parachute—*right now!*"

And thus ended, on a lovely fall 1945 day in sunny south central France, my painfully short career as a parachutist.

Yes, It Really *Was* Rocket Science

On that beautiful June afternoon in 1952, I thought I really couldn't take time for anything other than preparing for an upcoming out-of-town trip to some now-long-forgotten meeting. Tooling across the Pentacrest, however, through Old Capitol and south toward the Woodburn Radio Shop on College Street to buy some accessory for my portable tape recorder, I stopped short, almost literally stumbling over a collection of aluminum tubes perhaps eight to 10 feet in length and four or five inches in diameter.

They lay on the lawn between the then-Physics Building and Schaefer Hall, looking like they had been carelessly dumped there along with what appeared to be packing cases. They were obviously destined to travel, but to where? And to what purpose?

Other people walked briskly by, taking no apparent interest in the matter. But my natural curiosity and my responsibilities as News Editor in the University Information Service forced me to take time to find out more about this particular collection of hardware, with its new packing cases on which the varnish still hadn't completely dried.

I stopped several passers-by to ask what they might know about this strange cargo, only to be told that they had no more idea than I did. Someone did suggest that they might belong to the Physics Department, housed in those days in the north end of what today's Hawkeyes know as McLean Hall. So I started my search there, thinking that this might also be an opportunity to introduce myself to the then-almost-new head of Physics, a Professor Van Allen. He had recently come to the campus from the East Coast Naval Research Institute, as successor to former department head Professor Charles Wylie. My Information Service was overdue to interview him.

Making my way to his office. I first asked the receptionist there if anyone could explain that strange collection of aluminum pipes and packing cases outside on the greensward. I also ventured a question about the possible availability of Dr. Van Allen for a short get-acquainted visit.

She said that Van Allen was in his office, checked to see if he could give me a few minutes, and advised that he would be exactly the right person to answer my questions about the artifacts on the lawn.

So I met the new physics head and had a few minutes of pleasant conversation with him before I asked about his interesting collection of lawn ornaments. He then explained that together with several faculty members and graduate students he was about to fly to Churchill, Manitoba, on Hudson's Bay, where they were going to attempt some upper-atmosphere research. The aluminum tubes, he said, would become rockets when suitably packed with solid fuel, wired to fire when they received a radio signal to do so. In the noses of the rockets would be instruments to measure radiation in the upper atmosphere, and miniaturized radio transmitters to report those radiation readings back to their research base on Hudson's Bay.

"Huh?" I must have said, at least by the look on my face, for he continued his explanations. The rockets would first be hoisted by balloons as high as possible into the earth's atmosphere, Van Allen explained, then fired into the much thinner upper atmosphere where they would roar upwards to carry their radiation readers to heights never achieved by balloons or airplanes alone.

"Is this a new departure in high altitude research?" I asked him.

Not completely, he acknowledged, and explained to me that in the previous few years he and others from the Naval Research Institute had been experimenting with rockets "liberated" from the German army less than a decade previously. These experiments had taken place on a western desert, and had demonstrated the feasibility of using rockets for such research.

"Our next step is to try launching our balloons and rockets from a point almost at the top of the world, near the North Pole," he said.

"This will surely add to the world's knowledge of radiation in outer space," I said, fishing for a profound statement to put into our University news bulletin.

He casually observed that he viewed their forthcoming experiments as only the first step in really studying the upper atmosphere. "Someday before much longer we'll be able to put these radiation detectors in metal cases that will be lifted by big rockets so far above the earth that they will go into orbit, where they can circle continuously, taking measurements, and reporting back to us from outer space every time they get within range of our radio receivers here on the campus."

Who had ever heard of such a thing? I was almost glad that it was time for me to leave and resume preparations for my own forthcoming trip, for my understanding—and indeed, my imagination and credulity—had been stretched almost to the limit. As I left the building I imagined myself having had the nerve to end my interview with Van Allen with a "Yeah, sure, Jim—you just keep on dreaming. Balloons, rockets, maybe—but circling the earth every 90 minutes or so? Come on, what do you take us for?"

Barely five years later, of course, the Russians' first Sputnik satellite was doing exactly that, followed very shortly by the U.S. Explorer I. Van Allen's own name would become known world-wide, for the discovery of the "Van Allen Radiation Belt" that his Hudson's Bay experiments would explain. And I was glad to admit, to anyone who would listen, how limited my own imagination had been, the day I stumbled over those tubes and crates on the lawn south of Old Capitol.

Ocie Trimble

Ocie Trimble is a storyteller in the manner of O. Henry, James Thurber, and Paul Harvey. Ocie's life lessons are drawn from his experiences as a husband, father, neighbor, athlete, horseman, airman, salesman, track coach, and educator. He writes of a specific time and place, yet his wit and wisdom energize his memoirs with a universality that speaks across generations.

Hero or Goat

In late May in 1949, it was graduation day in Cedar Rapids, the sun was shining, and the world was good. Seniors from Roosevelt, McKinley, Wilson, and Franklin high schools were assembled for graduation rehearsal in front of the Memorial Coliseum on Mays Island.

Now Mays Island is in the center of the Cedar River—thus making it neutral ground as it is neither East Side nor West Side. Graduation was one of the few occasions when the students from our four high schools cooperated on anything by choice. We were rivals in sports, music, art, debate, state placement scores, etc.

This rivalry was exacerbated by our dislike of each other, justified by which school's boundary lines one's parents chose to reside in. In later years, we were amazed to realize there were actually people of worth who went to one of the other three schools.

At that time, Cedar Rapids had a new superintendent of schools. He wasn't all that popular with a lot of students, because he was a "director type" of man—one that would take charge and change things. Now we all want progress, but we don't like change. Thus a dilemma! During the afternoon rehearsal, the graduates-to-be realized that the graduation march had been changed from *Pomp and Circumstance* to *Spring Flowers* because the superintendent of schools wanted it that way.

All rivalries ended. A truce was automatic, and for the first time in my memory, the students from all four schools were unified. We wanted the power of *Pomp and Circumstance.* We wanted the emotion of *Pomp and Circumstance*, and what's more, we wanted to have our way! It was our graduation and how does this arrogant … have the gall to show up in his first year on the job and change our tradition?

We hastily formed a committee with a rep from each school and appealed to the new superintendent, but he wouldn't budge.

The programs were already made up, and so was his bullheaded mind! No change, No way—end of conversation! Frustrated, the committee reported back to their groups that there would be no change.

I was standing at the coliseum in a group of people who were about as distraught and despondent as 18-year-olds can be over unimportant matters. My girlfriend, a very cultured and proper young lady, uttered the first uncouth oath I'd ever heard from her lips. She suggested that this fatherless man of canine ancestry was not a heavenly candidate! She then said to me, "Do something!"

Now it just so happened that at that time of my life, I was riding on a wave of success that was capped with an 18-year-old's hormones—plus occasionally, I was a bit of a showoff. At that time I could, and worse yet would, do things I wouldn't later even consider once sanity and good sense set in. So I hopped up on the concrete railing of the coliseum, held my arms up and yelled, "Could I have your attention?"

A sudden hush went over the group and I said in my most authoritative voice: "Do you want *Pomp and Circumstance?*"

The students yelled back a resounding "Yes!"

Then I said, "Our group won't march until we hear *Pomp and Circumstance* and there will be no graduation for us unless it's played—are you with us?"

"Yes," they roared!

Now we were half-way there. Somehow, someway, I had to get the organist to go along with this revolt. To compound the situation, the poor woman's boss was none other than the superintendent himself! Now when you have only a few hours to find a person that you've never met, and once you locate her, sell her on being a key participant in a revolt against her boss's wishes, you find you've bitten off a pretty big bite. We tried calling her—no answer. We went to her house—she wasn't there. We spent the next four hours being master sleuths, but to no avail.

We were running out of time, and couldn't locate her. Finally, at 6:30 she appeared at her home to change clothes before she went to the coliseum to play for the commencement. She was sympathetic but unbending. She said she had to play *Spring Flowers* because her boss, the superintendent, said to "stick to the program"!

My mind was racing and I remembered what a master salesman once said: "Show them a way and make it the only logical way." So I said, "Ma'am, go ahead and play the program, including *Spring Flowers*. Then play *Pomp and Circumstance*, and that's when we'll march in."

She started to cry and I felt like a heel. I asked her if she had the music, and she looked up at me all teary-eyed and said, "I do, but I've played it for years and I don't need it. I know it by heart."

Two hours later, and not knowing if I was going to be a hero or a goat, we lined up for the graduation march. Parents, families, grandparents, and friends were inside proudly waiting, all cameras ready to capture this big event. I was trying to look confident as I reminded the first few columns of graduates that no one moves until they hear *Pomp and Circumstance*. Deep inside, I was a little sick, as the outcome of this rebellion was now on the line. I wasn't going to be popular with both factions, no matter what the outcome. I was sure hoping it was the superintendent that hated me and not everyone else in town. This had to work, because my neck was on the block.

The organist played the four songs on the program. Then she paused. The processional, according to the program, was *Spring Flowers* and the organist played it. No student budged, despite the people in charge trying to get them to start. There was another pause, she played *Spring Flowers* again, and once more, no one moved. The four schools' graduating classes were steadfast. Then there was one more pause—a long one, and the crowd sensed something was wrong because all at once you could hear a pin drop in that huge auditorium.

Suddenly, we heard a *clack, clack, clack* sound as all the stops were being pulled out on that giant pipe organ. The organist leaned forward and unleashed the thunderous power of that organ, producing a *Pomp and Circumstance* like none of us had ever heard before—or since! I swear, if the windows hadn't been open in that building, the strength and pressure of sound would have blown the roof off.

Down the aisle came the graduates—laughing, grinning, crying, and waving to their friends and family. The superintendent sat with his teeth clenched, and his baldpate crimson red. Then to our surprise, those of us who were looking his way noticed a big grin spread across his face. His defeat had turned into a success, and a successful commencement was what he wanted this evening to be—could it be that maybe he was ok?

After the ceremony, several of us went to thank the organist for her part. We were met with a big smile, and were shocked as she gave us a hug. Her eyes were sparkling and she looked younger than her years. She said, "That was the most fun I've had in ages."

I replied, "Yeah, me too, thanks to you!"

It was still the same day late in May 1949, the air was still warm following a beautiful sun-shiny afternoon, and the world was still good. I had lucked out and I knew it!

Horsing Around

At the end of World War II and for the next few years, the teenaged boys and girls of our area turned to horses as one of their favorite formss of fun and adventure. Cars had become an extinct item, as the war effort made gasoline, tires, and parts nonexistent. The old inexpensive cars that teenagers loved to fix up into "jalopies" had long been sent to the scrap yards to be melted down for the machinery of national defense.

At the same time, cavalry mounts had become a dinosaur in modern warfare. The War Department decommissioned these wonderfully bred and highly trained horses, and sent them to livestock auction barns all over the country just to get rid of them. Farmers had no need for them, and unfortunately, thousands of them ended up in the killer pens. Never have so many great horses been for sale at such a bargain.

These horses were mostly the crossbred result of thoroughbred stallions and very high-quality "grade" mares. The mares were selected to give a little more bone substance, as well as a less flighty disposition, than the thoroughbred has. The "get" was a very athletic, fast animal that was tractable and had good sense. They had been trained by experts to jump and respond to fingertip control. Because of this unique situation, U.S. cavalry horses became the mounts of 25 to 30 boys and girls of our area.

We rode them like a bunch of Comanche Indians. We raced them, we got into trouble with them, we swam in the river with them, and we bushwhacked and terrorized blanket parties on the golf course fairways at night. We even hunted rabbits off them. They were trained for combat, so of course, the "pop" of a .22 caliber rifle didn't bother them a bit. At night, we'd ride in groups of 10 to 15 riders. No lights or reflectors of course, and all it took was one guy to yell, "Charge!", and we'd be off in a wild race regardless of surface or footing.

One night, while foolishly racing on an asphalt surface, one of the lead horses lost his footing and went down. Suddenly the road was full of falling, stumbling horses, and bouncing, flying bodies of the riders, as the horses made a sickening pile-up. I was under the whole mess and squashed flat. There was a searing pain starting at my shoulders and going down along my spine to the bottom of my rib cage. I couldn't breathe, as all of the air had been crushed out of my lungs. I was conscious, but I was afraid my back was broken, since that was where the pain was coming from. The road was full of groaning boys, and scrambling and kicking horses as they regained their feet. One of the guys, Bob Dodd, noticed I was trying to breathe, but couldn't. He started raising and lowering me by the small of my back and said, "The wind's just knocked out of you." I thought, "My back's broken and he's going to kill me!" He did get the air back into me, but there was no doubt in my mind that I was hurt. What I didn't know was that I had five broken ribs, and several more separated from my spine.

I was in a fix. My dad had been after me to sell my horse because it was fall, school was on, and I was out for football. He said, "You can't do everything, so sell now and get another one when school is out in the spring." I didn't want to sell, but this would give Dad a good reason to push his will. Dad had been trying to separate me from this group of guys for some time without being dictatorial about it. He felt they "were trouble waiting to happen," and of course, looking back, he was right.

That night, I was unable to lie down. Anyone who's had broken ribs can attest to the impossibility of that. I sat on the edge of my bed all night, breathing very shallow. As the night progressed, I made my game plan as to how to get my ribs fixed and not blame it on the horse. I can truly say that this was one of the worst nights of my life. I thought it would never end.

The next day I made sure I was late for school. I didn't want any of my friends roughhousing with me like teenage boys always do. I would excuse myself from class early, go to the men's room, take over a booth, door closed, until the next class started and then repeat the procedure. I was hurt, but no one could know this if my plan was to work out. I took over a booth in the men's room during the whole noon hour, entered class late, and got excused early to go to the rest room so I could avoid everyone. I really felt that if I got bumped or grabbed, I'd die on the spot. None of the teachers questioned me about coming in late or leaving early, because I'm sure I looked sick enough to be "death warmed over." The last class I just skipped. I went down to the locker room and spent a very unpleasant hour putting on my football pads and pants. I didn't even try to get my jersey on—that was impossible. I walked out to the practice field, and when the first guys came out, I went back in to the coach's office.

I said, "Coach, I think hurt myself horsing around." Coach Carney checked me over and sent me to the hospital. My use of the words "horsing around" served as a rationale of honesty with the coach, if you sort of shrunk the words. Age and time of situation has a way of making deception funny—if you tell it right. After all, I didn't lie to my dad. I never did. I just let him assume. Dad got the straight story about a year later on the heels of some yarns about his teenage pranks. Timing, of course, is everything.

It was a little scary to learn later that if one of those broken ribs had punctured a lung, I might not have survived that night sitting on the edge of my bed. But then, youth has never been in league with good judgment.

On the positive side, my football career was over. Due to my size it would have ended anyway on graduation from high school, much as I loved the sport. My knees, hips, and ankles were still undamaged for the sports for which God gave me talent: track and cross-country. I really hadn't lied. Well, sort of hadn't, and more important to me at the time, I still had my horse!

Cattle Prod

Now it just so happens that I have had experience with electricity and livestock management. My uncle Ted[*] was always involved in something in his spare time: house building, livestock dealing, farming—always something. It made him feel vital to be learning and doing. This time, he and some buddies were dealing with cattle. As a result there were two electric cattle prods lying on his couch next to where I was sitting.

It was summertime, shorts were in, my sixteen-year-old cousin Sandra was there, and I was armed with not one, but two cattle prods. I had never been nailed with a cattle prod, but my curiosity was piqued. Besides, I wasn't always the nicest guy in town.

I waited for the perfect moment: her back turned, bending over to pick up a newspaper, and completely unsuspecting. "Ol' Two-Gun Trimble" gave simultaneous shots to both right and left sides, just about at the hemline. Bzzz-buzzz!!!

One hell of a scream! She demonstrated the vertical leap of an Olympic athlete and the dexterity of a gymnast as she turned mid-jump to face me on her way down. She came down with talons unfurled as she raked me, splitting my lip and laying my nose open, drawing considerable blood. Words came out of that girl's mouth that I didn't think she knew.

I had a date that night with a girl who knew Sandra, and I got no sympathy whatsoever from her. She said, "Is that *all* she did?"

---

[*] Ocie Trimble's Uncle Ted is the same "Ted" that Ocie writes about in "The Dream Boat – Or Viking Funeral" (p. 222) and Sandra Hudson writes about in "A Man of Contradictions" (p. 99), her memoir about her father, Ted Chermak.

Electric Fence

As a young man, I found myself wasting time enjoying horses. At that time I kept my stallion, a magnificent horse of beauty and animation, at Bob Lane's acreage. Bob had a big barn, and a pasture, and there were areas to ride in. This is hard to imagine now, as what was once a quiet country road is now paved and is the site of many a traffic bottleneck. Bob also had two children. The older one was a son, Lester, who did a lot of the work around the place. The other was a bright-eyed and mischievous sister, Lori, who was about four years younger.

Now it just so happened that Bob had strung up a single-wire electric fence to divide his pasture. Lester wanted to cross the pasture and he was carrying some stuff. Lester set his load down, walked over to the barn, and shut off the power. What Lester didn't know was that his grinning little sister was watching him from her hiding place in the haymow. She watched him as he picked up his load in one hand and grabbed the wire with the other. The power was, of course, off. Lori waited until Lester swung astraddle the fence and then she flipped on the switch. Now the fence was about waist high, so as Lester swung over the fence, he was pushing down on the wire. Lester was nailed! He dropped the tools he was carrying and let go of the wire. The wire immediately sprung back and Lester was quick to learn they were both bad places—worse than bad places—to get jolted.

I watched this hilarious performance and laughed so hard I hurt. He went through about four go-arounds of grabbing the wire, getting a charge in the hands, letting go, and catching a worse shot as he rode this electric bucking bronco. Finally, in desperation, he made a dive and got off. Lori was no longer laughing: She was running for her life! Lester roared, "Where is she!" Lori was learning at a young age that she had track talent. She won the race to the house and locked herself in the bathroom till the folks came home. By that time, Lester wasn't mad anymore, but he never told her that. He let her spend the afternoon in a small room with no reading material.

The Dream Boat – Or Viking Funeral

About forty years ago, and living on the water, I had great plans to build a cabin boat: glistening white, with an inboard engine, sleeping facilities for four, and a biffy. I had just built my first house and re-built two others. I was no stranger to carpentry tools, nor was I short on energy and dreams. I was as ambitious then as I am lazy now. In those days I could and did work about 15 hours per day, and then went out for a five-mile run. This was my seven-day per week sched-ule, holidays included. I had hit full-stride in the dangerous worka-holic syndrome, and my wife, who prefers play to work, was sick of our lifestyle.

About this time my Uncle Ted had acquired the hull of a lake boat, cedar strip in construction, five feet in depth, nine feet across the beam, and 28 feet long. There was no dry rot and it was 100% sound! I wanted this monster that weighed about a ton. It was going to be the basis of my dream boat. Uncle Ted wouldn't sell it to me, but he said, "What do you have for a swap that *I* can use?" It just so happened I had a walk-behind Sears tractor that had a double-bottom shallow plow, a harrow and disc, and a four-foot sickle bar. I had bought it at a farm sale and *didn't know why*. He didn't know I didn't want this piece of equipment, and I wasn't about to tell him I'd had no luck in selling it or giving it away! I didn't know he'd offered several people the hull *for free*—but, no takers, and he was tired of mowing around it and having it take up space. We dealt, we argued in fun, as we countered our "valuable" offerings with anything except money. We finally made a straight swap on the condition I trans-ported the boat out the next weekend (I had to rent the trailer) and he'd provide the muscle for loading it via a group of his always-pre-sent friends. I also had to haul my equipment to his farm not far from the Canadian border, about 500 miles each way. The other stipulation was that I hang up my hammer for a couple of days and go fishing with him on the 7th Crow Wing Lake and not think of work or "hurry" for the entire time.

I brought this "treasure" home and put it in one stall of my 30-foot-long garage. It barely fit. As luck or destiny would have it, Janet and I decided to build another house, and all my spare time and effort for the next year and a half went into that project. The boat only sat there in the way and became a "catch-all." When the new house was completed, we sold the one we had lived in, and the boat had to be moved. We hauled it over to our side lot, turned it upside-down, blocked it up, and there it sat for *17 years*. It was in the way and something to mow around, just like it had been at Ted's. I had lost interest, and my hyper-lifestyle was waning.

I tried to sell it, but couldn't find a buyer. I tried to give it away, but no takers, because by now, all boats of this type were fiberglass. As time went on, it went into disrepair. Every time I looked at it, I had a guilty feeling. I offered my boys and their buddies $50 to haul it to the landfill and out of my sight!

The guys thought about it and said, "We won't take it to the landfill, but if you'll let us, we'll give her a 'Viking Funeral' and do it for free."

Now those who are not savvy to a "Viking funeral" should know that it is burial by incineration at sea and at night (besides, they said *free*). The guys got very busy with patching pitch, and plugged up all cracks. They covered the drive shaft openings and sealed them, flipped the hull right-side up, and with the aid of rollers, and a bunch of young muscle, moved the boat the length of our side yard, about 300 feet, and positioned it on the river's edge for launching. They then filled it with dry firewood and waited till a little past midnight. They loaded two five-gallon cans of gasoline, christened it with a bottle of beer over the bow, and pushed her in. She floated beautifully, and the guys climbed aboard the boat, then moved downstream for its first journey in probably forty years, and the final trip forever.

The plan was to ignite it by the Sigma Chi House and let *them* explain if the police and fire department didn't think this was a good idea. There was our audience on the Hancher side of the river though, because half of our neighborhood "just happened" to be taking a stroll that night about 1:00 AM along the river across from the fraternity houses: an amazing coincidence.

The guys placed a dummy on top of the firewood, and doused it all with the 10 gallons of gasoline. Mark struck a match and threw it as he and a dozen forms dove for the water's protection from the expected inferno. Nothing! The match had gone out as he threw it! Undaunted, Mark climbed back in, picked out a small piece of the gas-anointed firewood, lit it, and threw it on the pile. No problem this time, as the fumes had spread. A loud "ka whoom" was heard as the gasoline exploded. Mark dove as he threw, but the flames hit *him* before *he* hit the water! All hair on the back half of his body was a thing of the past. The swimmers reached the bank in time to look back and see a beautiful gasoline fire in the middle of the river with flames 15 to 20 feet high that gradually burned down until my dream boat at last disappeared and settled into its eternal resting place at the bottom of the river. I can't help but feel that the ancient "ark" was happy with its final ride. I'm sure she was probably smiling about ending her last earthly day in a blaze of glory instead of being unceremoniously dumped in a garbage pit.

The "swimmers" all jogged through the park and swam across the river to our house to avoid drawing the obvious suspicions from the DNR, the fire department, the city police, the sheriff, or the campus security.

The next day's newspaper had a mention of the "phenomenon" of a fire on the river—and the beautiful reflections on the water. It was assumed to be an "art happening"—not an uncommon thing in Iowa City.

Janet, my good wife, missed out on the celebration and the demise of our long-time lawn sculpture. She wouldn't grace us with her presence or dignify the fact boys are just that: boys!

She was also upset that sometimes boys had gray hair. She's come of age now, and has a lot more fun being one of the guys. That makes life easier for both of us—most of the time.

Broken Antenna In Wind Storm

One of my favorite workout routes in Iowa City included the river walk past the old Hancher Auditorium and the University Art Museum. There were outdoor displays of modern sculpture there made of all types of things like stone, pipes, cable, chain, or gears. Some of these creations were a bit of a stretch, but a lot of it was "kinda neat."

At this time, my sons Mark and Matt had started a one-horse construction company for their summer job. They called it "M and M Construction" and did driveways, sidewalks, patios, roofs, trash cleanup, or whatever else their customers needed done. They hired several friends and the boys really did well.

Now hang in there with me if it seems I wandered off the river walk path. I really haven't.

The boys worked late one Saturday, and when they finished they had a truck full of junk. It was already past closing time for the landfill, but they needed this truck for some Sunday plans they had. The small stuff could be put into dumpsters, but what about the 30-foot, triangular-shaped TV antenna, the tractor wheel rim, and other large pieces of junk? I made a suggestion: be a "group of artists" and make an innovative sculpture, right in line with those on display at the Art Museum on the river walk.

Oh yeah, and the all night mission was started. They dug a three by five-foot by one-foot deep foundation, dumping the dirt over the riverbank so as not to be detected as a prank. Several of the boys spent two hours bending materials and figuring out how the sculpture should look. The finished product was an antenna, neatly bent to a 30-degree angle—log chain holding a rusty tractor wheel rim that swung back and forth, a blinking traffic signal, and various other junk. Some of the boys mixed concrete on the truck in our driveway and then drove to the Art Museum parking lot from where they moved the concrete by wheelbarrow to fill the sculpture's base. Matt found a piece of brass plate, polished it, and using a metal stamping set, stamped in the title: *Broken Antenna In Wind Storm*. He drilled a hole in each of the plaque's four corners, inserted long brass screws, and mashed it down into the newly troweled base. It really looked professional.

The boys finished the project about 3 A.M. and somehow didn't get arrested. I told them "if I get a call from my old friend, the police chief, I'll lie and not know who you are."

The boys fully expected outrage from the art department. They were amazed that it wasn't ripped out the next day. They were dumbfounded it was still there when school started a month later.

Summer sun and fall colors faded into winter snow, and *Broken Antenna in Wind Storm* was still on display the following 4th of July. We saluted the creators of *Broken Antenna* every time we ran that route, until finally it disappeared along with the rest of the creative displays of modern sculpture.

Maybe the art professor had a sense of humor and figured that he wouldn't dignify this bit of "gooning". Or was he waiting for the engineer of this masterpiece to come forth and be nourished. Or was be biding his time to find out who did it, and give him a well-deserved "prat" kick?

Shouldn't have been too hard to solve—after all, any native of Iowa City, age 18 – 22, not involved in the esoteric field of artistic sculpture, knew the whole story.

Robert Wachal

Rhetoric is Bob Wachal's forte. He keeps his fellow writers on their toes and is a valued editor to our group. Bob's writings enlighten the Midwest experience, many taking place in Nebraska, North Dakota, Minnesota, and Wisconsin. Bob loves to write about controversial topics that make his readers think. Many will be familiar with Bob's op-ed articles in the *Iowa City Press-Citizen*.

My Uncle Emil

His name was Emil, the E being pronounced like the A in 'say'. He was the youngest son in a family of five and my mother's baby brother. He was the gentlest man I have ever known. Once when I was five, I painted one side of his new car yellow with some paint I found in his garage. Although a well-nigh executable offense, he somehow found it amusing. I think the paint job was caught while still wet and therefore cleanable.

He got married and had a son. He worked in a steel and iron works. His wife wanted him to be a bank clerk or at least something white collar. He wouldn't seek a new job, and she divorced him, but not, perhaps, entirely for that reason. She may have seen early signs of his impending schizophrenia without knowing exactly what was wrong. Perhaps that was why my mother never blamed her for wanting the divorce. He moved in with us.

Like others with schizophrenia, he heard voices, which he believed were transmitted through electrical circuits. We never found out what the voices were telling him, but the result, seemingly very tough for him, was benign for the rest of us. He remained a totally gentle and kind person.

After we moved to Fargo, North Dakota, he lived with his father and kept house for him. He lost his job when the men he worked with became spooked by his mad mumblings. When I was fifteen, I spent the summer with them—uncle and grandfather. On Friday nights the three of us went down to the Czech hall to play bingo. One night I won a big basket of fruit and other goodies including a gallon of Virginia Dare port, a wine of choice among our kind. I was allowed one small glass an evening. Alcohol was a drink of pleasure in my grandfather's family and no one ever abused it.

Some years later after my father died, my mother moved in with her father and brother in the Omaha house where she lived when first married. I've often wondered how she felt about that, but one didn't ask about the inner lives of others. You learned only what they chose to tell you. She and Emil got along very well, but sometimes when he thought she was asking too much of him, he would say, "Sure, and why don't I shove a broom up my ass and sweep the floor while I'm at it." This struck us as so funny that it became the family mantra to be uttered whenever we felt overburdened.

There were painful times too, like when the entire family would sit down with Emil and try to argue him out of his madness, over my protestations. The tendency to view mental illness as an aberration rather than a sickness was not uncommon in those days, the early 1950s.

Emil's life was mostly unhappy due to his demons, but luckily he had a home with those who loved him. I am not sure how old he was when he died: probably in his 70s or 80s. I attended his funeral and burial, and I wept.

Robert Wachal

Catnaps

Are catnaps the only kind of nap that cats take? I read not too long ago that cats are always light sleepers, ready to awaken at the slightest signal from their environment. This is not always true of my own cats when they sleep indoors, but outside, they are always in "sentinel" status.

I always awaken very slowly, becoming aware of sensations from my skin, muscles, nose, and ears as my inner self rises gradually out of the deep recesses of my brain. My closed eyes alert me to whether my surroundings are dark or light. Then dim shapes and colors begin to form and finally to clarify as my eyes open. At some point early on in this process, my first awareness is of my location, even if that location has been the same side of my own bed for the last 40 nights and more. Infrequently, I have awakened in a strange bed—in a hotel room, at the home of a relative, or the home of a friend.

But this time it was different. As my consciousness rose out of its depths and even before the mists of semi-awareness began to clear, I knew instantly that I was in a new and strange world. Fleetingly I thought I might be in a dream place. The first clues to this new reality were the absence of familiar background smells and the presence of new, unidentifiable smells. The birds of home could not be heard, and I knew that I was shut away from the out-of-doors.

I suddenly remembered that I would awaken in the surgical intensive care unit. I heard footsteps and an occasional moan or whimper, presumably from a near-by someone. I tried repeatedly to clear my throat, before realizing that something was stuck in it. I started to panic and then remembered I had been told that there would be some kind of tube stuck down my throat. Oh, yes, and that there would be two wires sticking out of my chest, just a bit below my breastbone, and I was not—absolutely NOT—to try to pull them out! I did not want even to imagine the damage that might be done to my viscera if I pulled at those wires, and I could not feel them anyway nor even get at them, feeling all weak and swaddled as I did.

231

I heard a metallic swish and opened my eyes to see a curtain being pushed back and a white-garbed man coming to my bedside. I motioned toward my throat. He said he knew that the tube caused some discomfort ("discomfort" being the medical term for pain and terror), that it was there to ensure my breathing, not to block it, and that the tube might have to stay in place until the next morning. At that point, the tube depriving me of speech, I tried to gesture and look pleadingly. He said he would see if it could be taken out later that evening but couldn't promise. I once more did the distraught and pleading routine as best as I was able without the power of speech, and he left.

I dozed fitfully until the scent of a familiar perfume pierced the veil of my semi-awareness. My eyes popped open to see Jane, my wife, who looked a bit distraught herself and for good reason. It was now about 4:30 in the afternoon and she had been waiting since bringing me to the hospital at 5:00 a.m. Finally they were allowing her a brief visit. Months later she told me that not only was she exhausted but that before I opened my eyes, I looked near death, hooked up as I was with an oxygen tube, several IVs, a catheter, and monitoring equipment. She told me that my operation, a triple heart bypass, had gone well and that she had spoken to one of our friends who does heart transplants and who assured her that the operation was a complete success. While that was gratifying, all I could think of was the damned tube down my throat. She said the male nurse attending me had noted from my records that I had obstructive sleep apnea and was supposed to wear a special mask at night. He wanted to know if I had brought it to the hospital.

I had as much power of speech as a cat, but at least I had the power of understanding. I squeezed her hand twice to indicate yes. She asked if that meant yes, and I again squeezed her hand twice. A voice from beyond the curtain told her that she had to leave but she could come back briefly in the evening if she wished. She asked me if I wanted her to return, and I squeezed her hand twice again. When we had parted early that morning as I was to be wheeled into the operating room, I told her not to wait around, that the operation was scheduled to take four hours and she might just as well go home and rest or go to work. She looked at me as if I had totally taken leave of my senses and assured me she would be nearby and see me as soon as it was allowed. But I was too doped up to consider any feelings but my own, and, feeling extremely vulnerable, I wanted her by me as much as possible. Like a cat's owner, she was my anchor to home and to all that was good in life. She said she would come back, and she did.

And when she wasn't there, I catnapped—in sentinel status.

What Kind of Lexicographer Am I Anyway?

During the latter part of my career as a specialist in matters of the English language, I turned to lexicography because it doesn't involve a lot of intellectual heavy lifting. Of course I'd much appreciate it if you did not quote me to any lexicographers you just might happen to know. They are good people and justly proud of their important work.

After several years of giving papers at dictionary conferences, I was given a chance to produce a small dictionary of abbreviations for the American Heritage dictionary series. I stopped after the first edition and suggested that they do revisions for new editions in-house. The reason was that I would otherwise become a slave to the project. Every time I encountered an abbreviation I did not recall listing, I would need to boot up my computer to check.

There were more interesting things to do. For example, I recently finished a biographical dictionary of noted Czechs and Czech-Americans, contracted for by Iowa City's Penfield Books.

Not long ago, I was asked to review a proposal for a third edition of *The F-Word*, a listing of all combinations of the F-word with other words, for which I was paid a small but adequate sum. But you ask, "Why Bob Wachal?" Well, some years ago I presented a paper at a meeting of the Dictionary Society of North America on the subject of taboo words. I based the paper on a newspaper writer's claim that words dealing with body functions and body parts are becoming less tabooed, and words that are ethnic slurs are becoming more tabooed. However he gave no evidence to support his assertion. So I began a hunt through dictionaries published during the twentieth century to see how, over time, the strength of taboos might have changed. Essentially I proved the reporter's claim.

Somehow, this paper got me categorized in the minds of folks in the dictionary publishing business as "the dirty word lexicographer." So when Oxford University Press wanted an outside opinion on whether they should do a third edition of *The F-Word*, they turned to me. I was very gratified to be asked though I felt just a bit sheepish about it. I was reminded of the time when a Canadian lexicographer tried to rope me into jointly authoring a paper claiming that dictionaries were anatomically incorrect concerning a part of the female body that I am not allowed to specify here. I concluded that although from a strictly anatomical point of view, he was correct, dictionaries were merely reflecting the common misuse of the term, as indeed they should. Thus I barely escaped becoming known as the V-word lexicographer.

Sometimes specialization is not a good thing.

One Sweet Moment of Life

For most of us, great moments of life are rare. The few that occur are mostly expected—my marriage to Jane, my Ph.D., my gaining tenure, my retirement. Some, however are quite unexpected; they come springing out of a seeming nowhere and giving great joy. Such is one that happened to me the evening of Wednesday, March 24, 2004.

It began ordinarily enough, when Jane and I went to Prairie Lights Bookstore, mainly because our friend Ed Folsom was to talk about Walt Whitman's sense of "the good life," and because I wanted to see Robert Hass, my favorite contemporary poet, who was speaking. Hass told of his wife's Baptist insistence on tithing, not just with money at church but also in volunteering time in one's community. After remarks by Folsom, Hass, and Kate Geller, the audience members were invited to share their views of what constituted the good life. After a number of people spoke, I felt that the good life was in danger of being equated with the noble life.

I raised my hand. I wished to speak, I said, in defense of hedonism and to put it in a particular context. Surely the noble life is a good life. But there are other ways of living the good life and the practice of hedonism is one of them. When I retired, I began volunteering at the Senior Center. With so much free time on my hands, how could I not? This community tithing allows me to live a hedonistic life free of guilt. My main hedonistic activities are writing poetry for the sheer joy of it, eating good food, and drinking fine wine. That was all I said, and I thought it articulate enough but otherwise unremarkable.

After adjournment, I went up to Hass and thanked him for the pleasure I got from his poetry. He thanked me and said that my remarks on the good life were eloquent. I was astounded, almost turned to stone. Me? Eloquent? To be labeled such by a great poet and former U.S. poet laureate was something I'll always remember. For me, it was a great moment, a sweet moment, a moment to treasure forever.

Meeting Celebrities is
an Uncommon Pleasure

I do not collect autographs, and I have never gone out of my way to meet celebrities, but when it has happened, I have very much enjoyed it. When Hancher Auditorium brought in Gene Kelly to answer questions after a showing of *Singing in the Rain*, I was lucky enough to be invited to the reception for him at the home of the UI president. I talked to him for a bit then gave way to the next person who wanted to chat. When I noticed Kelly getting antsy, I interrupted as if I had not yet had my turn. We played this rescuing game throughout the evening. It was fun.

Since my field is linguistics, it is not surprising that we had Noam Chomsky over for a party after his talk. He was much impressed by the architecture of our house, designed by local architect Bill Nowysz.

Then there was the evening when Gregory Peck and his wife and his assistant came to dinner. They were originally slated to go to the Amanas, but Peck said to his wife, "Jane has gone to a lot of trouble to prepare dinner for us dear, so let's stay here." And they did.

There was a time when the university library held a series of chats with mystery novelists. Usually they gave a talk and a reading, but Robert B. Parker wanted to be interviewed, and I was selected to do the job before a standing room only audience. I had asked to spend an hour with Parker just before the public session. Our chat ranged from why he hated university English departments to what kinds of questions he liked or didn't like. The interview went well, and I had a good time with it.

But my all-time favorite celebrity meeting occurred at an annual meeting in Chicago of the American Institute for Wine and Food founded by Julia Child and Robert Mondavi. The theme was sustainable agriculture. I was sitting in the front row of a large auditorium waiting for a panel discussion to begin. In from a side door came a gofer for a large publishing firm, probably Knopf, escorting Julia

Child, who was recovering from a double knee replacement operation. The gofer led the famous TV chef to a seat right beside me. I
was ecstatic!

She said, "Hi, I'm Julia Child."

I responded, "Very pleased to meet you Mrs. Child; I watch all of
your TV shows."

"Call me Julia," she warbled.

We own all of her cookbooks and cook from them frequently, the
pleasure always enhanced by the memory of that meeting.

Why Here, Why Now in Winter?

As January ebbs into February (and sometimes in August) I ask my-self, why do I live here in this atrocious climate? Well, there are rea-sons, of course. My wife owns a real estate firm and the building that houses it. Iowans are nice people. Iowa City is the writing capital of the English-speaking world, and, as a writer, that means a lot to me. And most of our friends live here.

But let's face it, the winters here are not getting any better—so much for global warming! I suppose that most places have their drawbacks. I'd like to live in Santa Cruz, just south of San Francisco. They do have the occasional earthquake, but that's better than snow and sleet and freezing temperatures in my estimation.

Still, an 80-plus-year-old fogy can only be expected to put up with so much that is undesirable or worse. I am tired of winter at this point and would gladly put up with the fits and starts, the nagging uncer-tainties of spring. But I guess this is just a case of pull up your socks and get on with it.

Some nice things do happen about now. The Iowa Summer Writ-ing Festival puts out its preliminary list of offerings. I got it just the other day. That arrival is to me like the arrival of seed catalogs to an avid gardener. I mark a number of possibilities and wait to see what the teachers have to say about their offerings when the full catalog arrives. I have rarely been disappointed. Of course one of the great things about this program is that it happens in summer, the only rea-sonable time of year.

Well, yes, fall is nice and football is interesting. But there is noth-ing as nice as being warm. Perhaps it has something to do with being old, with having bones that need coddling.

But aging is not all bad. My wife has just decided that I am not competent to manage my own financial affairs. She has taken all of my finances over and will manage them far more ably than I have ever been able to do. What a relief!

Living by Rules – Most of the Time

Don't most of us have rules that we live by, and follow, mostly? I do. Some are trivial—like I never ask my wife to make me a drink because she will deliver only half a drink. So I always pour my own.

My main serious rule is, if you say you will do something, well, by God, you do it. That's what makes you a real person and not some kind of jerk. That is not just my personal rule but it is a rule I expect others to follow and if they don't, I judge them to be people not worth bothering with. There are a lot of them out there.

Many of our rules are taught to us while we are young. Like look before you leap. Or he who hesitates is lost (a bit of a conflict there). How about never judge a book by its cover? That's a good rule. Sometimes when you meet someone, what you first see is what there is. But usually it is not. Don't we all have something beneath the surface? I sure as hell hope so.

I have some rules. Treat with sympathy those who are younger than I or dumber than I or less sure of themselves than I. Otherwise I would be acting like some kind of overly intellectual goon. That's a simple rule and easy to follow, unless you are suffering from low self-esteem.

Another rule is to arrange your life so most of the time you are doing what you most enjoy. In my case that is writing—poems, essays, whatever. Life is best lived by doing what we enjoy. For me, sometimes that is drinking a vodka on the rocks, at other times it is writing these essays.

I hope you find what works best for you

More Things I Don't Understand

I've written before about things I don't understand. But there are more. They keep coming at me. I don't understand why we don't have daylight savings time the year round. Changing all those clocks is a huge pain in the rear end. But getting rid of that pain would require an act of Congress. And are we fools enough to expect rationality from those yahoos? I think not. Who do you think brought our economy to its knees?

I don't understand how we got to have such a bunch of incompetents for the Board of Regents. They forced David Skorton out as UI president for defending the university against the rapacious Blue Cross people. That I can understand, because contrary to the principle of conflict of interest, the board has people on it who are shills for Blue Cross. It is as simple as that. The Board of Regents is morally corrupt and not all that bright as well. I don't understand why Governor Culver doesn't clean house and get some decent honorable people on the Board who are not brain dead or venal.

I don't understand all the complaints from members of Congress about the huge bonuses AIG and other poisonous corporate entities have voted themselves. Congressmen are the ones who gave out the money without proper safeguards. I realize members of Congress are not geniuses. Fine. But they appear to be totally inept. And I don't understand why. But maybe their actions are more driven by greed than by stupidity. Who knows?

John Calvin, the founder of the Presbyterian Church, had caused Unitarians to be burned at the stake as heretics, and in one account, may have lit the fire himself. Given that and Calvin's pernicious doctrine of predestination (if you were rich, you were pre-saved; if poor, not), it would seem that Presbyterians would not name churches and colleges after him. Surely there are more deserving murderers to honor. I just don't understand. Perhaps I am being too idealistic to expect so many people to be rational. I write as a disappointed long-time member of the Presbyterian Church.

I also don't understand why so many prominent and intelligent people lost most of their money to Bernard Madoff. Even I, a man of modest means, use two stockbrokers rather than entrusting all of my investment funds to just one.

And why do we force names on places that the people who live there don't use or want? The local names for Germany, Ireland, and Prague, to name just a few, are Deutschland, Eire, and Praha.

People often say of someone that he is so smart he can do the Sunday *New York Times* crossword puzzle in ink. Well, since it is in the magazine section and on glossy paper, it would be quite difficult to do it with a pencil. The *Times*, like the *Press-Citizen*, starts each Monday with an easy puzzle and they get more difficult as the week goes on. Will Shortz, the *Times* puzzle editor, has said that the Sunday puzzle is a bit harder than the Wednesday puzzle but not so difficult as the Thursday puzzle. It is simply its size that makes it appear so daunting.

And why all the fuss about Michelle Obama wearing a dress that showed off her arms? Given the amount of brouhaha, one would have thought she was baring her breasts. In the recent Frost/Nixon film, Nixon is portrayed as saying, "If the President does it, it is not illegal." Well, I say, "If the first lady wears it, it's not improper." Besides, doesn't the Second Amendment guarantee her the right to bare arms?

Section II

Members From The Early Years

Dean Andersen

In his book, *Praise the Lord and Pass the Penicillin,* Dean Andersen wrote of his experience during World War II. For a little over three years, he served as medic in the Pacific. In his words it was "a time of youth, war, and of the human feelings—fear, loss, anger, hate, patriotism, and solidarity—common to soldiers of every era." Following the war, Dean completed his education, and entered the field of medical research. He culminated his career as head of the University of Iowa Pediatric Research Laboratory.

Praise the Lord and Pass the Penicillin[*]

On June 7, 1944, I was sent with a doctor and a squad of litter bearers to an outpost about 20 miles into the foothills of the mountains. We started out early in the morning. We had packed our backpacks with our usual supplies and extra medical equipment. I had my pack filled with three days' rations and three units of plasma. I also carried a surgical kit and a box of morphine Syrettes. Of course, I had my rifle and plenty of ammunition. Between us we had to carry several litters.

The morphine Syrette was a disposable single injection dose that we used on the wounded to prevent shock. The liquid was encased in an aluminum tube about one inch long. The sterile needle was encased in a coverlet. After use the whole piece was discarded. The plasma unit was in a small box with two bottles. One bottle contained dry blood plasma in a vacuum. The other bottle contained the liquid. The kit contained a two-way needle. By placing the one end of the needle into the liquid bottle and then pushing the other end into the plasma, the vacuum would draw the liquid into the plasma. A sterile intravenous kit, which included needles and tubing, was packaged in the box.

We hated to leave the comfort of the beach headquarters area, where a tent city had been established. Our destination was a native settlement called Afua. This was an important location along our lines of defense. All of the jungle trails between the ocean and the high mountains went through Afua. Control of Afua became an important part of the conflict that was to follow.

(We did not know that June 6, 1944, was "D Day" for the forces landing on the beaches of Normandy. Later, when asked, "Where

---

[*] Excerpted from *Praise the Lord and Pass the Penicillin: Memoir of a Combat Medic in the Pacific in World War II* © 2003 Dean W. Andersen, pp. 98-102, by permission of McFarland & Company, Inc., Box 611, Jefferson NC 28640. www.mcfarlandpub.com

were you on that historical day?" I could reflect on the trip to Afua, New Guinea.)

The jungle hike to Afua was guided by a squad of eight infantry-men. Four men led the procession and four followed in the rear. We were accompanied by four natives. The native volunteers carried loads of supplies for us to the remote areas. One of the natives had been designated native police. He was given an army issued officer's cap, a rifle and a belt with ammunition. This was his clothing except for the usual loincloth. All of the natives walked everywhere without shoes.

As we entered the thick jungle, the trail narrowed and we had to walk single file. The trail was muddy and going was slow. We had gone a short distance when we met a group of New Guinea natives. They had been out searching for food and their baskets were full.

The trail through this jungle tropical rain forest was very dense in most places. Occasionally we would come to a clearing where the sunlight could penetrate and the ground was not muddy. In this clear-ing we could move about and inspect banana trees and papaya. There must have been places where pineapples and melons grew. The na-tives had some of these in their baskets.

After leaving the clearing, we came to a more muddy and swampy area. The trees were very tall and there was little sunlight. In places the mud was so deep that we would get stuck and need help to pull our feet out. We tried to stay out of these sinkholes by walking on roots and rocks that protruded above the waterline.

This whole area was a fantastic tangle of vines, creepers, ferns, roots and giant trees. The vegetation was covered with giant ants and occasionally we came to large mounds of large, crawling insects. We saw giant three-inch-long wasps flying from huge nests hanging in the trees. There were huge, hairy spiders hanging from webs strung between the trees. Some of these were four inches across and of black and yellow colors. Snakes crawled up and down the trees and we kept our eyes open for any that might be too close.

Mosquitoes and flies were everywhere. The dampness and the humidity along with the high heat made travel very slow. The stagnant water pools and the decaying vegetation made for a very nasty odor. Some large birds could be heard high up above us in the trees. We could hear the call of the kookaburra and the screech of the cockatoo. Looking up, we could glimpse black, yellow and red feathers as they moved about.

Finally we came to an open area and the trail went to a steep climb up a hill. The ground was slippery with a cream colored clay. It was very hot and the sun was directly overhead. We all were sweating profusely and had to stop and catch our breath.

Just ahead of me was a native boy carrying a large radio that must have weighed a couple hundred pounds. He never slowed from the weight or from the heat. His feet were large and wide. I couldn't help but notice how his bare toes curled under as he climbed the hill. His toes acted like claws digging into the clay. He had never worn shoes and the bottom of his feet were as thick as shoe leather. These people were really adapted to living in this environment.

After going up and down two of the hills, Captain Gunderson, our medical officer, asked for a rest. "I don't think I can go on," he said, "I'm exhausted." He was much older than the rest of us. I would guess his age at about 30.

After we rested about ten minutes, I asked him, "Can you continue if we carry your pack?" I knew that we had to keep going if we were going to reach Afua before dark.

His response was, "I'll try."

We took turns carrying the officer's pack and arrived at our destination as it was getting dark.

The place called Afua was a native village on the top of a large hill. The area was sparsely covered with trees and vegetation. This place had a military advantage because it was high and overlooked the lower valleys in all directions. All of the trails for miles around terminated at this hilltop. Whoever controlled the hill had control of the area for miles in all directions.

"What are you doing, Ruby?" I asked.

"Picking leeches off of my boots," he answered, "Those little devils will crawl right up your ass."

I replied "We need a bath, but it is too late in the day. All we can do at this time is sponge out of water in our steel helmet. Then we better find a safe place to bed down for the night. It is getting dark."

The native huts were built of bamboo poles with the floor elevated four or five feet above the ground. No one was living in the huts. The native population moved out when our soldiers moved in. That is, except for our native police and the volunteers who carried for us. Our soldiers had built bunkers all of the way around the perimeter of the area, and again another row of defense farther down on all sides of the hill. Our battalion headquarters was located near the summit.

"The huts are empty," said Charles Ruby, "Why not sleep inside one of them?"

"They would be dry and a shelter from the weather," I observed, "But I wonder how many lice are inside."

We decided that it was dry and comfortable underneath the huts. After eating our ration, we bedded down for the night. It's amazing how much lower the temperature gets after the sun goes down. I lay my plastic poncho on the ground and curled up in a blanket. When it was dark I began to feel something crawling over my feet. I pushed it away and discovered it was a rat. It was too late to move to a better location, so I just rolled up in my blanket and poncho. I could feel them crawling about all night long, but my clothes dried from the heat of my body. I was exhausted and slept, even with the rats. In combat we learned to sleep every chance we had even in the worst conditions.

During the night we were awakened to the sound of an explosion. It was about what would be expected from a grenade or a land mine. The natives were beating on drums and in the far distance other drums were answering with more drum beats. We had our breakfast ration and then proceeded to find a better place to bed down away from the rats. We dug double slit trenches—wide enough for two people to sleep side by side below ground level and deep enough for protection from shells and bombs.

After we were settled in, I went to our battalion headquarters to check in. Major Morris, commanding officer, asked what he could do for us. "I think the most important thing we need right now is to wash up and clean our clothes. How far is it to the river?"

"The river is three hours' walk, but there is a small stream with clean, fresh water about twenty minutes away. I will send guards along with you, as you will have to go through our lines and gun emplacements," he said.

"What was the explosion during the night?" I asked.

"We placed booby traps on all of the trails leading into this camp. Some are grenades and some are mines fastened with a trip wire. I guess some wild animal must have tripped one in the night. Probably it was a wild dog."

I asked about the drums. I was told that the native could communicate with the drum. They informed us where the Japs were located and their movements.

I gathered together my men and we were escorted to the nice cool mountain stream. It was great washing away the mud and sweat from the long hike out to this place.

Sam Becker

Sam Becker was a man who cultivated his roots, whether those connections were to family, the University of Iowa, or his academic discipline of communications. As a Gray Hawk memoir writer, he reflected upon those connections. In the short memoir printed here, he honored his Russian-born mother and Polish-born father. Sam's 'stairway' metaphor is memorable. It will invite you to recall, relive, reflect, and perhaps even communicate through a memoir of your own. The Samuel L. Becker Communication Studies Building at the University of Iowa is a testament to Sam's outstanding scholarship, teaching, and administrative talents.

The Front Stairs

If there's one metaphor that encapsulates the Becker household in Quincy, Illinois, from the 1920s through the 1940s, it's the metaphor of stairs. In this case, the front stairs that connected our shoe repair shop downstairs to our flat upstairs. Those stairs symbolized a style of life my family lived at that moment in time, as well as a vision of other lifestyles for their five children for which my parents strove.

Immigrants from Eastern Europe, they believed with all their hearts in the American Dream. How many times did each of us kids watch the store while Pop grabbed a bite in the kitchen upstairs, hoping to finish his lunch before being called back down to take care of a customer. That hope was seldom fulfilled. There always seemed to be someone we couldn't take care of, and who was in too much of a hurry to wait a few minutes. So, we'd open the door from the shop to the stairway, and yell "Pop" as loudly as we could, so it would echo up the stairs and down the hall to the kitchen. Almost immediately we would hear the heavy tread of Pop's feet running down. It evidently never occurred to him to insist that he had to finish eating his herring, borscht, or kosher salami sandwich before he could come down, that his lunch was just as important as whatever the customer thought he had to rush to.

At the Star Shoe Repair Shop the customer was always right. Satisfying a customer was more important than the risk of indigestion, or legs tired from standing at his shoemaker's last all day, and running up and down those stairs. It was not unusual for Pop to hustle up and down a number of times before he could get through a simple lunch.

Mom, too, made countless trips each day up and down when business became brisk and Pop needed help, or when her special talent at the heavy sewing machine was needed. It was never clear to me how, between all of those trips up and down the stairs, she managed to get meals prepared, our clothes washed and ironed, and the house cleaned.

I suppose those steps had a healthful effect on each of us. They certainly must have strengthened our legs. They strengthened our lungs even more as we yelled forcefully up the stairs to get Pop's attention. I think my sister Esther and I must have benefited most from that vocal exercise. At least we turned out to be the loudest members of the family.

I credit those stairs with my ability, years later, to lecture to a class of more than 300 students without benefit of microphone. Interestingly, none of us ever thought of the possibility of a buzzer. But that's probably a good thing. I'm not sure what would have then replaced our yelling up those front steps in our memories.

Those stairs also played a special role at night and on Sunday when company came. There were two entrances to the foot of the stairs, one from the shop, and one from outside on Main Street. There was a special sort of suspense when the outside doorbell rang, and someone ran down to let the caller in. The rest of us stood at the top of the stairs by our large windup Victrola to see who it was, never knowing for sure until whoever answered the door returned to fill us in, or until the guest or guests came up the steps far enough to reveal their identity.

I also have a delightful memory, which may or may not be accurate, of Esther falling down the steps one time. What in hindsight seems potentially serious, at that time struck me as wonderfully humorous. Esther and I were at the age when an accident befalling the other was a source of great hilarity. That age, it seems to me, lasted throughout the years we were growing up, until she left home for nurse's training in St. Louis. The day of Esther's departure was a sad one for me. It left me without anyone to fight. My oldest sisters, Mary and Zelda, had already left home, and the seven years that separated Bill, the youngest member of the family and me, were too much to make fights challenging.

The front stairs—I still see them ever so vividly—all brown, a rubber tread on each step, worn from heavy use. It reminds me of how hard Mom and Pop worked for us, as they climbed what must have amounted to hundreds of miles of steps over those years.

They also remind me of my parents' ambitions, not for themselves, but for their children—Mary and Zelda, Esther, Bill, and me. They climbed those front stairs, so that we could climb, and they took great pleasure in every step up we made, in school, in music, in scouting, in almost everything we did. As they said in one of their frequent reversions to Yiddish, it gave them *nachas*—great joy—the sort that one can only get from the achievements of one's children.

Another dimension of that metaphor of the front stairs is "living above the store." In this, Mom and Pop were following the great tradition of the immigrant family that had taken one step up that stairway toward its dream. The stairs represented the independence that came with being one's own boss, although it was never clear to me whether Pop was the boss of the Star Shoe Repair Shop, or the shop was the boss of Pop. I should say whether Pop and Mom were the bosses, or it was their boss. But the store was a joint operation.

In any case, their lives were largely ruled by that shoe shop—the Star Shoe Repair Shop—but they loved it. They were tremendously proud when the large sign in the shape of a shoe was hung from the front of our house out over Main Street, heralding not only the name of the enterprise, but its owners: Nathan and Rose Becker, proprietors. They never got over that pride, Pop especially. He would stand working at his last by the front window, happily and proudly waving at all of the people who walked by and waved at him. He took pride in the fact that so many people knew and respected him and his family.

He enjoyed looking out on the world wandering up and down Main Street, just as he enjoyed that world looking in on him, and he loved it when customers in the shop would tell us what a fine person he was, or would tell him how proud he must be of us kids.

Pop was a wonderfully gentle, loving man. He was dedicated to climbing those stairs, lifting his five children ahead of him, but never at the expense of anyone else.

George Bedell

George Bedell provides the reader a glance back to the 1950s in the Department of Internal Medicine at the University of Iowa Hospitals & Clinics. That was a period before he developed the university's pulmonary training program and before he became Director of the Division of Pulmonary Medicine. He served the University Hospital for 50 years, while simultaneously serving 45 years on the staff of the nearby Veterans Administration Hospital. George was a devoted family man. He loved pursuing and talking about sports with his ten children. We have included a memoir about 1930s baseball that he liked to share with them. As a political activist most of his adult years, George always had an interesting tale to tell. Here you will find only one small snippet.

Department of Internal Medicine 1950s

During the 1950s, the physical facilities of the University of Iowa College of Medicine and the hospital changed only slightly. The medical research building, built in 1955, was located between the east part of the hospital and the west part of the medical laboratories building. It provided space for the biochemistry department on the first floor, and research space on the second, third, and fourth floors. Several laboratories and the metabolism unit moved into the research wing during the 1958-59 year. The medical cardio scope room was located on the third floor of the general hospital with new audiovisual devices.

At the time of my promotion to associate professor, I was granted tenure in the Department of Internal Medicine and in the College of Medicine. I had expected this. I had committed myself to academic medicine and I was happy with my choice. Subsequently I have had no doubts about my career and never explored the possibility of going into private practice.

At this time, salaries still came from appropriated monies and the commutation fraction. A significant number of staff members were supported by the Veterans Administration Hospital, and their duties were for the most part at the VA. Grants had expanded greatly since 1946 when I had come to Iowa as an intern. These grants went to individual faculty members for their research efforts. At this point in time support of departmental salaries from research funds was minimal. The duties of faculty members were teaching medical students and residents, research, and the care of patients, both indigent and private.

In terms of teaching, the medical school size had remained stable at about 120 students per year. There was an increase in graduates, from seventy in 1950 to one hundred by 1953. The residency program in Internal Medicine had expanded slightly from 15 residents to 22 residents. Funding for the residents came from the hospital. Residents' stipends were modest.

Yesterdays

The faculty members in Internal Medicine taught medical students in the junior and senior years. Teaching in the first two years was by the Science Department faculty. We were starting to develop a course—Introduction to Clinical Medicine—which would be taught in the second year. Eventually this course expanded to take up the second half of the second year—squeezing back time allocated to the basic sciences.

The teaching of residents was an important function of the department. During the 1950s, those who completed the residency tended to go into practice in the state of Iowa, and they formed the backbone of medical practice in their communities. Our trainees located in Dubuque, Davenport, Burlington, Fort Madison, Cedar Rapids, Ottumwa, Marshalltown, Des Moines, Mason City, Sioux City, and Council Bluffs—all the major cities of Iowa. The Iowa Chapter of the American College of Physicians met regularly so that we retained contacts and friendships with these Iowa-trained internists. These physicians were and are proud of their Iowa training and have returned regularly for post-graduate courses.

The size of the department had increased from 16 faculty at the assistant professor level or above to 24. While six of these individuals were primarily at the VA Hospital, and paid by the VA, they did make substantial contributions to the Department of Internal Medicine at the university. They were involved in teaching medical students and residents. The patients on the VA ward were used for teaching and research, significantly augmenting the number of patients available for teaching and research efforts.

Most of the additional faculty had started at Iowa as residents and then stayed to become faculty members. The department was a comfortable place for good people to develop, and the administration encouraged their efforts. We were vigorous individuals who would make significant contributions to education, research, and the practice of medicine in the next 10 years. I saw us as a family, and for the most part a happy family.

258

Baseball

During the 1930s the national pastime was baseball. The two major leagues were the American League and the National League. They each had eight teams. The Cincinnati Reds were one of the National League teams. Cincinnati was extremely proud, although they had been in the cellar (last team in the league in the standings) for several years in a row. Things were always going to get better, and they eventually did when Cincinnati developed the Big Red Machine, which was famous in the 1960s and '70s.

But this was the 1930s. Cincinnati always opened the season against St. Louis and the game was played at Crosley Field. Dad liked to take Don and me to the opening game. We would drive down to the vicinity of Crosley Field, which was located in a Cincinnati slum, and park on one of the streets in the area of the baseball diamond. Little black boys, age 7-10, would watch your car for $1.00. The purpose of this was to make sure you didn't have a flat tire when you returned after the ballgame.

Opening day would be packed. One year the opening-day pitcher for St. Louis was Jay "Dizzy" Dean. He and his brother Paul were famous because they had pitched the St. Louis Cardinals to the 1934 National League pennant and the World Series. Dizzy Dean was a good pitcher and a showman. After it was announced that he was pitching, he would make an appearance and make a spectacle of himself, which the fans loved.

Carl Hubbell was a famous pitcher for the New York Giants, and I remember going down to get his autograph on a baseball when the Giants were in town. He was a very quiet and shy man, but he did sign my baseball.

During the baseball season, the games were announced on the radio. Every store in town had the radio on so that everyone was aware of what was going on. One of the things I remember about the 1938 season is that was the year that Johnny Vander Meer pitched two no-hit games in a row. The first game was in Cincinnati. Don and I had gone to that game and sat in the bleachers, which I believe cost 50 cents in those days. The second game was in Brooklyn. It was a night game. Most major league teams allowed play-by-play descriptions of the game over the radio, but for some reason the Brooklyn Dodgers were not allowing this. The score could be announced only at the end of each inning. Cincinnati was comfortably ahead, but I stayed up late to learn the final outcome and was very surprised to hear that Johnny Vander Meer had pitched his second no-hitter in a row. The next day the headlines in the Cincinnati papers went all the way down to the fold, as impressive a headline as the bombing of Pearl Harbor three years later.

I now live in a college town, and football and basketball are big here, but I don't think they match the intensity of feelings of the whole city that the Cincinnati Reds had in the 1930s.

Iowa vs. Notre Dame

As early as late 1958 the Democrats were gearing up for the presidential election of 1960. John Kennedy came to Iowa City and he gave a short address in the Student Union on Saturday morning before the Iowa vs. Notre Dame game. I was in the audience at this time and although the election was two years away, it was amazing to me that such a big crowd had showed up. Kennedy obviously had charisma. Something about him just made your spine tingle. In the question and answer session, somebody asked him whom he was going to root for at the game. He answered quickly, "I'm going to root for Iowa and pray for Notre Dame."

Mirriel Bedell

Mirriel Bedell lived for more than 60 years in Iowa City. She currently resides in Port Townsend, Washington, and is celebrating her 94th year. Mirriel's memoirs simultaneously inform and amuse, a knack she may have developed while raising 10 children. For this anthology, Mirriel has selected stories that will appeal to all ages. When you share "The Milkman's Horse" and "Starting School" with your children, grandchildren, or great-grandchildren, we believe they will generate lively discussions about "then and now."

The Milkman's Horse

The earliest home that I can remember was a gray, two-story house in Morgan Park, a suburb on the southwest edge of Chicago. It was the most disreputable looking house in a comfortable middle-class neighborhood of homeowners. It was the mid-1930s, and we rented, and the rent was low in keeping with its appearance. My father was a saving man. The house occupied a double lot on the corner of 109th Street and Irving Avenue. The spacious side yard was shaded by a giant soft maple and bordered by flowering bushes along the sidewalk. The flowerbeds along the side of the house were tended by my grandmother with Mother's help. At the back there was room for my father's large vegetable garden and a tall apple tree. Although a cement walk served our front door, at the kitchen entrance a boardwalk led out to the sidewalk. Occasionally I have wakened from a pleasant dream to realize that it has taken place in some version of that old house and its setting. And recently as I have turned my mind to writing this memoir, I have been able to drift back in time and to inhabit it again along with the ghosts of my father and mother, two aunts, an uncle, a grandmother, and two sisters, all of whom lived there for at least a good part of my childhood.

* * * * *

Suddenly I am six years old again! The heat of July is on our backs and the buzzing crescendos of the katydids in our ears. Grasshoppers escape from the tufts of uncut grass along the walk and hot boards give slightly under our feet as Jean and I emerge from the back door and hurry down toward that strip of grass between the public sidewalk and the street (known to us as "the parking"). It is a wide area at first almost level and then steeply sloping down to the street, a place where the lawnmower seldom ventures. Out there, just beyond our wooden walk, is a shallow depression left by the removal of some old tree. Lined with leaves and grass, it is just the right size to become a nest for our young bodies, a focal point for imaginative play. Today we have a mission. It is Wednesday and the milkman will soon be here. In the summertime he delivers the milk early in the morning before it is light, but on Wednesdays he and his horse and wagon make the rounds of the neighborhood to collect from his customers. The milkman is our good friend, but it is his horse that compels us to this weekly tryst. Occasionally Mother will spare us a single carrot or half an apple, but food is not abundant and today we know exactly what to do. With the vigor of six-year-olds we attack the tall grass beyond the sidewalk, ripping out great handfuls of the fragrant hay and heaping it into the nest. We are careful to avoid certain rank herbs that experience has taught us are not acceptable. As the horse pulling the white wagon turns the corner, we are ready with quite a sizeable pile.

This large gentle animal knows exactly where to stop. Our friend the milkman has looped his reins around a post in the wagon's cab when he first entered the neighborhood and busied himself with his collection book. Dobbin needs no guidance—experience has taught him his role. Our excitement mounts as he clop-clops into position along our curb and, with an up-down motion of his head and a good shake, loosens the traces to his comfort. We have Mother's permission for this one activity to step into the street and we do so now, our hands full of green offerings for this most noble animal. We have learned over the summer to present each handful of grass in a position that enables the great bared yellow teeth to get hold of it without including our fingers. We thrill to the whiskery feel of the giant lips against our palms. He flares his nostrils and breathes a gentle snort when we reach high to pat his long forehead-nose, and we take care to keep our sandaled feet well away from the heavy iron shoes. He enjoys our fresh hay treat. His manner is mild and he is well behaved.

The milk wagon was not the only horse-drawn vehicle that came to our house during those long summers. The ice wagon required a team of two to draw its heavy load. We never really made friends with those powerful animals. They were a bit scary. The ice route brought them to our street at noon and their driver had "nose bags" filled with oats, which he fastened to their halters, and while he settled down to his sandwich and coffee, the horses enjoyed their lunch too. We liked to watch them toss their heads high to make the oats at the bottom of the bag slide down into their mouths. But the real excitement that gathered all the children in the neighborhood on hot summer days was the ice. With his heavy tongs the Iceman would slide a big 100 lb. rectangle of ice out to the back ledge of his wagon and, after a quick survey of the ice cards displayed in kitchen windows, he would divide it with skillful use of his ice pick into pieces of appropriate size to be carried in to each customer. Occasionally he would have a piece too small to sell, broken off or too melted away, and this bonanza he would bring up to the sidewalk, chop up, and deliver to our hot, eager hands and mouths. But usually we had to be content with handfuls of small chips tossed up for us to scramble after as they melted away. Only when the last discernible chips had evaded our fingers and turned to wet spots on the sidewalk did we heed our mothers' calls and hurry in to lunch.

Starting School

Mother and both of her sisters were schoolteachers, the only appropriate job for an educated woman in those days. "You can always get a job wherever you go" was Auntie Rue's theme throughout my childhood and adolescence. As a result, during my college years, I avoided all courses that led to a teaching certificate. Aunt Doris escaped into journalism for a few years, but reverted to teaching eventually. Mother got married. So it was not unnatural that when I, her eldest child, began to show some sign of a developing intellect, she should teach me to read.

My only clear memory of this is a bright summer morning out under our big maple tree with several of the neighborhood preschoolers gathered. It must have been about 1924. Mother in a long white dress was standing in front of an easel with a pointer in her hand, turning over large sheets of paper with the letters of the alphabet and large illustrations as we recited "A, Apple." It must have taken hold, at least for me, because when she finally decided to send us to school, I apparently was already reading.

I remember the first day at school well. It was certainly not the first day of the semester, nor did we arrive on time, for by the time mother had walked Jean, who was to start that day also, and me the five blocks to the Morgan Park Elementary school, the playground was deserted. Inside the ancient, square, red brick building several wooden steps, deeply hollowed to fit our feet, led to an empty hallway. It must have been a sunless day because the light that came through the tall windows in the two opposite stairwells gave the hallway a gloomy atmosphere. A luminous glow from four frosted glass windows drew one's attention to the closed doors at each corner of the square hall and a gentle murmur of voices that floated in the still air.

Did Mother seat us on a bench outside the principal's office while she consulted him? I must have been too busy marshaling my inner forces against what was happening to record that. But surely he or someone must have escorted us to that far door on the right and introduced us to Mrs. Abbott, the first grade teacher in room 1A. Or perhaps Mother had talked to the authorities earlier and knew where to take us? In any event, Mother abandoned me at the door, and Mrs. Abbott waved me to a seat as a silent class followed me with their eyes.

It was a relief when, not much later, Mrs. Abbott summoned me to her desk and, presenting me with a book, pointed to where I was to read. It was an easy assignment and I must have performed adequately, for in a few minutes she closed the book and beckoned me to follow her. We went out the door and in the next door where I stood in front of another silent staring class while the two teachers conferred. My senses numbed, I was led to a seat halfway back in the second row. Gradually as I loosened up, I began to take in my surroundings and realized that I had skipped the first half of first grade. And thus I became a member of Miss Bernard's 1B class.

By recess time I had become warily observant. As the class, in single file and under our teacher's eye, marched out of the room to the playground outside, I was aware of screams and sobs coming from the kindergarten room. My sister, Jean, was not adjusting well to her first day at school. Mother was standing outside the closed door hoping for the best. I think in the end Jean had to be taken home for the rest of the day.

That old Morgan Park Elementary School had a distinct smell that brings back memories of old dark wood, wet galoshes in dark cloakrooms, and the repressed whispers of children moving from the joyful clatter of the playground to the orderly behavior imposed by adult supervision. In each classroom the desks were arranged in rows, with eight seats to the row. Each desk had a varnished hardwood seat and a matching desktop with an open shelf beneath for books and papers. The desktop displayed a round hole, which in the more advanced grades held an ink bottle, and a shallow groove to keep pencils and

"Crayolas" from sliding down the sloped workspace. Chair and desk-top were bound firmly together by a rather ornate cast iron frame-work and bolted securely to the floor. As one moved up year after year from grades one through twelve, the size of the desks grew as well. Children, usually boys, who could not master the rigid curriculum, were held back until they were successful and had to suffer the scorn of their classmates as well as the discomfort of desks that were much too small.

The classrooms were square with the teacher's desk facing the class. Tall windows lined the two outside walls. They could be opened from the top for ventilation using a long pole with a hooked end; the same pole was used to raise window shades that rolled up from the bottom of the windows. The other two walls were covered with long chalkboards above which hung portraits of George Washington and Abraham Lincoln. In our fifth grade class, we also had a large picture of the sailing ship USS Constitution, won as a result of contributing the greatest number of pennies toward her restoration. Two doors opened out into the hall and one into the cloakroom, a long dark narrow room lined with numbered hooks where we hung our coats.

In each grade we received report cards at regular intervals. Not only did these inform our parents of our progress, they also determined the seating arrangement in the classroom for the next grading period. Thus we were ranked from the first seat in the first row for the student who had achieved the greatest number of "A" marks to the last seats in the last row for those who felt lucky if they got a "C" or two, or avoided "Fs". This of course established our social ranking in the class as well. The first row was usually filled with girls while the big older boys (last year's failures) lolled uncomfortably in the last seats in the last row.

Lane Davis

Lane Davis delighted us with childhood stories of growing up in a small company town in Alabama in the 1920s and early 30s. The love he developed in that longleaf pine country for the woods, water, and wildlife stayed with him for a lifetime, and is evident in the detail of many of his memoirs. Lane was on the faculty of the University of Iowa for 41 years. Students in the fields of political science, literature, science, the arts, and the Unified Program benefited from his award-winning teaching and memorable stories.

Remembering Anncie

I'm going to tell you about Anncie, but I've got to begin by saying something about Long Leaf, where she lived most of her life. Unusual and out-of-the-way things were always turning up at Long Leaf. By the time I was six, I had learned that this settlement in the backwoods of southern Alabama was more than you first expected it to be.

For instance, my Grandpa Matt's big old house was a place full of things I had never seen before. There was a mysterious cistern in the backyard and two strange, grave-shaped mounds in the front yard, heavily banked with pink verbena and half-hidden by the woods. White and purple wisteria partly hid the long columned gallery that encircled the front and sides of the house. Ancient arbors of scuppernongs hung over the back fence. Moss roses dotted the hedge that ran to the front gate, and the sweet olive tree planted in memory of my grandmother spread fragrance from its place by the front steps.

On spring evenings, the place looked peaceful and romantic, but in the daytime Long Leaf was altogether different. Life buzzed around the back gallery, the garage, the woodshed, the chicken yard, the barn, the laundry, the kitchen, and various other workplaces. I could hear the chuffing of the sawmill in the distance and smell the burning pine sawdust. Cars, trucks, and wagons rumbled by on the red clay of St. Stephen's Road and the roar of trains was a familiar sound.

Though the people of Long Leaf were always busy, everyone—both black and white—found time to talk. They all had opinions, usually strong ones, and were ready to express them at the slightest provocation. But even more than opinions, they had stories. If you wanted to know Long Leaf—if you wanted to know its people—you listened to their stories.

Some of the people were in my family: my Grandfather Matt, who had built Long Leaf from scratch and ran the lumber mill around which Long Leaf turned; Miss Edwill, his second wife, whom I dearly loved; my great-aunt Georgia and her nieces, Sarah and Margaret; and a considerable population of other relatives.

Most of the people at Long Leaf, who looked after me and who made up my childhood world, were black: John, my trusted pard from the moment he helped me down from the Pullman at age two; Clemmie, John's wife; Alec Mason, peerless teller of tall tales; Aunt Lou, Lillie Mae, Louisa, Walter Reed, Uncle Charley Aaron; and my very own confidant and guardian, Anncie. They all had tales to tell and I heard most of them at one time or another. They made me a part of their world by telling me their stories, especially Anncie.

Anncie had joined my grandfather's household to be my father's nurse long before I arrived on the scene. She stayed on to spend her life at Long Leaf. Her babies included all of my father's generation and when I arrived, me as well.

When Anncie came to the Livingston household, she was a short, chunky, dark-brown, active young woman in her late teens. Her eyes were gentle, her manner quiet, her voice soft and low, her observations on people and events penetrating and realistic. When I became her charge years later, she was a clear and often devastating observer of the world, from toad frogs to bishops and ghosts to salvation, and a teller of tales from her own simple life. Quiet and dignified, she had become a respected figure of authority in her domain.

If you would know Anncie, you listened to the stories she told.

Fring-Ding-Dum

I first heard about Fring-Ding-Dum one day when Anncie was iron-ing clothes in the ironing-room and I was keeping her company and telling her about the latest thing on my mind.

"I'm trying to get Daddy to find me a dog," I told her. "Something like Remus, the hunting dog he had when he was a boy. He said he'd see what he could find. Wouldn't that be keen?"

"Yes, indeed!" she said. "It surely would. I do like puppies."

I was glad to hear that Anncie agreed with me on dogs. I had a feeling that Daddy wouldn't go far to find me a puppy if she didn't approve.

"Anncie, why don't you have a dog if you like puppies so much?"

"I don't know, child, I really don't know," she said and went on ironing slowly. When her iron began to cool she reached down on the hearth for a fresh, hot one. "Maybe what happened to Fring-Ding-Dum has something to do with it," she said, and told me his story.

When Anncie was a young girl, it seems she went with five other young people on a basket picnic to Chunchula about five miles up the road from Long Leaf. There she found herself adopted by a scrawny, half-fed little white mongrel that nobody claimed but whose name everybody knew: Fring-Ding-Dum.

She had never owned a dog. But after the affection shown by kindly Anncie, reinforced by picnic scraps, Fring-Ding-Dum fol-lowed her from a distance, and then suddenly appeared beside Anncie a mile out of Chunchula on their way home to Mauvilla, a mile or so south of Long Leaf. They tried to run the dog back, some of the boys even throwing pinewood knots at the dog, but Fring-Ding-Dum, in-stead of retreating, came to Anncie and crouched at her feet for pro-tection. She picked up the frightened animal, determined to take it home.

The sun was setting low and the trail they were following passed near what was called "Alligator Pond," a small, almost round sheet

273

of water of abysmal depth. The water was crystal clear, but the pond always appeared black, as it was surrounded by spreading cypress trees that kept it in everlasting gloom. It was a spooky place where no call of wading birds interrupted the silence, and as the little party came to the bank of the pond, the atmosphere stilled their voices.

Now one of the boys in the group was a joker and a show off. He snatched the dog from Anncie's arms and, stepping to the pond's edge, yelled, "I'm throwing him to the alligators!" He flung the little creature far out over the shadowy black water. As the little dog came to the surface and made a first stroke to return to the petrified Anncie on the bank, a creature rose to the surface from the depths.

"It was ten feet long and blacker than the pond!" Anncie told me. "Its tail looked like a crosscut saw. Its mouth was open, and longer than your arm."

"What happened?" I asked, my eyes wide.

"Fring-Ding-Dum called to me, just one lone call to his only friend! Then there was foam and blood, and after that only ripples. My dog was gone. He had liked me. He had trusted me. He had followed me only to die, and I still hear his last call . . . I've heard it ever since."

Anncie held the hot iron above the shirt as she talked. "I could have killed Charley Love. He threw my dog to his death. For the first and only time in my life, murder was in my heart and hands. But I had no knife to cut his throat, no gun to shoot him, no axe to split his head open. I cried all the way home."

"What became of Charley Love?" I asked.

"He started running, and kept on running as far as I know. He went on down to Mobile and didn't come back."

Anncie reached down and picked up a fresh iron. We sat there silently together as she ironed. There didn't seem to be anything more to say.

Mr. Rabbit and the Singing Alligators

Anncie loved to tell stories—all kinds of stories.

One day I was sitting with her out in the laundry. She was scrubbing clothes on a washboard and I was stirring the soapy clothes with a stick in a tub of rinse water. We were talking about something, I can't remember what, when Anncie said:

"Things weren't always just like they are now. When I was a little girl, there were singin' alligators and dancin' rabbits. Did I ever tell you about that?"

I remembered every story Anncie had ever told me and was sure I had never heard anything about singing alligators and dancing rabbits.

"How could alligators sing?" I asked skeptically.

"That's what I'm goin' to tell you 'bout," said Anncie. "Long ago, back in slavery times, they sang, not like people, but way down in their throats, like bulls and lions."

"And rabbits danced?" This seemed pretty unlikely to me. "Rabbits run and jump. They don't dance."

"Now you sit there quiet," said Anncie, wringing out a shirt and tossing it into the tub. "Keep stirrin', and I'll tell you what happened way back then, even 'afore the war, even 'afore Anncie was born."

Stories were what I liked best. I did what I was told and paid attention.

"Well, there was Miss Lucy," said Anncie. "She was a beautiful young white lady over in Baldwin County whose papa had the biggest watermelons in southern Alabama 'afore the war. Miss Lucy had a pet. He was a smart rabbit. Just like a natural rabbit 'ceptin' he was mighty smart. Maybe he was the smartest rabbit in Baldwin County. Miss Lucy done learned that rabbit to skip rope and to dance when she played on the piano. She tied a yellow ribbon 'round his neck with a big bow. She said that ribbon was his stock. That's what they called things 'round your neck in those days.

"Well, that rabbit was mighty stuck up and proud for a rabbit, what with his yellow bow and his dancin' and his rope skippin'. Miss Lucy give that rabbit a name—Mister Rabbit—and that made him even prouder. He done swelled up with pride. See, he don't know any better, not being a church member.

"Miss Lucy say, 'You such a smart rabbit, I could take you to church or show people your tricks on a theater stage.'

"But Judge Abercrombie, he was a friend of Miss Lucy's papa, heard her say that and he didn't like it. He believed everything should stay in its proper place, and church or a theater stage wasn't the proper place for a rabbit, no matter how smart he was.

"So he told Miss Lucy, 'That rabbit of yours would look better in a stew pot than sittin' all dressed up with his yellow stock on the mourners' bench or dancin' round on a theater stage doin' those tricks of his.'

"Miss Lucy, she got right mad. She say to the judge, "So would *you* look better in the stew pot than on the mourners' bench? You haven't even got a yellow stock. And you can't dance or skip rope no how.'

"That done it for the judge. He shut his mouth and didn't say nothin' more about Mister Rabbit.

"Well, one moonlight night in June, Mister Rabbit went out sparkin' in the woods with his big yellow bow and all his fancy ways."

"What do you mean by 'sparking'?" I interjected. "What's sparking?"

"Don't interrupt, child," said Anncie. "You'll find out about sparkin' soon enough. Sparkin' means men paradin' 'round with young girls. That's what sparkin' is."

I was still puzzled, but I knew enough to let it go. Anncie liked to tell a story without interruptions. She tossed the last of the laundry into the tub, emptied the soapy water down the drain, and sat down on an overturned tub.

"When Mister Rabbit went sparkin'," she said. "He and his lady friend took a walk down to the bayou, and that's where he made his big mistake. The bayou was where Old Man Alligator and his wife, Beulah, lived. They been a-watchin' their alligator eggs all the livelong day. She's been a-singin' near the nest all day long to make the little alligators hurry up and hatch out of their eggs, and he's been a-roaring like a bull to let her know that it's past time for the hatchin'.

"Well, the sun was about to set when all the little alligators come a-bustin' out of their shells, a-snappin' and a-cheepin'. When that happened, their mama started yellin', 'Run for your lives, children! Run to the water! Run for your lives, children! Papa's a-comin'!

"So the little alligators started runnin' for their lives, obeyin' what their mama said. Little alligators have to run 'cause the big alligators want to eat 'em up. And Old Man Alligator sure was hungry. He'd been a-workin' and a-roarin' all the livelong day."

"What was he working on, Anncie?" I asked timidly.

"Buildin' nests for more little alligators, and huntin' somethin' to eat," said Anncie. "Old Man Alligator is always hungry. He likes fishes and frogs, but he likes big fat rabbits best of all.

"Now by the time Mister Rabbit strolled down to the bayou with his lady friend, it's night and the moon is out. Old Man Alligator and his wife are still a-huntin' for food, but Mister Rabbit says he's not worried about alligators.

"So his lady friend says to him, a-waggin' her cottontail, 'I'm more scared of 'gators than anything in this wide world! How'd you get so brave? What can you do that other rabbits can't do?'

"'I can run faster than a fox and eat more side meat than a bear,' said Mister Rabbit, just a-braggin'. He always talked biggetty when he went a-sparkin'.

"'Let's see you eat more side meat than a bear,' said the lady rabbit.

"'Ain't got no side meat here to eat,' said Mister Rabbit.

"'Well then, what else can you do that no other rabbit can do?' said the lady rabbit, still waggin' her tail.

"'I can dance to music and skip rope,' said Mister Rabbit.

"'Let's see you dance,' said his lady friend.

"'Ain't got no music to dance to,' said Mister Rabbit, 'If I had music, I'd dance in a big ring circle, like I do when Miss Lucy plays her piano.'

"Old Man Alligator heard him a-talkin', so he says, 'Me and Beulah will make you music, Mister Rabbit.' Then he began to roar out the sweetest tunes you ever heard, while he and Beulah kept a-beatin' out time with their long saw tails. This is what those alligators sang:

> The bears can climb,
> The pups can jump,
> Clean on over
> The old pine stump.
> Row Wump, Row Wump, Row Wump, Row Wump,
> Row Wump, Row Wump, Row Wump, Row Wump.

"Mister Rabbit started dancin' just like Miss Lucy showed him. And the alligators just kept on singin':

> Rabbit eats meat
> From a fryin' pan,
> He do his eatin'
> Like a 'portant man
> Row Wump, Row Wump, Row Wump, Row Wump,
> Row Wump, Row Wump, Row Wump, Row Wump.

"Now Mister Rabbit was gettin' prouder and prouder, just like a 'portant meat-eatin' man, and he was a-dancin' closer and closer to those two hungry alligators, who kept on singin', their mouths a-waterin':

> Rabbit so friendly,
> Rabbit so smart,
> Out-eat a bear,
> Right from the start.
> Chee Rup, Chee Rup, Ching-a-Ringah,
> Chee Rup, Chee Rup, Ching-a-Ringah.
>
> Rabbit eat meat,
> Bear he's starvin',
> Rabbit eat meat,
> Bear he's starvin',
> Chee Rup, Chee Rup, Ching-a-Ringah,
> Chee Rup, Chee Rup, Ching-a-Ringah.

"Nearer and nearer danced Mister Rabbit, just like a 'portant meat-eatin' man. The young lady rabbit was sittin' on a stump, sayin', 'You dance beautiful!' And the mama alligator was sayin', 'Dance a little closer, Mister Rabbit, we want to see those fancy steps you're cuttin'.

"Mister Rabbit is prouder than ever, and he dances closer to show off his fancy steps. The alligators keep on a-singin' a dance tune, their mouths a-waterin' and their tails a-twitchin':

> Chee Rup, Chee Rup, Ching-a-Ringah,
> Chee Rup, Chee Rup, Ching-a-Ringah,
> Rabbit eat meat,
> Bear he's starvin'.

"And then …" Anncie paused. "You want to know what happened?" she said to me.

"What happened?" I asked weakly. I was sick at my stomach, for I was sure I knew what was going to happen to Mister Rabbit.

"Now don't interrupt while I tell you," she said.

"I won't," I promised miserably. I had to know the worst.

"Well," Anncie continued, "Old Man Alligator, his mouth open three feet wide, his long teeth a-showin' and a-drippin' for fat young rabbits, whipped out that long saw tail of his, like a curved sword 'cept it come from his hind side, and give it a mighty swing. Swish! Splash! Mister Rabbit is gone from there.

"The lady rabbit sittin' on the stump gave a scream. ' Mister Rabbit been kilt! Alligator done cut him in two and et him up! Mister Rabbit is dead!'

"'No I ain't,' called Mister Rabbit, already halfway up the hill. 'He missed me. Missed me a mile. I jumped his tail like a skippin' rope, just like Miss Lucy learned me.' And Mister Rabbit busted out a-singin':

> Skip 'gator's tail,
> 'Gator done missed me.
> Skip 'gator's tail,
> Like Miz Lucy learned me.
> Swish! Wump! Swish! Wump!
> 'Gator done missed me.
> I's too smart for him.

"Was he still alive?" I asked, not trusting my ears.

Anncie was smiling her wonderful smile. "Of course, child. How was he goin' to get halfway up that hill and bust out a-singin' if he wasn't 'live and well? You know better'n that. Good people always goin' to outsmart bad ones, 'specially when good people look out for alligators lying 'round, like Mister Rabbit did. He knew what Old Man Alligator want to do. Mister Rabbit was too smart for him.

"And after that," Anncie said, "There was no more sparkin' outside the picket fence that Miss Lucy's papa long time ago built round the yard. Mister Rabbit ought to have stayed inside the yard in the first place, and not scared us all to death. Sparkin' and dancin' got

Mister Rabbit in trouble, but skippin' sure got him out. He never went sparkin' again, least not 'till the next time."

We sat there quietly for a minute or two. I was thinking I liked the way the story ended. Maybe it would be a good idea if I learned how to skip rope. Never could tell when it'd come in handy.

Anncie got up. "Got to hang out this old laundry," she said.

I went over to the corner and got the basket of clothespins while she wrung out the clothes. Then we went out in the chicken yard together to hang up the clothes to dry.

Meeting the Devil

Long before I knew Anncie, when she had been my father's "nurse, guide, and policeman" (to use his words), Anncie was—as she described herself—"a wicked and unredeemed woman" who knew she needed salvation and was actively looking for it.

Toward the end of this search, Anncie told my father all about how she had been seeking salvation. He was about eight years old at the time and hadn't the slightest idea of what the word meant, beyond the fact that it had something to do with Anncie and that it was apparently something important.

What was salvation? Was it like "the pomps and vanities of this wicked world" which he had been told to renounce, especially by his Aunt Georgia? Never one to stand back when his curiosity was aroused and a means at hand to satisfy it, my father turned to Anncie for explanation.

"What is salvation?" he asked.

"Salvation," she said, "is something you've got to find. You ain't born with it. To find it you must seek it with a pure heart; you just don't stumble on it. It ain't like fishing. It ain't like guessing at a riddle. You got to pray for it."

"What is it?" he persisted. "Why do you look for it? What good will it do you when you get it?"

Though Anncie must have been surprised, even outraged, by my father's ignorance—this was something he surely should have known—she was patient and instructive.

"Salvation," she said, "means being saved, saved from eternal damnation, through God's forgiveness of your sins and the promise given to you that you are saved from Hell and will live in the Kingdom of Heaven. When you've found salvation you live a good and happy life, and then go on to greater glory when you die."

My father was puzzled. What was "eternal damnation"? What did "greater glory" mean? And why did you need God to forgive you if you hadn't done anything wrong? He was sure Anncie had done no wrong. He sat thinking for a while.

"I didn't understand it then and I don't understand it now," my father told me much later. "But there didn't seem much point in arguing about it. And, of course, Anncie might be right. She usually was. So I asked her some more."

"Can you lose salvation after you've found it?"

"Yes," she replied sadly, "if you backslide, sin, and consort with the devil."

My father pressed his inquiry: "And can you get salvation back if you lose it?"

"They tell me you can," she said, "if you pray and God wills it. But, once old Satan gets you a second time, your ears don't hear good the voice of God and your eyes are half-blind to the light of heaven. Satan got you by the throat, dragging you down."

Now this talk of the devil brought my father back to familiar ground. He had heard of the devil and all his works before.

"Anncie, have you ever seen Satan?" he asked nervously, glancing around, torn between skepticism and anxiety.

"Yes, I was a-coming to that," she answered him. "I seen him last night, just as plain as I see you now. I was praying for religion down by the spring and the moon was shinin' bright as day. He stepped out from between two bay trees. I got to my feet. His eyes were like coals of fire, his hair stood straight up, and his nose bent down like a fishhook. He was clean-shaven and dressed in black. And then he said to me in a sweet deep voice like bass fiddles at a dance, 'Annie Sanders, don't waste your time anymore praying. God won't hear you because there ain't no God. Men's souls are mine; mine, now and forever, forever more.'"

Chills ran up and down my father's eight-year-old spine; this was more than he had bargained for. "How did you know that was Satan talking to you?" he asked.

"How did I know? Because there were little horns in his head, like a goat. Plus I saw one foot. It wasn't a natural foot; this'n was cloven like a cow. And sticking out behind, twitching like a cat charming a bird, was a long tail, like a bull's tail."

"What did you do?" my father choked out, thankful for the afternoon sunlight and the familiar back gallery.

"I said, 'Go away. Go away! I seek God and salvation. I believe in God! I believe! I know that my redeemer liveth! My soul is God's, not yours!'

"And then a calm voice, just as clear as a church bell way off, somewhere up in the air, said, 'Annie Sanders, I have heard your prayer. You believe in me. You have reached the salvation path that leads to paradise. Your redeemer liveth, and welcomes you. You will enter into the glory of your Lord.'"

"I fell on my knees," Anncie continued, "and I looked toward the voice, but all I saw was a bright light bigger'n a star shinin' above me. I looked toward Satan, but he wasn't there. Then I smelt something like gun smoke, but I wasn't afraid."

And then, as my father told it, Anncie began to rock uncontrollably from side to side and shout out, "I know that my redeemer liveth! My redeemer liveth! He liveth!"

To say that the boy was frightened would be putting it mildly. "After all," my father told me many years later, "I'd just heard a first-hand account from a lady who'd seen the devil in the flesh, had spoken to him, had seen a light from Heaven, and had heard the voice of Jesus. And now she was beginning to speak and act like I had never known her to speak and act before. It was all very real to me and very strange."

My father paused. He seemed inclined to end his story at this point.

"So what happened?" I pressed him, knowing I'd never have the gumption to ask Anncie.

"The women in the kitchen heard the noise," he said. "They ran to the back gallery, put their arms around Anncie, and led her away. She was weeping as she went in the house."

"And then?" I asked.

"Anncie and I never spoke of salvation and the devil again," my father said. "And though it wasn't my business to ask, I'm sure she never lost the salvation she found by the spring that night." That was the Anncie I would grow up with, looming large in my life.

Bob Kremenak

Bob Kremenak played the clarinet and a bit of saxophone as a youth growing up in a small Iowa town, and for a dance band while in college. Then there was a hiatus of nearly fifty years during which he served three years in the Navy with trips to the Arctic and the Antarctic and a flight over the South Pole, married and nurtured four children, and had a rewarding 30-year career of teaching and research at the University of Iowa. This memoir is about the unusual circumstances that resulted in his dusting off his saxophone case, and the experiences that followed.

The Saxophone Episode

I had a phone call in January from a young woman in the Alumni Affairs Office at Doane College in Crete, Nebraska. I'd attended there from the fall of 1949 until the spring of 1951 before coming to Iowa City for dental school. The young woman said she was calling to invite me to play alto saxophone in a dance band that Gene Harding was organizing for a dance to be held in Butler Gymnasium on July 17th. The occasion would be a reunion of old Navy veterans who had been at Doane for officer's training in the V5 and V12 Programs from 1943 to 1946.

I was flattered to be asked. I told her I would call Harding to talk about it. She gave me his phone number. "He still lives in Crete, up on the hill by the College," she said.

This was interesting, I thought, but there were some things that troubled me. Not the least of these was that I had not picked up a saxophone for almost 50 years—since 1951, to be exact, when I had played briefly with the same group Gene Harding had then. I was not sure I could relearn the sax quickly, or even if I wanted to. I had mainly been a clarinetist in college, learning only a bare minimum of sax, and had only recently begun working on the clarinet again after I retired. Despite the similarities of the two horns, learning to play sax again would be a chore.

Also troubling me was that Gene Harding hadn't called me himself. Maybe he was still upset with me for leaving him and our other friends in the lurch in June of '51 when I, unexpectedly for all of us, suddenly moved to Iowa City to fulfill a course requirement for dental school. Preoccupied with my own problems, I was sure I hadn't taken care of loose ends back there in Crete. I may not have even said goodbye.

Now I felt awkward and embarrassed about making the phone call to Gene Harding. I kept putting it off. I didn't forget. I just stewed about it.

Yesterdays

In February I went out to West Music and rented an alto sax to try out. I began getting reacquainted while continuing on my clarinet. I aimed for an hour a day on each horn but often settled for less. At one of my weekly clarinet lessons I told Himie Voxman, the retired Director of the School of Music and my teacher, about the invitation to play sax in Crete in July. He said, "Oh my God, you didn't say yes, did you?"

This didn't help my confidence. I kept working, though, and finally called Harding sometime in March. "Hi," I said, "I hear you're looking for an elderly alto saxophone player."

Harding, even a little older than me, didn't mention anything about carrying a 48-year grudge. He said four of the other guys from our 1951 band were coming and he hoped I would too. I said okay, but that while my clarinetting was good, I was just learning sax again. He said not to worry and that he'd send music, including some with clarinet parts. I could practice, he said, and it would all be fine.

The music came in the mail in a few days, an inch-thick bundle of yellowing, mostly third-sax parts with a few that had clarinet solos. Gene had found a library of old music from a 1940's dance band. He had lots of old standards like *In the Mood* and *Tuxedo Junction*, and songs I'd never heard of like *Idaho* and *No Love No Nothin'*. There were 52 in the bundle, and he said we'd probably play only about 20. Deciding which to practice was a problem. And I was still working with a saxophone fingering chart on one stand and the music on another.

Himie Voxman had demurred about helping me much, but he relented. "I haven't touched a saxophone in years," he said, but he still seemed to remember all the normal and alternate fingerings. Ken Hubel, a long-time acquaintance and retired medical professor, also turned out to be a good coach. He had never stopped playing saxophones since receiving a lesson from Ellington's great Johnny Hodges when he was still in high school, and he played regularly in

288

the Doc's Big Band of local fame. He helped me get back a little of the old swing feeling I was having trouble with.

The weeks raced by. I worked hard and worried, and woke up in the middle of nights having dreams about forgetting how to finger C sharp. I became grouchy about having my life dominated by this silly obligation to play the saxophone for two or three hours in the middle of July in the middle of Nebraska. "You can still back out, you know," said my wife Nellie sometime in June. But by then it seemed too late. I plunged ahead and felt obsessed and oppressed much of the time. Sometimes I was sure I was deluding myself about being ready in time.

Finally crunch time was upon us, and Nellie and I drove to Nebraska. We got there a day early and everyone was friendly. My old buddies didn't even seem to remember that I had walked out on them in 1951. Nellie fit in nicely with the other wives, two of whom were also librarians. We practiced all one evening in the basement of Harding's big old house and, amazingly, it seemed to work. We sounded good and I was pleased and surprised that we could all still do it. Another practice session the next morning, the day of the dance, and we were ready. There were seven of us in the band ranging in age from 68 to 72. A 30-year-old local music teacher named Mike Morris announced and sang and played a little trumpet, but it was still Gene Harding's 1951 band with Gene out in front on tenor sax, backed by Earl Green and Paul Hedge on trumpet, Joe Chapman on alto sax, me on alto and clarinet, Gene's wife Maggie on keyboard, and Joe Swoboda on drums.

Big old Butler gym was mercifully air conditioned on that hot July 17th. About a hundred and fifty of the old Navy guys were there, most with wives. They looked to be eight or ten years older than we were, and I thought they'd probably just sit and listen. But they danced! And danced, and danced, and still danced some more. There was even jitterbugging. Whenever they stopped and stood and watched, they still whistled and clapped and appreciated our performance. The sound system didn't squeal, the acoustics were fine, and we sounded almost like the old days. Maybe better. The college had even sprung for a free bar along one side of the gym floor. There were tables on one end of the basketball floor, and a dance floor and our band on the other.

We played *In the Mood* and *Kiss Me Once or Kiss Me Twice* and *To Each His Own* and *One Dozen Roses*. And we played corny things like *Strip Polka* and *Mairzy Doats*, and *In Der Fuehrer's Face*. The crowd seemed to love us and we had a good time. I didn't make a fool of myself after all, none of us did. It all made me feel pretty good. Worth the trouble.

Nellie Kremenak

Nellie Kremenak is an ardent diarist. Her fellow memoir writers admire the manner in which she mines her diaries to add authenticity and rich detail to her memoirs. Nellie credits her parents with engendering in their children with a love of words and sentences, and a strong commitment to family. As the eldest of six, she was aware of her parents' struggles to take care of a growing family despite financial and other difficulties. In "The War Comes to Des Moines," Nellie shares her reaction to one of those difficulties.

The War Comes to Des Moines

In the background of our semi-rural life in Des Moines, the radio opened an amazing window to the wider world, in the mornings bringing "Stella Dallas" and "Backstage Wife", and just before supper "Terry and the Pirates" or the wonderfully stirring "William Tell Overture", that signaled stories about the deep-voiced, mysteriously masked Lone Ranger and Tonto, his faithful Indian companion.

In the evening, the radio got less interesting to my interiorized self. At certain moments though, something would change; Mother or Daddy would quiet us, and we would all listen intently to the harsh, angry, almost hysterical diatribes of Adolf Hitler. The English translator's calm voice followed on the heels of each sentence and, in between, we heard the distant roar of Hitler's followers. Other times, we heard Winston Churchill's sonorous tones, my own language, but shaped differently, deliberate and compelling. Mother and Daddy grew serious, listening gravely to these voices, and shushing my brother and me so that we listened too, though without really comprehending, those voices rising and falling, surging and fading, moving toward us across the ocean floor. Their dissonance washed over us, slowly changing our world in infinitesimal and unobservable ways until suddenly, a couple of years later, we found ourselves re-situated, in the same world but viewed from a different aspect. For me, childhood was beginning to be over.

Although I took no notice of it, in the fall of 1939, as I began kindergarten, the Germans invaded Poland. The rescue at Dunkirk came in May, 1940, the month of my sixth birthday. In early November, the Armistice Day blizzard abruptly ended a school day in early afternoon, and my father appeared miraculously in the schoolyard, emerging out of the blowing, blinding, whiteness just as my brother and I pushed open the heavy metal doors of the building, bedazzled by the whirling snow-filled air, oblivious to its threat. My father took us and some neighbor children home in a borrowed car; the blizzard killed the apple tree in our front yard.

Sometime during that same year, my father left his part-time work taking care of the ponies and the baby elephant at the State Fairgrounds. He took a new, better-paying job at a place we always called "the ordnance plant," but that his Army discharge papers name as the United States Rubber Co. The change brought new luxuries to our lives. We now had electricity, light bulbs replacing kerosene lamps, and a telephone, the only one on our hill, so neighbors sometimes came in to make important calls.

In December, 1941 our baby sister Carol, one year old and nourished from her inauspicious beginnings by milk from our small flock of goats, rose to her feet, her large green eyes shining in her pale pointy little face, and for the first time walked by herself across our cozy living room. In that same living room, that same wintry December Sunday afternoon, my brother and I, excitedly urging Carol to perform her amazing feat over again, were shushed again for radio voices, and heard the ominous "We interrupt this program to bring you the following special announcement ...." We learned that the Japanese had attacked Pearl Harbor, a place we'd never heard of, on the other side of the world, yet somehow important to us, part of who we were.

Still, our lives seemed to move forward peacefully. By 1943, my parents' relative prosperity and the arrival of our sister Margaret, brown-eyed and sweet-tempered, transplanted us to a larger house on a paved street, Watrous Avenue. With pale brown shingles on the outside, and an upstairs and a downstairs, the house seemed grandly spacious to my nine-year-old self. In the basement, a coal furnace blasted hot air through big pipes into all the rooms. Upstairs, besides two bedrooms, we had a bathroom with porcelain stool and tub; in the kitchen, a gas stove and an electric refrigerator; and in the living room, a small fireplace with a lovely little gas grate whose small symmetrical blue flames turned its pale ceramic shapes a rosy pink.

A smaller piece of land than we had had at Bell Avenue meant no more goats, and our dear big white Newfoundland dog, Duke, was exiled to a farm to help mind the Fairground's ponies. We still had room for a vegetable garden though, and chickens, and a cat with kittens, and a rabbit in a cage.

In the spring of 1944, only a few months after our move to the Watrous Avenue house, my life—all our lives—changed abruptly. My father, still holding down his good-paying job at the ordnance plant, was drafted into the United States Army. We had all been a bit startled and uneasy a few weeks earlier when he had received the familiar message in the mail, dreaded but still the topic of jokes on the radio comedy shows: "From the President of the United States, Greeting:" Why just a single greeting instead of "greetings"? It had a tight-lipped, unfriendly sound to it.

Despite the grim sound, and the fact that Father was ordered to report to Camp Dodge for his physical examination, to my brother and I, at least, there seemed no possibility that the letter could change our lives. We couldn't imagine that he would have to leave us. He was 37 years old. He had rheumatism and flat feet. After years of problems with his teeth and a bout of pneumonia, the dentist had pulled them all and replaced them with dentures. And, he had four children!

I don't know what my mother thought. She read the newspapers. She must have known, after three years of war, how desperate the government was for more soldiers.

On the appointed day, we waited anxiously. By the time my father finally returned from Camp Dodge, it was almost suppertime and getting dark. With an unsettling, almost silly manner, he announced to us that he had passed the physical and would be inducted into the Army. We couldn't believe it; we thought he was teasing.

He showed us the paperwork as we stood around him in the kitchen. Our faces froze, our hilarity dissolved. He had been classified 1-A. My brother and I were stunned, and I suppose my mother was too. What would happen to us? What would happen to *him*? Such a serious frightening moment in our family's life, and I think now, in retrospect, that my father was a little drunk. He seemed delighted that he had so grandly surpassed our expectations; despite our low estimation of his fitness, Uncle Sam *wanted* him! Perhaps I was unsettled as much by his reactions as by the event itself. He didn't behave like a grownup, but like a giddy child. I wanted to be reassured and comforted. He seemed to want to celebrate.

That moment brought me a hard lesson. Without quite articulating it, I sensed that I could not rely on him to be a shield against the scary world. It seemed to me that he was not to be depended on for emotional support and maybe some other things as well. And I suppose, after that, perhaps unfairly, I did not look for that kind of support from him again.

Hal Mulford

Hal Mulford wrote about survival: his own, and other people's. Hal's World War II memoirs are remarkable. A Midwesterner who did not know how to swim, he was a sailor on three ships that sank. After the war, he took advantage of the GI Bill. Hal received his Ph.D. from the University of Iowa in 1954. He returned in 1956 to become the Director of Alcohol Studies, a position he held for the next 37 years. Hal's compassionate and thought-provoking memoirs about people's trials and tribulations in surviving their addictions provide great insight.

Miss Bainbridge

Miss Bainbridge was a pleasant-looking young woman with short wavy black hair. She was plump and sturdy, and physically fit. She was my fifth grade teacher back in 1932 when I attended school in a one-room country schoolhouse. The school was located in Henry Township, Plymouth County, in northwest Iowa. It was my school for the first eight grades. The 16 students were of various ages and were distributed in various grades.

Our farm home was located almost directly across the dirt road from the school. However, some of the students walked as far as two miles around the square mile to school, unless they cut across farm fields.

The white schoolhouse was not much larger than a modern-day family living room. We entered through a small anteroom where we hung our coats and hats and lined up our overshoes along the wall. The building was heated with a pot-bellied coal-burning stove standing beside the teacher's desk at the front of the room.

On winter mornings Miss Bainbridge arrived early to start the stove. Students stood beside the teacher's desk to recite their lessons. Behind her desk was the blackboard, covering the entire front wall.

While one student recited, the rest of us were expected to work on our own lessons. However, we sometimes learned much from listening to those in higher grades recite their lessons.

Miss Bainbridge tolerated little nonsense and no misconduct. She did not use a hickory stick on naughty children. She used a two-foot-long end of a leather bullwhip—which she kept prominently displayed on a nail above the blackboard. She rarely used the whip, or needed to.

One day she did use it on Ole Olson. He had misbehaved and she told him, "For that, you may not go out for morning recess." He said that he would if he wanted to, and called her a "fat old cow." She grabbed the whip, and Ole felt the sting of it on his back. He decided that going out for recess that morning was not such a good idea after all.

Ole was one of the school's three "big boys," the three oldest students in the school. They would not have still been in school had not the law required children to attend school until either they successfully completed the eighth grade or they reached the age of 16 years. All three of those big boys were closer to 16 than they would ever be to successfully completing the eighth grade. This was because their parents had kept them out of school a few weeks every fall to help harvest crops, and then kept them home a few more weeks again in the spring to help plant new crops.

They were more bullies than scholars. They often entertained themselves at recess time by slapping us younger kids around when Miss Bainbridge wasn't looking.

When she rang the bell ending recess, Miss Bainbridge expected students to promptly go inside and be seated. However, this school year had hardly begun when we boys developed a bad habit. We took the sound of the ringing bell as a signal to line up behind the coal shed and pee before going inside. After only two days, this bad habit came to a sudden halt when Miss Bainbridge came charging around the corner of the shed with whip in hand. She cut off our water and sent us scurrying for our seats without taking time to button our pants.

One morning recess, Alvin, a fellow fifth-grader, and I got into another fight. We fought a lot when Miss Bainbridge wasn't looking. It was a cold, cloudy and windy fall day. Alvin grabbed my cap and threw it over the schoolyard fence into a freshly plowed field. I grabbed his summer straw hat, and threw it over the fence. As we were climbing over the fence to get our hats a strong northwest wind gust caught his straw hat and carried it far, far across the field and out sight. Alvin said that I should get his hat. I didn't agree. We began to scuffle. I had him down on the ground sitting on him and rubbing some of that plowed field dirt into his face when the bell rang. We ignored the bell until Miss Bainbridge appeared, whip in hand and broke up the fight. She ordered me to go find Alvin's hat, while she grabbed him by the ear and marched him inside.

I thought it unfair that I should have to retrieve Alvin's hat, since he started it. Instead, I went across the road to my home. I was not sure how my parents would react. They usually sided with the teacher, as was the custom in those days. However, in this case, I thought they would agree with me. After all, that's where I got my sense of fair play.

They decided that I should stay home until noon, then return to school and see what happened. I did that and nothing happened. At least nothing has happened yet. And, for all I know Alvin's hat is still sailing before the wind.

One misty, moisty spring morning we were out for recess and were playing on the steep hillside beside the schoolhouse. Only recently we had been sledding on the snow down that hill. Now it was covered with lush green grass. This day the wet grass was nearly as slippery as the recent snow cover. Miss Bainbridge was watching us play when she saw first-grader Kenny, Alvin's little brother, hit a little girl—making her cry.

When Miss Bainbridge ordered Kenny inside to his seat he stuck his tongue out at her and started running away down the hill. Miss Bainbridge was close behind. As she grabbed Kenny's coat collar about halfway down that slippery slope, both feet slipped from beneath her and she slid down the grassy hill feet first on her rear end. Still holding tight to Kenny's collar and sitting there on the wet grass she laid little Kenny across her lap and spanked him, and spanked him, and spanked him some more. For the remainder of the day, when we saw her from the rear we didn't laugh aloud, but we did smile. We called her "grassy butt," but not so she could hear it.

Nukualofa Tongatapu

Following several weeks at sea, and the battle of the Coral Sea, my USS *Astoria* shipmates and I looked forward to some well-deserved shore leave. Recently, on May 7-8 1942, we had engaged the Japanese Navy in a unique sea battle in which not one shot was fired between enemy surface ships. The battle involved only carrier-based planes. During the two-day battle, our planes sank one enemy aircraft carrier and severely damaged a second. We also sank an enemy light cruiser and brought down nearly twice as many of their planes as we lost. Enemy bomber planes did fatally damage the U.S. *Lexington*, one of the two U.S. carriers that the Astoria was escorting. The explosions on the *Lexington* killed many men. However, the others safely abandoned ship before two torpedoes from one of our destroyers sent that majestic ship to the bottom of an otherwise calm tropical sea under a clear blue sky. Anti-aircraft fire plus our fighter pilots' skills saved our second carrier, the *Yorktown*, although she was slightly damaged.

With that behind us, we anchored ship in the harbor of the tiny village of Nukualofa Tongatapu, ready for shore leave and some R and R. Nukualofa is a small seaport on the island of Tongatapu, one of the many Tonga Islands. They are located just south of the equator and east of the 180th meridian, about 5,000 miles southwest of San Francisco and about 2,000 miles east of Australia. When Captain Cook explored the islands in the 1770s, he called them the Friendly Islands due to the happy, carefree ways of the Polynesian natives. They subsequently came under British rule, took on the English language, and missionaries converted the population to Christianity, mostly Methodism. The island's government was a monarchy. While we were there, the Queen came aboard our ship to have dinner with the ship's officers. Her skin was light brown like that of her subjects. However, she was no swivel-hipped Pacific Island beauty. She looked more like a 400-lb. sausage tube encased in a long, loose-fitting, flowery red muumuu dress. She could not climb the ship's steep, narrow gangway, so a crane hoisted her aboard on a cargo platform.

Beyond a name that delights the tongue, Nukualofa Tongatapu held other delights. We had barely arrived on shore when a young native on horseback approached me and invited me to join him and his family for Sunday dinner. I could not turn down what promised to be an exciting new experience. He had no saddle, and had only a rope tied around the horse's neck to control him. That appeared to be sufficient. The horse seemed well trained. Like the pony that I had left back in Iowa, the youthful high spirit and exuberance that horses begin life with had turned to resignation.

My new friend guided his horse up beside a rock and gave me a hand up. I settled down behind him and we set off down a trail through the lush tropical jungle of dense foliage and tangled vines. We soon came to a small clearing, which he said was the island's jail. All I saw was a couple of broken strands of wire strung around some trees to make an enclosure about 50 feet square. It was empty of prisoners. He assured me that prison escapes were no problem. Anyone put in jail stayed there, he said.

Farther along the trail, we came to one of the island's few wooden buildings, from which emanated some beautiful choir singing. It sounded much like Negro spirituals. I wondered why my host was not in church, but was not so impolite as to ask.

I was also beginning to wonder what the dinner menu might include. Nothing along the path gave me a clue. I saw no vegetable gardens or other evidence of cultivation, except that I did notice two rows of pineapple plants, perhaps two dozen plants all together.

We eventually came to his home, a hut made of coconut palm leaves located in a small clearing. We stopped at another hut where he introduced me to his grandmother. She was sitting on a palm leaf mat on the ground puffing on a roll-your-own cigarette. The cigarette was about the size of my thumb, and appeared to consist of locally grown coarse tobacco leaves rolled in what looked like a piece of a brown paper sack.

There were no children or neighbors in sight, though the two nearby huts might have belonged to neighbors. My host's wife was tending a wild pig roasting in a pit of hot coals. Although that was not the way that I had seen Mom prepare pork, the aroma of the steam seeping up through the palm leaves covering the pig made my mouth water. I suppressed my drooling, wiped my chin, and wondered what next?

My host's wife went off into the jungle, but soon returned with a double handful of roots. She ground the roots between two rocks, mixed them with water, and served me some of the mixture in half a coconut shell. It looked and tasted like muddy water. He asked me if I felt anything. When I said no, he said she put too much water in it. They called it Tonga Kava. I have since learned that kava is a narcotic from the roots of a shrub that is a member of the pepper family. I wonder now what delight I might have missed due to that extra water. A woven palm leaf mat covered the hut's dirt floor. Dinner was served on individual mats. That was the extent of their furniture. The roast pig was delicious, although it needed salt. The menu also included breadfruit, bananas, oranges, coconut meat, and a couple of other exotic fruits. Coconut milk was our after-dinner drink. I watched, amazed, as my host shinnied—almost walked—up a 25-foot coconut tree in his bare feet, cut loose a coconut, and slid back down to the ground. He then husked the nut by driving the thick husk onto the point of a stick anchored in the ground. We shared the milk, and he then cracked it open with a rock and we had some more coconut meat.

We talked mostly about their lifestyle, how nature provided most of what they needed, including everything on our dinner menu. Even the usual Sunday roast pig roamed wild in the jungle. He told me about their unique mail service, called "tin can mail." Due to the shallowness of the harbor water, cargo ships could not get closer than about a mile of the shore. The mail was sealed in tin cans and dropped off in the water as the ship passed the island. The natives rowed their canoes or swam out to gather the cans. I purchased a couple of the special tin can postal stamps as souvenirs, but lost them when my ship was later sunk.

Soon after dinner, we mounted our trusty transportation and headed back to my ship. We had not gone far when my digestive system suddenly signaled an urgent need for a bathroom. It was telling me that it was not accustomed to so much exotic, albeit very tasty food. We had no trouble finding a bathroom, one evidently designed by the same architect who designed the jail. We found a very similar bathroom on down the path when the need arose a second time. Fortunately, this Iowa farm boy was quite aware that while a piece of Charmin tissue paper and a handful of poison ivy leaves can serve the same initial purpose, they have much different long-term consequences.

I arrived back aboard ship on time and without further mishap. The day had been a welcomed break in the boredom of sea duty between battles. It was also an unforgettable experience for one who, before joining the Navy, had hardly been farther from home than the distance he'd travel to hunt rabbits.

In Need of Swimming Lessons

On August 7, 1942, amidst some of the heaviest sea battles of World War II, I was aboard the USS *Astoria*, a warship covering an American marine landing on Guadalcanal, a Japanese-held island in the far southwest Pacific. The Astoria was a heavy cruiser armed with nine eight-inch, and eight five-inch cannons. As per orders of the day, all hands had shaved, showered, put on clean clothes, and were at their battle stations.

While we were still some miles from the target beach, a delicate perfume aroma wafted in on a warm offshore island breeze. The Captain assured us that there was no need for gas masks. Rather, we should enjoy the exotic fragrance of the island's flowers as we were entering battle.

No grass-skirted native women greeted the marines as they waded ashore under our protective gunfire, but neither did they meet much enemy resistance.

The next day our task force repelled an attack by some 30 to 40 enemy planes, coming in only about 50 feet above the water. As our task force patrolled the bay that day, we little suspected, but would soon learn, why the bay was about to become known as "Iron Bottom Bay."

At 1:45 the next morning, from my battle station, I saw distant gunfire. Then I saw our two sister ships, and an Australian cruiser, all ablaze from stem to stern. The hundreds of shell hits on my own ship had exploded the fuel storage tanks located amidships. Our ship was still afloat, but the ship was dead in the water with both her engines and her guns silent.

My battle assignment was to operate the ship's rangefinder, a 25-foot-long stereoscopic binocular. I used it to estimate the range to the target and to help aim the ship's guns. It was located on a small, open-air platform about 10 feet above the main stern deck.

The captain, on the ship's bow with about half of the crew, had lost communication with the second in command (the executive officer), who was on the stern with the balance of the crew. Unaware of the captain's decision to remain with the ship, the "Exec" judging the ship to be in imminent danger of sinking, ordered those of us on the stern to abandon ship.

Although I could not swim, I judged floating in the sea in a life jacket was preferable to being sucked to the bottom by a sinking ship. As I cinched up my life jacket ties I wished that instead of those Arthur Murray dancing lessons that I had taken in Seattle, I had gone next door to the YMCA and learned to swim. To reach the ship's rail and jump into the sea, I climbed down the ladder from my battle station to the main deck. There I made my way through dead and dying bodies and the many body parts littering the deck. If I stopped to help the wounded, I would only accompany them to the sea bottom.

I reached the rail, climbed over it, and plunged into the Pacific Ocean some 25 feet below. I paddled furiously to get away from the ship as far and as fast as possible, that it not suck me down with it if it sank. The night was pitch-black, and it was raining so hard that I could not tell sea from not-sea. However, the raging fire aboard the ship told me which direction to paddle.

Once safely away from the wounded ship I drifted alone for a couple of hours. With the heavy rain washing the salt water from my eyes, I eventually spotted several shipmates clinging to a small life raft. I joined them to find one man losing touch with reality and shouting ominous nonsense.

I picked up a life raft paddle prepared to lay him out if his antics threatened the group's safety. However, he soon fell silent.

As our raft drifted we saw an approaching searchlight playing on the water's surface, and then heard machine gun fire. We thought it might be a Jap ship shooting some of our fellow survivors. If it came closer I would slip off the raft into the water hoping that might offer some little protection. Later we learned that it was one of our own destroyers shooting sharks around some of our men. To stop to pick up the men would have risked a torpedo hit.

Dawn revealed land on the distant horizon. We had no idea who controlled that real estate, but we agreed that regardless of the slant of the owners' eyes, any dry land was preferable to drifting farther out to sea on a raft with no food or water.

A couple of hours later another destroyer came bearing down on us. It was the USS *Wilson*. She pulled alongside our raft and lowered a rope ladder. No one hesitated to accept the gracious invitation to climb aboard.

After shaving, showering, and donning clean clothes, we lined up to pass before a medical corpsman standing beside a 50-gallon wooden drum full of sulfa powder. As we passed by, he slapped a handful of the powder on all open wounds. That included the shrapnel laceration on the front of my right leg, for which I was later awarded the Purple Heart.

Throughout the ordeal, my mind was too preoccupied with the rapidly shifting demands of the moment to panic, or to be overly frightened. I was too busy doing to feel. Moreover, at the age of 20, I had a strong sense of denial and invulnerability. It did not occur to me that something *really* bad could ever happen to me.

Some three years later, and a year or so after having also survived the Normandy Beach invasion aboard a destroyer, the USS *Thompson*, I finally took those swimming lessons. I even qualified to become a Red Cross-certified lifeguard. Better late than never.

Clayton Ringgenberg

Clayton Ringgenberg grew up in Newton, Iowa and graduated from Cornell College in Mt. Vernon, Iowa. He went to graduate school at the University of Denver in a special program called government management. His early employment was in Boston and Providence, Rhode Island. Clayton returned to Iowa in 1955 and became the first employee and director of the Iowa State Legislature's newly established Legislative Research Bureau in Des Moines. He later moved to Iowa City to work at the University of Iowa Institute of Public Affairs, where he became the director in 1975. Clayton also spent a valuable and professionally fulfilling year on the staff of Governor Bob Ray. His hobbies were golfing and "orcharding."

The Great White Supper

It was one of those ordinary, Thursday night, husband and wife suppers. Just the two of us. At least that was what it was supposed to be—ordinary, that is.

This event took place in our cozy, dark, one-room apartment in Brookline, Massachusetts. Brookline, a suburb of Boston, was where we lived when I began my first professional job, as a researcher on the staff of a special legislative commission for the Commonwealth of Massachusetts.

Both Helen and I recall the darkness of that apartment, caused primarily by the fact that there was only one small window, and it faced north. So we had to have the lights on all the time, even in the middle of the day. We had been married a little more than a year. But we were still inexperienced newlyweds, and a long way from home in good old Iowa, where both of us grew up.

Helen was still learning to cook. Before marriage, she had not cooked a meal. So her inexperience was fairly evident in the culinary part of living, particularly because both of our mothers were excellent cooks, and both Helen and I were used to tasty, well-prepared food. But I was hopeful about the future for Helen's cooking. I was optimistic that some of our mothers' cooking skills would trickle down to her. But it was taking a while. For good or ill, I had picked up some cooking tips from my mother which helped us survive. And I sometimes passed on these ideas to Helen, or helped prepare some food, particularly at those times when Helen was close to tears from the results of her inexperience in the kitchen.

So it was that memorable, dark October evening when we sat down to enjoy a pleasant, if ordinary, supper for two. I took one look at what was on the table, and began to wonder, almost in disbelief. Then I took another look. It was amazing, at least I was amazed.

What was I seeing? I saw pearly-white mashed potatoes, cauliflower with dripping white sauce, turkey breast with gleaming white gravy, white apple salad with adequate white mayonnaise, and white bread. I think the décor was completed with white napkins!

I was speechless, which is somewhat unusual for me. But I was speechless primarily because I just didn't know what to say! There was a moment or two of silence. I was thinking hard, stunned by the scene on the table.

Should I break the silence by asking, "Are we going to have chocolate milk?" What to do? I decided to peek into the kitchen to see what was for dessert. Sure enough, there sat a light-colored cake with mountains of white frosting. This scene was getting to be too much for me. So I simply commented that things looked nice on the table, that everything was so clean, and pure, and white. Helen looked at what she had prepared, then she looked at me, then looked at the table, then she glared at me. Then we both started giggling, and then burst out laughing. Then we ate. It was great—the food and the relationship!

An hour later, we could barely sneak a glance at each other without giggling and laughing. We just didn't know what to say or what to do, so probably the giggling and laughing was the best thing we could have done.

We considered making popcorn, but we dared not look at a pan full of white popcorn. That would have been anti-climactic.

So we went to bed.

We were tickled "pink," a colorful pink. We were tickled that we had handled a ticklish situation so well. It had been a colorful evening. As I recall, the sheets and pillow cases were—you guessed it— light blue!

Guidelines: Gray Hawk Memoir Writers Group

- **The benefits of these guidelines:**
  - Active involvement by more people, and greater diversity for listeners.
  - A short enough piece that analysis can be more meaningful.
  - Part of the fun of a workshop is listening to fortnightly installments.
- **Suggested guidelines for discussing members' readings:**
  - Maximum size of group: 14. If more people want to join, start a new group.
  - Reading from published memoir or writing advice before member readings: reading for 8 minutes, discussion for 2 minutes.
  - Write at least a paragraph for each meeting.
  - Readings and discussion, for those who are ready: reading for 9 minutes, discussion for 5 minutes.
  - At the beeper, you may finish the paragraph you are reading and then stop. Continue reading from this point next time. If only one additional paragraph remains, you may finish that too.
  - *Authors are encouraged to read only works on which they are currently working. Once a work is completed or published and is no longer under revision, authors are encouraged to start something new. Current rewriting or reworking old stuff is okay.*
  - *A work once published is eligible as "Reading from published memoir or writing advice."*
  - Comments during critique should be focused on the writing, not on personal experiences.
  - Oral comments about the memoir by the author during discussions need to go into the revised memoir.
  - Write down your personal experiences suggested by the reading.
  - Support opinions with analysis.

- Discussing specifics will help you to bring general principles of writing to light.
- Positive environment for encouragement; reinforce things you like in another's work.
- Suggest specific changes for things you believe could be improved.
- Clichés that are part of family stories are appropriate to use in family memoirs.
- Personal essays, academic pieces related to memoir, fiction, and poetry are permitted.

Index

Made in the USA
Charleston, SC
11 September 2014